D1031232

AMERICAN
NATURE
WRITING
1997

Books by John A. Murray

The Indian Peaks Wilderness

Wildlife in Peril: The Endangered Mammals of Colorado

The Gila Wilderness

The Last Grizzly, and Other Southwestern Bear Stories

The South San Juan Wilderness

A Republic of Rivers: Three Centuries of Nature Writing
from Alaska and the Yukon

The Islands and the Sea: Five Centuries of Nature Writing
from the Caribbean

The Great Bear: Contemporary Writings on the Grizzly

Nature's New Voices

Wild Hunters: Predators in Peril

Wild Africa: Three Centuries of Nature Writing from Africa

Out Among the Wolves: Contemporary Writings on the Wolf

A Thousand Leagues of Blue: The Sierra Club Book of the Pacific

American Nature Writing 1994

The Sierra Club Nature Writing Handbook

Grizzly Bears

American Nature Writing 1995

The Walker's Companion (with Dave Wallace, and others)

American Nature Writing 1996

Cactus Country

Alaska

American Nature Writing 1997

Desert Places

AMERICAN NATURE WRITING 1997

Selected by John A. Murray

SIERRA CLUB BOOKS
San Francisco

The Sierra Club, founded in 1892 by John Muir, has devoted itself to the study and protection of the Earth's scenic and ecological resources—mountains, wetlands, woodlands, wild shores and rivers, deserts and plains. The publishing program of the Sierra Club offers books to the public as a non-profit educational service in the hope that they may enlarge the public's understanding of the Club's basic concerns. The point of view expressed in each book, however, does not necessarily represent that of the Club. The Sierra Club has some sixty chapters coast to coast, in Canada, Hawaii, and Alaska. For information about how you may participate in its programs to preserve wilderness and the quality of life, please address inquiries to Sierra Club, 85 Second Street, San Francisco, CA 94105.

http://www.sierraclub.org/books

Copyright © 1997 by Sierra Club Books

All rights reserved under International and Pan-American Copyright Conventions. No part of this book may be reproduced in any form or by any electronic or mechanical means, including information storage and retrieval systems, without permission in writing from the publisher.

Pages 267–269 are an extension of this copyright page.

ISBN: 0-87156-395-9
ISSN: 1072-4723

Production by Janet Vail and Robin Rockey
Cover and book design by Amy Evans
Composition by Wilsted & Taylor

Printed in the United States of America on acid-free paper containing a minimum of 50% recovered waste paper, of which at least 10% of the fiber content is post-consumer waste.

10 9 8 7 6 5 4 3 2 1

For John Haines

To Marc
with love
for making a difference.

Carol

*The views of nature held by any people determine
all their institutions.*
RALPH WALDO EMERSON, "English Traits"

Men perish because they cannot join the beginning with the end.
ALCMAEON OF CROTONA, "Fragments"

*We all move on the fringes of eternity and are sometimes
granted vistas through the fabric of illusion.*
ANSEL ADAMS, *Autobiography*

Contents

Preface

Many years ago I set out to know a country, to settle in it as deeply as I could. And, as it turned out, make of that living knowledge a book. As a writer, I could do nothing else. In the end I could not separate art and nature, the country and the writing. They depended on each other, and with good fortune would make a single work.

John Haines, *Fables and Distances*

It seems just a short while ago that the first Sierra Club nature annual was published. Four years have passed, and the fledgling series has taken root and flourished. I thank all of you—readers, reviewers, booksellers, nature aficionados, English teachers, public radio commentators—who helped spread the word and ensure the success of the first three volumes. With this book, nearly one hundred nature writers have been published in these pages, including a former American president (Jimmy Carter), an Alaskan salmon fisherman (Nancy Lord), a California surfer (Dan Duane), an Idaho sheep rancher and seasonal firefighter (Louise Wagenknecht), and such best-selling authors as Barry Lopez and Jane Smiley. As in previous volumes, selections by women are alternated with those by men, to create a natural rhythm that will hopefully add to your reading pleasure. In the 1997 annual, you can hike to the bottom of the Grand Canyon with Ann Zwinger and her daughter Susan, go hunting on Gooseberry Marsh with Gretchen Legler, explore the Mississippi backwoods with Don Schueler, or get to know the Wisconsin countryside with John Hildebrand.

Earlier this year the folks at Educational Testing Service contacted us, requesting permission to use a portion of an essay in a future S.A.T. test. It is nice to know that high school seniors, during that tedious rite of passage, will at least be able to relax a little by reading about nature. It says something, too, about nature writing, which in just a few decades has leapt from relative obscurity to become one of the major nonfiction genres—as I recall, when I took the examination twenty-five years ago, the literary excerpts tended more toward the dense turgid prose of Thomas Carlyle and the fatuous ramblings of William F. Buckley. Much has changed in our society, and will continue to change. In thirty months from the publication date of this book we will enter the twenty-first century. Environmental writing can only become more essential as the human population grows and conflicts with nature increase. To paraphrase William Kittredge, nature writers are concerned with power and injustice, and through their writings drive light into the political darkness at the heart of society.

The 1997 annual is dedicated to John Haines, whose essays have been published in this series several times. From 1947 to 1995 Haines lived on a homestead in northern Alaska and practiced the self-reliant philosophy of Thoreau. Many readers know the seventy-two-year-old Haines as the "Edward Abbey of the Far North," and the dedication acknowledges my great love and admiration for this accomplished naturalist, master nature writer, and environmental activist. When I was a professor at the University of Alaska, I always told my students that if they wanted to read the most perfect short nature essay in the English language, they should read Haines's "Ice" (from his essay collection *The Stars, The Snow, The Fire* [Graywolf, 1988]). I would further recommend to readers *Fables and Distances* (Graywolf, 1996) and *Living Off the Country* (University of Michigan, 1981). Haines is also an award-winning poet—Edward Abbey called Haines's *News from the Glacier* (Wesleyan University, 1980) the finest book of poetry to come from Alaska.

Because book publishers generally focus on proven authors, the Sierra Club nature-writing annual provides an important venue to lesser-known writers. Last year I featured ten such individuals, and this year I've included the same number. I am dedicated to making the selection process for this anthology democratic and open, and to including as much diversity—by region, style, theme, gender, ethnic background—as possible. The sole criteria, beyond strong natural content, is literary excellence. I will consider any submission, from any person, in any genre, about any theme related to nature. I always hope for the best, and am always looking for stellar new talents. One of the dreams of every editor is that he or she might locate and nurture a talent powerful and original enough to transform the landscape of literature and human thought. Every submission that I receive is opened and read with that hopeful expectation. If you have a selection, or know of a selection, that you believe will contribute to the anthology, by all means send it to me in care of Sierra Club Books, 85 Second Street, San Francisco, California 94105.

I have many thanks to give. First, the writers, their agents, and their publishers have been wonderfully cooperative in securing permissions and I thank them all; no anthology is possible without such quick and enthusiastic assistance. My editor, Jim Cohee, as ever, has provided constant good cheer and steady guidance as we brought this collection into being. All authors should be blessed with such wise counsel. I must thank my readers, whose correspondence, phone calls, and miscellaneous packages (home videos, newspaper clippings, fresh cookies) always brighten my day. It is for you I work. Many thanks to Verne Huser of Albuquerque, Diane Grob of Seattle, Ray Novotny of Youngstown, Kim Steiner of Olympia, Carlene Cross of Bothell, and all the others who have written in warm friendship. Finally I give thanks to the Murray family for their love and support, especially my son, who, when he is not playing with his Power Ranger toys, loves to frolic in the wilds with his dad. One of these days soon I will take him for his first trip to magical Cumberland Island.

J.A.M.

Introduction

Island in the Stream
I.
The vessel in which I was to embark for East Florida, being now ready to pursue her voyage, we set sail with a fair wind and tide. Our course was south, through the sound, betwixt a chain of sea-coast-islands, and the main. In the evening we came to, at the south end of St. Simon's Island. . . . Next morning early we again got under way, running by Jekyl and Cumberland Islands, large, beautiful, and fertile, yet thinly inhabited, and consequently excellent haunts for deer, bear, and other game.
William Bartram, *Travels*, 1791

1. Cumberland Island is a barrier island along the southern coast of Georgia. Eighteen miles long, two to three miles wide, with fifty feet of vertical relief, the island has few human inhabitants. It is warmed by the Gulf Stream and enjoys a climate best described as perpetual spring. Three major ecosystems are found on the island—salt marsh, maritime forest, and beach. Wildlife ranges from alligators to white-tailed deer. East of the island is Gray's Reef, the largest live-bottom reef north of the Florida Keys and a designated National Marine Sanctuary. Since 1972 Cumberland Island has been a national seashore, but it is a unique national park in that the number of visitors is strictly limited. Currently that number is three hundred per day. In this respect, Cumberland presents a vision of our larger na-

tional parks—Yosemite, Grand Canyon, Yellowstone—in the future, when such restrictions become more widespread.

Naturally I had to visit the place, and see how the system works, for one day we will have it in the West.

II. Eighty miles south of Atlanta, en route to Cumberland Island, traffic on Interstate 75 came to a halt. What was pouring from the sky was not rain. It was a biblical effusion, a drenching bottomless deluge, a thundering waterfall that would if unchecked soon flood iniquity from that province of the world. Somewhere in the atmosphere above a black anvil cloud was climbing toward outer space. Down the center of that column poured the heavens. Never in North America had I seen such a violent monsoon. And, of course, a few people continued to drive. Everyone else was pulled over on the shoulder. Eventually the dark colossus rolled east toward the sea. In its wake, the road under water in low places, traffic cautiously crawled forward. A half mile ahead, a red sports car with bald tires and Florida plates was wrapped around a white oak tree. A state trooper had just pulled over and was about to earn his pay.

That did it. I had no idea where I was, but I was getting off. I exited at the next interchange. The Georgia highway map told me the road was U.S. 341. It was headed in generally the right direction—south and east toward Cumberland Island—and the slow pace of the fugitive byway was agreeable. It was classic Southern farm country. Cultivated fields of soybean and tobacco, planted sections of corn and peanuts, neatly aligned groves of peach and pecan trees. And everywhere woodlots overgrown with kudzu and wild grape vines.

Gone were the Carolina parakeets and ivory-billed woodpeckers. Gone forever.

As the miles added up, the cotton fields became more abundant, the cotton bolls several sizes larger than those in Mississippi and Alabama. About every third or fourth crop had been harvested, the loose cotton piled in enormous white stacks. The stacks were approximately the size of a city bus. From this raw field cotton would come flags and funeral shrouds, dress shirts and pleated skirts, beach towels and bed sheets, tablecloths and wedding dresses, hospital linen and baby diapers.

By the time I'd driven through Pulaski County and Dodge County and passed through the villages of Jaybird Springs, McRae, Scotland, and Lumber City (founded 1837), I was no longer in the Georgia Midlands. The country was flatter, with black tupelo swamps spreading wherever the land was low. Mud turtles rested on half-sunken logs and wood ducks patrolled and bull frogs chanted. Stout papyruslike cane grew to heights of ten and twelve feet wherever the mud had gathered and started to form land. The air was hot and sticky and I was reminded that Cumberland Island is at the same latitude as Cairo, Egypt.

Water, water everywhere, and the faint odor of decay.

Okefenokee Swamp an hour to the south.

And the flora was changing. Around the houses, and in just the space of a few miles, there were suddenly banana trees, pomegranate trees, orange trees, and palm trees. I had crossed a border and was now in the subtropics. Nearly every home had its own giant live oak tree, a venerable behemoth with a trunk as massive as a corn silo. On the recumbent branches grew fertile gardens of resurrection fern, green moss, and trailing wisteria, and over the entire tree were draped hundreds of yards of Spanish moss, the long gray strands forever waving like ghosts reluctant to leave the place.

The overall impression was of strength and grace, of a tree that was not just a tree but a self-sufficient ecosystem.

The homes along U.S. 341 were of two varieties: unpainted wooden shanties that appeared to be held together with nightly prayers and rambling white-columned affairs of the sort that inspired Margaret Mitchell's epic tale of Tara. The former outnumbered the latter by a factor of about one hundred to one, a ratio that brought to mind ancient Mayan society prior to the mysterious collapse.

At a little town called Hazelhurst, county seat of Jefferson Davis County, I got some gas and turned south on U.S. 23.

Tired of solitude, I turned on the radio.

On a fading FM rock station from Macon there was a live interview with Georgia native Chuck Leavell, former keyboardist for Macon's own Allman Brothers Band and now playing for the Rolling Stones on the Voodoo Lounge tour. The Stones would perform in Atlanta later that week. In a thick southern accent, Chuck told picaresque tales of touring with the band. Mick Jagger loved Atlanta, Leavell chuckled, for two reasons: the blues clubs and the strip clubs. "What are you most proud of in your career?" inquired the interviewer. Leavell's answer was surprising. Not playing with slide guitar genius Duane Allman, or providing backup on Eric Clapton's *Unplugged* album, or touring with Keith Richards and company. He was most proud of having been voted the 1994 Georgia Tree Farmer of the Year. Leavell, it seemed, owned a 1,200-acre tree farm in the country south of Macon.

Georgia has more planted trees than any state in the union, and tree farming was big business in U.S. 23 country. Everywhere there were cultivated stands of loblolly pine, known locally as Rosemary pine because of the sweet-smelling resin. Some of the stands were young and not yet thinned out. Others were mature and cleared and soon to be converted into houses and paper. Others were past their prime—perhaps a benevolent owner was letting them change slowly to hardwood forest.

By the time I reached Folkston and turned east on State Route 40, cypress trees were growing thickly in the swamps on either side of the road. Cypresses are strange, ancient trees dating back to the age of dinosaurs. The way they evolved—a tall straight trunk and then a weirdly shaped flat crown with branches sharply angled—suggests that at one time they were heavily browsed by long-necked animals. The brontosaurus is gone, but the cypress remains. All you need is a little imagination to picture those immense vegetarians splashing ponderously among the cypress. The only relict of the dinosaur age remaining in the swamps today is the alligator, a tenacious egg-layer that somehow outlasted tyrannosaurus and the rest of that cold-blooded bestiary.

Fifteen miles from the coastal village of St. Mary's, where I would spend the night, I smelled the ocean for the first time. Actually I smelled the salt marshes. The odor was sulfurous, reminiscent of the valley of the Firehole River in Yellowstone. It is a smell that conjures up memories. Every drop of our blood contains the same percentage of salt as sea water. In the womb, along about the fifth or sixth week, we carry facial gills, our breathing apparatus from ages ago. Women's monthly periods are timed to the lunar tides in which our predecessors once lived and procreated and died.

Coming back to the sea, as they say, is coming back home.

Just this side of St. Mary's I passed the entrance to the King's Bay Naval Submarine Base, home of the Atlantic fleet of Trident nuclear submarines. A marine guard was busily saluting all the incoming cars with blue officers' decals, and I pitied him that piece of duty, four hours on, eight hours off for days on end. A little farther on was the Gilman Paper Company pulp mill. It was an imposing structure, though one not designed by Frank Lloyd Wright or any architect who has ever been seriously influenced by Wright. On the other side of St. Mary's was the waterfront of saltwater bars and seafood restaurants, and the fishermen's dock where I would catch the ferry. The ranger at the Cumberland Island visitor's center had good news and bad news. The good news was that my reservations for the ferry and campground were duly registered in the logbook. The bad news was that the mosquitoes and sand fleas were at a five-year high, a result of the recent drenching rains. The other bad news was that a local teenage gang was breaking out the windows of cars in the visitor's overnight parking lot and stealing everything they could get their hands on.

My first stop was the local police station, just down the street. Looking for advice, but no one was there. It was Sunday, and the sign said if you had a problem to call 911.

Next stop was the Goodbread House, a yellow-painted Victorian home that had been converted into a bed-and-breakfast. I was greeted there by Betty and George Kraus, sitting on the porch with their nine or ten cats. She was a retired junior high school teacher and he was a retired forester for the state of Georgia. They were friendly as Georgians are, and she seemed to like me because we had both worked as teachers. Within minutes the situation was resolved. I would spend the night in their restored 1885 home, and they would watch the car for the three nights I'd be on Cumberland Island.

That night after Betty's poached flounder and candied yams I went upstairs and stacked the pillows and read the book I had brought: William Bartram's *Travels Through North and South Carolina, Georgia, East and West Florida,* which was originally published during George Washington's first term. William Bartram was the son of John Bartram, the colonial botanist, and undertook some of the earliest surveys of southeastern flora for his father. I read through the first two chapters, as the naturalist arrived in Savannah, Georgia, and traveled south by horse, and fell asleep shortly after he reached St. Mary's, which was at that time "the utmost frontier" (his words) of settlement. The Okefenokee Swamp, the source of the St. Mary's River, Bartram spelled phonetially as "Ouqquaphenogaw," which suggests the pronunciation may have changed over time. The swamp, he wrote, was an "enchanted land" where "the daughters of the sun lived."

III. At breakfast I was introduced to Lauren and Paul Saxton, who had arrived late and would be going to the island with me on the morning ferry. Lauren was about fifty, with short gray hair and a sharp nose and a serious, intense quality about her. Paul was physically her opposite, about the same age but full-fleshed and fat around the waist. He was bald, wore a beard not yet fully gray, and had an edge to him. The first thing he said after shaking hands was, "This is the first time in a month I haven't felt like killing someone."

Lauren asked me what I did and I told them. Then it was their

turn. They were from Plainfield, New Jersey, Lauren a family practice attorney, and Paul a former corporate executive who now owned
his own computer consulting company, which in these days is the accepted way of describing a state of professional unemployment.

After wolfing down his cheese omelet and rasher of bacon and
homemade biscuits Paul sighed sadly and said he always forgot to
bring something and this time he had forgotten to bring his folding
knife.

I always carry two on camping trips, and so I gave him one. He
opened the blade and saw the blood stains and asked about them. I
told him that I had last used the knife in August to skin a caribou in
northern Alaska. A look of horror passed over his face.

"You hunt?"

I nodded.

"With a gun?"

After I affirmed that yes, I indeed hunted, they excused themselves and ran upstairs to pack their bags.

We met again at the dock.

The place was swarming with people. There were two groups: a
mob of eleven- or twelve-year-old children, attended to by a pair of
frantic teachers who had lost control of both themselves and their
class, and a boisterous crew of river rafters from "French Broad
River Outfitters" in western North Carolina.

Paul had a slightly panicked look on his face.

"We've been coming here for twenty years and I've never seen
anything like this before. It's like a carnival. Where do these freaks
come from?"

"Calm down, honey," his long-suffering wife implored.

"But Sea Camp will be a zoo. Look at this. Cases of beer. Banjos.
Guitars. They've even got CD players for Christ's sake."

"Just relax."

He actually looked as though he might have a fit, and she glanced
at me for help, and so I set my backpack and cooler down beside
their four duffel bags.

After a brief orientation by a ranger we were herded onto the boat. I found myself sitting between Paul and Lauren on the starboard side, facing the tangled green bank of Florida, three or four hundred yards distant. Every time the wind died the air vibrated with the music of mosquitoes and sand fleas. I mentioned something about the musical quality of the insects and Paul launched into a lecture on atonal music. It went on and on, with references to obscure European composers you and I have never heard of.

With a grinding of gears and a belching of diesel smoke, the *Cumberland Queen* got underway. We were at last headed down the tannin-colored St. Mary's River toward Cumberland Sound and beyond that Cumberland Island. The tide was coming in and the captain announced the trip would take a bit longer than usual.

Paul was still rambling on about atonal music. I was watching one of the members of the French Broad River group as she pulled her T-shirt up, wondering what she was doing. Someone handed her a baby and she began to feed it.

"You two ever catch a Springsteen concert?" I asked, hoping to get Paul to shut up about atonal music.

They looked at me as if I'd just spoken Greek.

"You know, from Asbury Park, New Jersey?"

"We know who he is," said Paul. "We just don't consider what he does to be music."

It was going to be one of those trips.

It being late November, the cordgrass salt marshes had lost their summer green and turned a rich golden color. There were long-legged birds, herons and cranes, stalking in the golden marshes. Even as I watched a crane stabbed a silver fish, a mullet probably, in its beak and then flew off to feed at the top of a sabal palm.

Midway down the St. Mary's River one of the North Carolinians, who had been drinking a can of beer, exclaimed, "I think I'm going to hurl," and then fulfilled the prophecy.

"I'd like to hurl him is what I'd like to do," exclaimed Paul, loud enough so everyone at our end of the boat could hear.

"Paul," whispered his embarrassed wife.

"I don't care. I may have to use some of my New Jersey rudeness before this trip is over."

Toward the end, after we turned into the blue waters of Cumberland Sound, a pair of dolphins appeared and followed the boat. You saw their triangular dorsal fins and their gray backs and then suddenly their rounded contoured heads, and then they would dive under the waves and resurface somewhere else.

One of the deck hands, a darkly tanned man made of solid muscle, stepped from the cabin to watch the dolphins. After a moment he pointed to a distant pair of enormous concrete bunkers to the north.

"That's where they keep the warheads."

I asked him about a sizeable naval vessel a mile up the Sound, surrounded by floating docks.

"That's the *Canopus*. A submarine tender. That's one Clinton decommissioned."

"I voted for Clinton," said Paul defensively.

The deck hand indicated that he had served on the *Canopus* before the budget cuts.

"What's the fishing like around here?" I asked.

"Sea trout are moving up the rivers to spawn. I caught a couple of them last night on the bridge."

The captain called and the man stepped back into the cabin. We were nearing the dock at the Dungeness Ruins on Cumberland Island. The 200-year-old ruins were not visible from the dock. All you could see was the dock and the jungle. There was no one waiting at the dock, and so we continued on to the Sea Camp visitor's center, which was a large cypress cabin set among enormous live oaks and a thick brush of sawtooth palmettos. Cypress is the ideal wood for cabins because it is naturally oily and resistant to rot.

Paul and Lauren were among the first off the boat. The first people off, Paul had confided, got one of the pushcarts. The pushcarts made it easier to move gear to the Sea Camp campground, half a mile distant. They sat near their pushcarts, pretending not to guard them. No one was permitted to leave until after the orientation lecture by the ranger.

One of the children, a boy with thick Buddy Holly glasses, a lad who reminded me of myself at the age, was solemnly informing a group of girls that they were now in Jurassic Park and that there were dinosaurs everywhere. Just then a red-haired ranger in shorts walked by. His freckled white skin, peeling and burned, seemed not to like the light of the subtropics.

"Is that true, mister?" asked one of the girls.

"What?"

"That there are dinosaurs on Cumberland Island?"

"Well, there are alligators."

"Are they big?"

"Some are. There's a female on Raccoon Key over ten feet."

The little boy beamed.

After a while I walked over to the visitor's center. On the porch was a small outdoor museum. Under glass were fossilized shark teeth, the strange extraterrestrial-looking skull of a loggerhead sea turtle, the big-domed skull of a dolphin, various seashells, a pair of white-tailed deer antlers, miscellaneous mammal vertebrae, shed snake skins, pressed beach wildflowers, bird feathers, a scorpion in a bottle, a baby alligator hide, a stuffed screech owl, and other novelties. It was a sort of pre-Linnean *wunderkammern,* or cabinet of curiosities, and the informality was refreshing. Something was lost, as well as gained, when we began to precisely catalogue and organize nature.

The orientation was held outside because of the size of the group. We were warned about ticks (one young man on the Willow Pond Trail came in with 500 on his person), tick fever, chiggers, Lime disease, scorpions, centipedes, fire ants, poison ivy, poison oak, standing pond water, amoebic dysentery, malaria, rabies, brown bats, rattlesnakes, water moccasins, alligators, barracudas, sharks, sting rays, sea urchins, wild horses, wild pigs, changing tides, sunburn, sun stroke, and so on. The only time the crowd took serious note was when the ranger gave directions to the clothing optional beach. When it was over we were assigned camping spots.

Paul and Lauren led the way. The hard sand trail was lovely, winding through a green tunnel formed by the overhanging branches of ancient live oak trees, all draped with Spanish moss.

When we reached our campsites on the far side of the oak forest—the sound of the surf coming from over the dunes—Paul and Lauren dropped everything and ran off to the beach. I stayed and set up my tent. When I was done I placed my cooler and food inside a chicken-wire box mounted on a wooden post. Before leaving for the beach I stopped to study the world's largest spider web, occupied by a golden orb spider as big as my hand. Trapped in the web was the partly consumed red carcass of what had recently been a green chameleon.

There was a boardwalk over the dune field to the beach. Reaching the steps at the top of the dunes I saw it was a magnificent wild beach running north and south into the hazy distance, the sand as white as field cotton, the cloudless sky one shade less blue than the sea. Once off the hot planks the sand was smooth and firm and warm underfoot. There were already a few people in the water and a few others were having lunch on the beach. Out beyond the breakers the sea was calm and blue, sparkling under the sun. You could see several boats, small fishing rigs and shrimpers and long container ships, sprinkled at random to the horizon. Although the tide was going out, there were a few lazy waves coming in. They came in toward the long beach slowly, gathering weight, and then broke over smoothly in the shallow water. I walked in the water and it was pretty much what you'd expect in November. A cool breeze was blowing steadily from the sea. Otherwise the beach would have been very hot.

As I said, the beach was all I'd hoped for. The cool breeze and warmth and open spaces and friendly people were a natural balm, a soothing medicine, the perfect antidote for urban civilization. Some people have therapists, medication regimes, behaviorists, weekly groups, and twelve-step programs. Others have places like Cumberland.

I walked north, to where the island curved to a point, with no other object than to find a place to lie down and spend the rest of the day doing as little as possible. I spent the afternoon among the dunes sunbathing, reading Bartram on the amazing crystal springs of Florida (the passage that inspired Coleridge's poem "Xanadu"), swimming whenever I became hot, and studying the changing colors of the sea and the way the shadows moved beneath the clouds drifting over the sea.

Lauren and Paul met me late in the afternoon on the beach and invited me to their place for dinner. Paul was a changed man, thoroughly sedated by a few hours on the beach, and I accepted. We cannot always choose our companions, but we can always make the best of it.

Sitting around the campfire that night, our faces more red from the afternoon sun than the fire, scratching our stomachs from a gourmet chicken teriyaki meal prepared by Paul, drinking beer from my cooler, we kept the conversation as casual as possible, saving the serious topics—the existence of UFOs, life after death, poltergeists, the future of the human race—for the next night.

Off in the distance someone with a guitar was singing old Grateful Dead songs.

After an hour of small talk it began to rain, at first gently and then not so gently, and so I retired to my camp. Several minutes after extinguishing the candle, a family of raccoons, a mother and her brood, began scratching insistently around the tent. This went on for a while, and so I finally offered them an apple, and they dragged it off into the night, clucking in religious ecstasy, and did not disturb me again.

As I drifted off into sleep a part of me wanted to run off into the night with them, climb the trees, explore the clearings, and wander the beach under the stars. Animals love the night in ways we humans have forgotten. But with the rain pouring down and the Jovian thunder and lightning I was just as glad to be sleeping peacefully in my nice dry tent.

IV. Islands. No man is an island. The universe is an island. An island is a universe. There are islands on the sun, and the sun is part of an island called the Milky Way. The earth is an island. There are islands where there was once sea, and beneath the sea there are sunken reefs that once were islands. Australia is an island. A desert oasis is an island. An iceberg is an island. A mountaintop is an island. Manhattanites live on an island. There are islands in the middle of crowded cities. You see them in the vacant eyes of people living without love, without faith, without opportunity, estranged from nature and themselves. According to William Blake every grain of sand is an island. Inside a microscopic cell there are islands. The isles of the pancreas produce insulin. Some historians refer to medieval Byzantium as an island. To a carpenter ant, your desktop is an island. When I think of my life, I think of times that were like islands, some like Cyclops and others like Calypso. Ulysses knew about islands. Excalibur rests at the bottom of a lake with an island called Avalon, and that lake is found on the island of England, and near that lake is said to be a stone that reads *Hic iacet Arthurus, rex quondam, rexque futurus* ("Here lies Arthur, who was once king and king will be again"). Shakespeare's last major play was about a shipwreck on an island and is based on what happened to Sir George Somers and his friends at Bermuda. Napoleon was banished to an island south of France. The ship that took men to the moon was launched from an island. Our national parks are islands. Some of our islands are national parks.

I was thinking about all this the next morning, lying on my back in the darkness, waiting for first light. It would be a busy day and I was planning it out carefully. A day well planned is a day well lived.

When the birds began to sing I ate my breakfast of Fig Newtons and put on my daypack and set out for the south end of the island, where I would spend the day exploring. I had the beach to myself, and it was the sort of brilliant red Homeric sunrise one might recall ages hence, sitting in a nursing home, reflecting on the high points of the journey.

All across the beach were scattered shells. Some were as small as your fingernail, others as big as your head. There were knobbed whelks, dogwinkles, periwinkles, augers, sundials, olives, limpets, scallops, cockles, coquinas, angel wings, and the less exotic clams and mussels. My favorite was the miniature half-inch auger, which resembled the detached horn of a three-inch rhinoceros. From the aperture each shell swirled in a tight logarithmic spiral from right to left in ever-narrowing circles to a sharp point. They were camouflage-colored either lemon yellow or light sandy brown. The soft, dead inhabitants had formerly made their living drilling into the shells of other gastropods and devouring the contents, or feasting on defenseless sea worms. Scattered among the treasury of shells were the remnants of hermit crabs, ghost crabs, fiddler crabs, horseshoe crabs, starfish, squid, sea cucumbers, sponges, sea fans, whip and star corals, sundry fish, and, in one case, a deceased seagull. After an hour at the high-tide wrack, my pack was a bit heavier and smelled of the sea.

The sun was well up from the sea now and I was sweating freely under the T-shirt I soon pulled off.

Two miles down the beach there was a trail to the west, and I followed it toward the largest dunes on the island. There were tracks everywhere: the sharply cloven tracks of white-tailed deer, sunken in soft places to the dew claws; the massive imprints of slow-plodding wild horses; the delicate humanlike hands of raccoons. Everything left its autograph here.

The dunes were covered with live oaks and cabbage palms, and some of the palms were surprisingly tall. The live oaks had all been shaped and sculpted by the sea winds, much like trees at timberline. Facing the sea, the branches were shortened, but on the inland side the branches extended normally. The elevation of the dunes provided a nice view of the distant sea, extending blue and flat beyond the green of the brush forest, and the cool breeze coming in from the sea grounded the bugs I knew would be a problem on the other side of the dunes.

Back on the trail I soon caught sight of Cumberland's most famous historical site.

The Dungeness Mansion, built by General Nathaniel Greene in 1783, was like something from a William Faulkner novel. It was a ruined four-story mansion of brick and mortar, a once busy country residence that now consisted of partially collapsed walls, woodless floors, empty windows, and bat-infested chimneys. The shingled roof had been blown off long ago by a hurricane. It was the sort of ruined place elegiac poets of the Thomas Gray school love. I tried to picture it in former days—the great parties with whale oil lanterns out on the lawn and linen-covered tables laid with venison and wild boar and sea bass, the silver platters of cheeses and fruits and cakes, the jugs of Madeira wine and kegs of Carolina beer. There were dances at Dungeness, and weddings, and horse races with fine stock whose descendants now live like the Snopses in the swamps. I pictured General Greene sitting outside in a hammock reading just-delivered, month-old letters from his friends Washington and Jefferson up north in Virginia, or perhaps the latest book on the vast unknown interior of Africa by Mungo Park or James Bruce, and I marveled at how much the world has changed in two centuries.

Out back of the mansion was a graveyard with antique faded headstones covered with green moss and fallen oak leaves and the glistening paths of garden snails. The inscriptions told of a loving wife, a Revolutionary war hero, a young daughter taken by God too soon, and others forgotten by time. I thought of John Muir sleeping in the graveyard up the coast at Savannah on his thousand-mile walk to the Gulf. The cemetery was, Muir wrote, the "ideal place" for the "penniless wanderer" to sleep, for naturalists, unlike the rest of the human race, are not afraid of ghosts.

As I left Dungeness Ruins there were wild turkeys strutting about the grounds, and it made a romantic picture—the gutted shell of the once great colonial house, the overgrown vegetable and flower gardens, the brick patios and promenades, the stately planted magnolias with bright green leaves, the royal palms imported from the Caribbean, the Spanish moss hanging from everything.

It was, someone said back at Sea Camp, an excellent place for a picnic.

Beyond Dungeness were the Indian middens, each pile of accumulated oyster shells representing centuries of Indian feasts. Here the first Americans had shelled oysters for 3,000 years. I tried to imagine what life was like on Cumberland before the Spanish and French and British, before the slave ships and the Dust Bowl days and the Trinity site. I thought about what Mark Twain said: "It was wonderful to discover America, but it would have been more wonderful to miss it."

Farther back was the salt marsh and a deer trail out to the far southwestern point of the island, where I spent two hours waving off mosquitoes and digging among the old dredge spoils for fossilized shark teeth, ray plates, sea drum teeth, and turtle plates. Most of the dredged fossils, according to the ranger at the orientation talk, were of Pliocene age, from 1.8 to 5 million years old. I had absolutely no luck at all, and could only marvel at the hundreds of fiddler crabs scurrying around the place in vast comical herds.

It was now afternoon, and so I returned to the eastern beach and sat down on the edge of an extensive marshland for lunch. There was a mosquito hatch ongoing in the marshes, but the sea breeze kept them from me, and the view of perhaps ten thousand swallows diving and feeding among the swarm was truly amazing. I took several photographs here, because I knew no one would believe me when I later reported there were ten thousand swallows. Throughout the lunch hour I was serenaded by dozens of frogs, but saw only one.

The southeastern tip of the island, with its view across the mouth of the St. Mary's River into Florida, proved an irresistible attraction, and among its jetties and dunes I spent the rest of the day. Here, on the protected side of the jetty I shed my clothes and swam in the clear warm lagoon as egrets and herons fished in the shallows. I probed among the rocks of the jetty for a time, examining trapped squid, crabs, starfish, shrimp, jellyfish, sea cucumbers, fish fry, and other fauna, and left after I saw what appeared to be a scorpion fish hiding with its venomous barbs in a pool where I'd almost stepped.

Following dinner that night, Lauren, Paul, and I sat around the campfire and solved all the riddles, mysteries, and lingering questions of human existence. Something about a campfire inspires the human spirit to such endeavors. Lauren believed the chief obstacle to human progress was the manner in which we treat children. So long as they are considered property, she insisted, the blights of the human condition would persist. In her practice she had dealt with this issue for twenty years, and spoke with the voice of experience. I asked her about Plato's suggestion in *The Republic* that children be raised by professionally trained people, rather than by whatever parents nature provides, and she recalled that this idea had been tried on some kibbutzes in Israel and in the old Soviet Union and hadn't worked very well. On the nature of the revolution we agreed. The details were left for others to work out.

Sometime after midnight the philosophers retired, and a short time later the raccoons, accompanied by curious armadillos, arrived.

v. The next day I spent walking to the far north end of the island. On the wide empty beach I felt variously like Robinson Crusoe, Gilligan, Prospero, the first man, the last man. The grueling trek at other times brought back memories of Parris Island, twenty years earlier, and the long death marches under the hot southern sun with me carrying the platoon colors. In the Willow Ponds, the Sweetwater Ponds, and Lake Whitney, I saw many birds, especially wading birds, but no alligators, otters, ospreys, wandering Florida panthers, or red wolves. The only excitement came just before lunch, when I snuck up on two white-tailed deer bucks drinking from a pool of stagnant water and startled them at a distance of about twenty feet by saying hello. I turned back at the north end of the island—ahead was an ominous swarm of mosquitoes and sand fleas rising from the waters of Christmas Creek.

After several hours of walking south there was a human form in the distance, and I waved and soon met a ranger on patrol. His name was Brian and he was from Utah, had a pregnant wife and two children back in St. Mary's, and was praying for a transfer to Zion National Park, which he said was the most beautiful place on earth. I asked him about local wildlife, and he said the most interesting animals were the Caribbean manatees that had taken up residence in the waters near the Gilman Paper Company, attracted by the warm water from the discharge pumps. They now lived around Cumberland year-round, and the company was working closely with federal biologists to ensure their safety. He said it was a good example of private-public cooperation, and I couldn't disagree. I asked him what the biggest management problems were on the island, and he said Greyfield Inn, a private inholding, and what to do with Plum Orchard Mansion, the old Andrew Carnegie place. We shook hands, and I bid him well on the reconnaissance.

As I returned to Sea Camp five miles later there was a small band of wild horses feeding quietly among the sea grasses. There were five of them: a gray stallion, three paint mares that appeared to be related, and a six-month-old gray foal. The stallion was a lean solid animal, always alert, flaring his nostrils into the breeze and turning his ears. On his back and neck were a constellation of white scars and partially healed bite marks.

It is a tough life, that of a stallion.

I got within thirty feet of them, and went no closer. The mares had no wounds and showed considerably more body fat than the stallion. The foal was happy and playful as are all young animals. I studied their feet, having shod my share of horses in my youth, and saw the sort of long-toed, heel-shattered, sand-cracked hooves that are a farrier's nightmare. The essence of a horse's health, and value, are in its feet.

It wasn't long before a dirty white stallion and a second herd of mares came trotting up a deer trail. Even as I watched, the new arrivals caught sight of the smaller band of horses at my side. The dirty white stallion assumed a tense, rigid position and whinnied a challenge. His mares stopped behind him. He was a big powerful animal, with more weight on him than the gray.

From beside me came the response, and at this point I climbed a dune to remove myself from the field of battle.

Indignant snorts and whinnies went back and forth. Much striking of the ground with front hooves and thrashing of heads.

The contest began with a thundering gallop to the water's edge, the dirty white intruder pursuing the gray stallion. When they reached the water the two horses stopped. Gulls and terns and pelicans scattered in every direction. The field of conflict belonged to the stallions. They stood perfectly still for a long moment. The tension steadily built.

Suddenly the fight began, and it was strictly a street brawl, with no rules, no time-outs, no ice packs waiting in the corner.

In the first confrontation the stallions reared up on hind feet and lashed with sharp front hooves. Each landed at least one painful blow in the initial exchange. When the fisticuffs were over the score was roughly even. After that the horses took turns at "finding the jugular." When they tired of that sport, both necks running red with blood, they played "try to castrate your opponent." This dangerous maneuver was attempted with teeth and hooves and involved undertaking defense and offense simultaneously. The heat of the engagement was now intense, both horses covered with blood and sweat. The gray was more nimble than the white and delivered several well-aimed kicks near the groin of the white. Just when it seemed the gray might gain the advantage, the white stallion pivoted on his front feet and landed a devastating blow to the most sensitive area of his opponent. The effect was immediate. The gray walked a few steps and collapsed as if shot. From that position, head down and legs tucked in under the body, the injured gray did not, could not, move.

Through all this the mares steadily fed, showing little interest in the outcome.

The victor walked over and stood beside his vanquished opponent as rigidly as he had in the earlier invitation to battle. The issue of who would keep the harem in question appeared to have been settled.

The little foal watched intently as his father lay defeated, absorbing another lesson in the world of adulthood. He alone among the equine spectators seemed affected by the scene.

The white stallion, snorting victory, then trotted over to claim his prize, the three mares and the bewildered foal, which he briskly escorted over the dunes to his waiting band of mares and foals.

But it was not over, not yet.

The dazed opponent shook the stars from his head. The sight of his mares and foal being led away roused his deepest instincts. He rose to his feet. Overhead the clouds were just then turning the color of watermelon rind. The whole beach was washed in red light. Ignoring evident agony, the gray cantered stiffly toward the white, vocalizing with a sound that could best be described as a roar.

The white stallion turned to face him. He snorted some sort of message to his mares and then trotted back to the open beach where there would be more room to move.

Another battle ensued, this one bloodier than the first but three times slower. It was like a prizefight in the fifteenth round, after the heavyweight boxers are exhausted and trying to remain on their feet until the bell sounds and the score is tallied and read by the judges. Only here there was no bell, no referees, no attending managers, promoters, physicians. This was nature in the raw.

On and on it went, up and down the beach. A run, then a tangle, then another run. Over and over. An irresistible force and an immovable object. A fight, it would seem, to the death.

Twilight descending, the clouds showing the last ruddiness on their bellies.

Suddenly all seven of the mares that had come to the party with the dirty white stallion looked up simultaneously and trotted as if responding to a distant call down the deer trail toward the swamp. The three foals in that group followed. The mares and foal of the gray remained behind in the sea grass pasture, milling about in confusion. To whom did they belong now? The white stallion broke off from savaging the gray in the neck long enough to whinny for his mares to stay. They did not heed his call. He whinnied a second time with the same result. The mares had apparently had enough of the spectacle, and were leaving. He hurried after them.

That, then, was the outcome: each stallion would keep his respective harem.

It seemed such a waste, but aggression is the force that drives nature and evolution, that separates the durable from the decrepit, the decisive from the indecisive, the destined from the doomed.

Suddenly it was nearly dark. The first star twinkled between the pale clouds.

Low tide had reached its ebb. The waves began inching back toward the high-tide wrack of last night.

I looked around and there was no one else on the beach. Everyone was back at Sea Camp preparing for tomorrow. It was just me and the sand and the sea. I sat on the dune, my back to the land, my eyes toward the sea, and chewed on the stem of a sea oat. The sand was warmer than the air, and the sea was warmer than both. I lingered, thinking about nothing, watching the sea under the stars. Eventually a rainstorm drifted slowly out to sea from the north Florida coast and I watched the lightning flash in the hollows of the clouds, illuminating amphitheaters and antechambers of darkness, and every so often the lightning reached down and touched the sea, and I never heard anything from this storm but distant thunder.

VI. Early the next morning I was awakened by the pounding surf. The wind had come up during the night, and the waves were crashing on the beach. With my ear against the sleeping pad I could hear the concussion of each swell. For a long time I lay in the dark listening to the sea. At five o'clock I lit the candle lantern and waited for the tent to warm. After several minutes the space was comfortable, and so I made a pillow of the sweater and read the last chapter of Bartram by candlelight. The chapter was just a few pages long and briefly described Bartram's return to Philadelphia after his expedition to the South. While passing through Savannah he had observed pack horses and wagons loaded with passenger pigeons. The previous night the local residents had taken pine-resin torches into the woods. Blinded and startled by the light, the "multitudinous" wintering flocks had dropped from the branches to the ground, where they had been beaten to death.

A week after Christmas, in deep snow and cold, the son of pioneering botanist John Bartram arrived at his father's house on the banks of the Schuylkill River.

There followed in the book an essay about the Creeks, Cherokees, and Choctaws of the American Southeast. William Bartram observed that "here the people are all on an equality, as to the possession and enjoyments of the common necessaries and conveniences of life." There was a "venerable senate" or council among each of the tribes, over which a chief presided. The chief was not born into the office, as with King George III of England, but, rather, earned it and was elected to it, as with the democracies of ancient Greece and Rome. Privileged classes were anathema in a society based on hard work and achievement. Among the "aborigines" there was less emphasis placed on private property than among those of European descent, but nevertheless each family was entitled to all the crops it had personally grown, while still depositing a portion in the communal area, from which less fortunate families could draw allotments. It was considered a disgrace and bad luck among the Indians not to help the poor.

Item: Bartram reported that the southeastern American tribes had invented a novel game they called "football," which was their "favourite, manly diversion." Football was played on "an extensive level plain" on which the players seized and carried the ball from the opposite party down the field and tried to hurl it "midway between two high pillars, which are the goals."

Item: Marriage was entered into "only for a year's time." Each year the contract between a man and a woman was renewed. Polygamy was permitted, and every man took as many wives as he could support, with the understanding that the first was "queen, and the others her handmaids and associates." After a marriage had been ended by either party, "the father [was] obliged to contribute towards [his children's] maintenance during their minority."

Above all, Bartram emphasized, the frontier southeast of his country was by no means a wilderness, but was the ancient habitation of populous nations that had built highways, canals, artificial lakes, pyramids, ceremonial mounds, walled cities, fortresses, cemeteries, and planted fields and gardens.

So concluded the Quaker Bartram.

At five-thirty I heard an unusual birdsong and put on my jeans and shirt and stepped from the tent. The sand and twigs and leaves were wet under my toes. Everything was wet. The air was heavy with the scents of the forest and the sea. Somewhere the bird twittered again. A local naturalist could name the species for you, perhaps even provide the Latin binomial. I cannot. I can only tell you the lovely melody was composed of seven notes. The lyric quickly dropped three notes and then went down four, but not all at once. It was like a stream that slides down a series of falls, each of slightly different height. Overhead there were still stars between the boughs of the trees. The air was cold and damp and still in the forest, and I walked quickly down the path. My eyes were accustomed to the shadows, and so I did not need the flashlight. No one was up yet. Sea Camp was uniformly still, but for the rumble of the surf.

Out on the wooden boardwalk the chill was suddenly gone and I could feel the warmth of the sea. It was like the warmth of a lover across the bed—a gentle heat that holds you near. The Gulf Stream carries with it a heat from far away.

The sky to the east held the faintest gray. All else remained black-

est night: stars, constellations, nebulae, galaxies. To the north was
the Big Dipper. To the west my old friend Orion held last watch. The
planet Mercury glistened like a spilled drop of plumber's solder on
the eastern horizon. A desolate world named for a dead god, forever
too close to the sun. Burned on one side and frozen on the other.
Similar to Milton's view of the afterlife, or travel brochures for Ice-
land.

The waves boomed and crashed rhythmically in three- and four-
foot swells. A steady wind blew from offshore. If you watched the
gray it did not appear to change, but if you looked away for a moment and then looked back you could detect the gray had lightened
a shade. It was like watching someone's spirits change very slowly as
you try to cheer them up.

As I walked along the dunes a ghost crab darted down its hole. It
entered backward, rear end first, claws last. There it would rest.
Anything that tried to roust it would be pinched.

Yes, the long nght was ending. The great day was beginning.

I walked up the beach into the wind, searching for the tracks of
the horses, but they were gone. The sea had washed them away. Because of the wind I walked over a dune topped with sea oats. Out of
the wind it was not so bad. When I looked back over the dune a bit
later I was treated to a wonderful sight. The eastern horizon was
glowing with all the hope that ever attended a birth in this world.
The sky was clear except for one small assemblage of clouds, coin-
cidentally floating above the exact point where the sun would rise.
Even as I watched, the distant cloud deck caught the first light. The
warm colors were like those my son brought with him from the
womb.

Out of the birth canal, into the world.

Then the sun, loving mother of nine planets, too bright for any
but the blind to look at.

Shortly after the sun cleared the water a flock of sea gulls flew by,
searching for treasures left by the tide. Then followed the terns and
pelicans.

Lauren and Paul suddenly appeared out of nowhere and asked me to take their picture. I remarked that they both looked ten years younger than when I first met them three days earlier, a statement that had the virtue of being true. They both loved to hear that, and after I took several photographs and wrote their address in my notebook and promised to mail them a nice print, they hurried off to finish packing.

After a while, I followed the boardwalk back toward camp and then at the last minute cut south along the dunes, found a place out of the wind, and laid down. I was not ready to leave the sea just yet. Who ever is? As I stretched out I heard the thump of deer. I never saw them, but I heard them thumping away. They must have been feeding on the lee side of the dune.

I stayed there on the white sand just this side of the dark wind-shaped trees for quite some time, soaking up the sun. If Cumberland Island were a glimpse of the future in parks, I was relieved. Rarely had I had such a fine experience in a park—no annoying cars, a manageable number of park visitors, plenty of solitude. For once people were compelled to leave the roads behind and use their legs and really get to know one small place well, rather than to drive frantically all over the country and actually see very little. For such an experience in Yellowstone or Yosemite I would gladly wait for a permit. When that day inevitably comes to the parks out West—which are islands as much as Cumberland—I will be the first to welcome it.

Finally the ferry boat horn sounded, telling everyone that the boat had arrived and would be departing shortly for the mainland. I left the island that day, but resolved to never leave it behind in my thoughts. In the end Cumberland, like so many of our finest parks, is too large to be folded in a map, captured in a photograph, or compressed into an essay. It is a place where the tides quietly rise into the brackish marshes and nourish the shrimp larvae, where the deer mice gather fallen acorns and the bobcats watch with eyes like polished topaz, where the river otters play in the freshwater lakes and the king snakes climb the mossy live oaks looking for treats, where the peregrine falcons rest on their migrations each September and the loggerhead sea turtles come to lay their eggs every summer. It is a place where the sun will forever rise on wild beaches that will never know the plague of mechanized development. It is a place to carry deep inside and hold close whenever you feel yourself in turmoil, and instantly be at peace.

II.

A society is a group of reasonable beings in common agreement as to the objects of their love.

St. Augustine, *City of God*

Much of the writing in this year's nature annual is concerned with wild places like Cumberland Island—how best to protect them, confer respect, celebrate beauty. Ann Zwinger takes us to one of the most heavily used western parks—Grand Canyon—as she and her daughter Susan descend on foot into the mile-deep abyss. They choose the ideal season: midwinter. Gone are the hoards of people, the lengthy strings of pack mules, the insufferable heat that can turn the journey into an ordeal at other times of the year. At the bottom of the desert canyon mother and daughter are surprised to find magnificent cottonwoods still holding golden autumnal leaves, yellow brittlebush blossoming as if it were spring, and water ouzels plying their trade as energetically as in midsummer. Here is a natural Eden, a permanent refuge, a protected sanctuary for the beleaguered human spirit. Upon reaching the snowy rim of the canyon days later, Zwinger is treated to an epiphany. She looks out over the gulf of canyons, ridges, amphitheaters, buttes, and mesas and sees "only a final stillness, only a beckoning, deepening cold, an absence, beyond which there is no more beyond."

Rick Bass has made a vocation of traveling to the wildest places in North America and elsewhere—Nepal, Japan, Romania. Of all those places, the one he holds closest to heart is Yaak, his home valley in northwestern Montana. For years, Bass has labored tirelessly to include parts of the Yaak in the Montana wilderness bill, a piece of legislation that is still pending at this writing. For him the beautiful, wild Yaak Valley is home, and such political battles are a necessary but difficult responsibility of good citizenship: "Many of us [in Yaak] are hermits, or shy, or reclusive because we simply live here for the solitude. Engagement in political struggles is, for many, not a healthy choice." And yet Bass and others, in Yaak and elsewhere, rise to meet the battle and charge into the breach, realizing that if they do not, no one will, that their futures are inextricably intertwined with the biota that sustain them and their children.

Other writers in this volume concerned with wild nature include Montanan Susan Ewing, who floats down the Snake River in Hells Canyon on the border of Oregon and Idaho; Alaskan Carolyn Kremers, who journeys into the snowy outback of the forty-ninth state with one of the last fur-trappers; and Minnesotan Gretchen Legler, who takes us on a duck-hunting trip with (of all people) her ex-husband. Legler admits to ambivalence with respect to the wild places of the earth and the spirit:

> Can I call this love? Can I say that I love the swimming greenheads in Lake of the Isles, when every fall I make an adventure out of killing them? Does killing have anything to do with love? What kind of language allows this paradox? . . . What does it mean, that in my body, helping to keep me alive, to make me joyful, to share joy with people I love, is the breast of a greenhead mallard that I shot down on a cool autumn day and scooped from the cold water with my hand?

Legler expresses perfectly the mystery and allure of these natural realms where our deepest instincts openly conflict with our highest impulses. That, indeed, is the essence of the wilderness, a place where the oldest, and the newest, elements of the human experience can creatively mingle.

The tradition of writing about pastoral nature is an equally distinguished one in American literature. It is often said to originate with the essays of Thomas Jefferson, who extolled the values of country living in much the same manner as the Greek and Roman writers who were his philosophical mentors. Jefferson was known to spend whole days personally planting and working in his extensive north Virginia gardens. He once observed that all he really needed for personal happiness was a vegetable and fruit garden, a cottage, and a regular supply of books (he also mentioned something about fresh ham steaks and imported French wine). In this volume, we have a number of writers who are concerned not with wild nature— the Valhalla of the northern Rockies, the vast wind-blown demesne of the Alaskan wolf, the otherworldly sculpted beauty of the Grand Canyon—but with the well-trod woods of home, the humanized nature where the largest predator is a red fox, the deer feed as much on orchard apples as on wild berries, and the local squirrels and rabbits have been given human names.

Along these lines, Don Schueler, in his book *A Handmade Wilderness: Untaming the Land*, tells the story of how in 1968 he and his companion Willie Brown bought eighty acres of logged-over forest in the sandhills of southern Mississippi:

> The dream that Willie and I had was to own land in the country. But not just any land. Not, for example, some cute little cabin in a resort development, and most definitely not the sort of "secluded" three-acre lot in the wilds of exurbia that is presently gobbling up even more of rural America than suburban sprawl itself. In its specialized way, our dream was more ambitious than that. . . . What we needed, obviously, was a pretty sizable chunk of countryside; enough space so we could be in touch with the natural world without moving it out when we moved in.

Over the years, the two men helped the scarred land to heal itself, restoring a nearly complete "handmade" ecosystem with patient and loving care. Along the way they had to face a cast of rural neighbors straight from a William Faulkner novel (with names like Hobit Bodner and Roddy Ray Janier), life without electricity and plumbing, and the surprising power of Hurricane Camille (which destroyed their first house). Eventually, Willie Brown died and Don Schueler, devastated by the loss, donated "The Place"—by then over 200 acres—to The Nature Conservancy as the Willie Farrel Brown Nature Reserve, a unique protected estate of live oaks and magnolia trees, white-tailed deer and gopher tortoises, alligators and armadillos, wild honeysuckle and rare bog pitcher plants.

In a similar vein, John Hildebrand, in his essay "Fences," writes about life in rural Wisconsin, near the town of Eau Claire where he teaches college. He spends the day on his farm removing old fences:

> A farm with a lot of fences is one that recognizes different kinds of land and different possibilities for them. A fence announces our designs upon the landscape; it imposes limits. Before fence laws were enacted in the last century, farmers fenced their crops to keep them from being trampled by horses and cows and hogs. Cowboys may have sung "Don't Fence Me In," but certainly not anybody who had corn or wheat in the ground.

One is here reminded of Robert Frost's poem "Mending Wall" in which the poet states that "Something there is [in nature] that doesn't love a wall." Walls and fences are humankind's way of dividing nature along property lines—a practical necessity to the farmer, but an artifical intrusion that nature often willfully ignores. Hildebrand's removal of the fence is an acknowledgment that such boundaries can have as many disadvantages as advantages.

Another midwesterner—Scott Russell Sanders—writes of his life in the fertile corn and cattle country of Bloomington, Indiana. Sanders's essay here concerns his relationship to his father, and to the original family home in Ohio. After thirty years of separation, he returns to the ancestral farm and is shocked at the change:

> At the bottom of a slope where the creek used to run, I came to an expanse of gray stumps and withered grass. It was a bay of the reservoir from which the water had retreated, the level drawn down by engineers or drought. I stood at the edge of this desolate ground, willing it back to life, trying to recall the woods where my father had

taught me the names of trees. No green shoots rose. I walked out among the stumps. The grass crackled under my boots, breath rasped in my throat, but otherwise the world was silent.

Like Sanders, I spent my childhood in rural Ohio—seventeen years of catching garter snakes, collecting fossils, and preserving woodland flowers in plant presses. I've returned just once to view the changes wrought on my native country by mechanized development. These places tell us, with a visual power greater than mere words, that we must save those areas not yet despoiled by industrial civilization, or risk losing them forever.

What all these essays about nature—whether wild or pastoral—have in common is love for the land. Nature for these writers provides comfort in times of grief, peace in the midst of turmoil, an alternative form of companionship in seasons of solitude, invigoration when fatigued, inspiration and guidance when lost, and understanding when faced with some riddle, paradox, or injustice. As a group of thinkers, these writers have found, as did the Stoics two thousand years ago when darkness began to fall on Rome, that—in disjointed times of violence and uncertainty—nature provides the "way" to enlightenment, to freedom from that which encumbers us, to a deeper understanding of the human condition, and to a fuller capacity for creativity and happiness.

III.

Man is not rational. There is intelligence only in what encompasses him.
Heraclitus

Never before has there been a greater need for the healing embrace of nature. Walk down any city street and you will see the empty faces of those living without hope, faith, or opportunity, estranged from nature and themselves. Everywhere people increase their belongings, but find themselves poor in spirit. We have mapped galactic clusters ten billion light-years from earth and catalogued the fine particles that comprise our physical forms, but no one can publish even the most rudimentary atlas to human consciousness. Our political institutions decay, crime fills our streets, and families struggle along without the support of traditional systems of belief. We have reached the point where the average adult in the United States now watches over twenty hours of television each week, time once spent reading, physically exercising, gardening, worshipping, and communing outdoors with nature. People have allowed their lives to be controlled and subverted in this manner because they have been presented with no alternative to the reality placed before them. The authors in this book are attempting to show people a different way.

Nature is a gospel without dogma, a scripture without words, a creed without colleges or cathedrals. It is not a religion, for there is nothing so unreligious as nature in the raw. It offers only refuge and restoration, eternal landscapes that are the natural abode of the spirit. In the end, the ancient thinkers in the mountains of Tibet and the deserts of Israel were right—the most important task in life is the care of your soul. All else is built on that foundation. The only way to save that most precious possession is through knowledge, and the best way to acquire knowledge is through the direct experience of nature. Knowledge is not, as Socrates believed, entirely the same as virtue, nor is it wholly synonymous with power, as Sun-Tzu espoused. Knowledge is most fundamentally a pathway to freedom, especially from suffering.

Camus stated that "One of the only coherent philosophical positions is revolt." In this case, the revolution begins with the simple act of walking outside and down the street toward the nearest woods.

J.A.M.

AMERICAN

NATURE

WRITING

1997

Gretchen Legler

Gooseberry Marsh

from *All the Powerful Invisible Things:
A Sportswoman's Notebook*

This fall on Gooseberry Marsh the weather is warm and the water is high. As Craig and I load the canoe on the grassy shore of the marsh, the sky is turning from rosy-gold to gray-blue. The blackbirds that make their homes in the reeds are singing by the hundreds, a loud, high, rocks-in-a-bucket screeching. Above us, lines of geese cross the lightening sky.

This is the first fall of our not living with each other, of living apart: Craig in the big house, me in a small apartment. But we decided to hunt together anyway, hanging onto this sure thing, hunting at Gooseberry Marsh, this thing we have shared for so many years.

We try in a polite and partly exhausted way to pretend that nothing is different, that we still love each other, but something subtle has shifted beneath us. It is more than the awkward and uneasy rearranging of our lives. In preparing for this trip, I bought *our* supplies with *my* money and brought the food to *Craig's* house. When we get *home* from hunting I will unpack *our* decoys and *our* coolers full of wet birds, do *my* laundry, and then I will leave for *my* apartment. We both feel embarrassed and sad when we catch ourselves saying, "Next time we should wear waders," for we both know there probably will be no next time.

But something more has changed. It is hard for me now even to reach out to hold his hand. The intimacy we had, the warm space between our bodies, has stretched so that it feels like nothing. Between us now is only this coolness, as we stand so close together on the shore of the marsh.

Even with the high water this year, we have to pull our canoe through the faint, watery channel between the forest of reeds that separates the two parts of the marsh. We both lean forward, grasp bunches of reeds in our fists and on three we pull.

"One, two, three, pull," I call. "One, two, three, pull." We inch along. This is maddening. I can't steer the bow. Because Craig is pulling so hard in the stern and not watching, the canoe gets jammed nose first in the reeds. We have to back out and start over. I twist around in my seat in the bow and glare at Craig.

"Don't pull unless I say so," I say.

"Just shut up and do it," he says, wearily, coldly. "This isn't a big deal."

A sourness rises up in me. The nape of my neck bristles. He has never said anything like this to me. Ever. He has hardly raised his voice to me in seven years, not even in the midst of my most dangerous rages. I am so startled I fall silent. As we move out of the reeds into the pond again, I say quietly, "You were a jerk. You should apologize."

"Okay," he says mockingly. "I'm sorry I hurt your feelings."

On the far end of the pond we see frightened mallards and teal rise up, quacking. We know they will come back later. The sky around us now is a faint pink. The day is fast coming on. We open the green canvas packs in the middle of the canoe and one by one unravel the lead weights and string from around the necks of our plastic mallards and our plastic bluebills, placing the decoys carefully in a configuration we think will draw ducks close enough to shoot— one long line to the right of the place where we will hide in the reeds, a bunch to the left, and sets of three and four scattered about. I reach into the pocket of my canvas hunting jacket to feel the hard, cold wood of my duck call. It has always been my job to do the calling.

After our decoys are set and we have driven the canoe into the reeds, pulled reeds down over us, stretched a camouflage tarp over us, we wait. We hear sharp echoes from hunters shooting far off on other ponds. The first ducks to come to us are teal. They are small and tan, only as big as a grown man's fist. They land on the water and we can see by the tinge of powdery blue on their wings that they are blue-winged teal. We have set some ethical guidelines to stick to, as we have every year. We will shoot no hens, and no birds sitting on the water. We don't shoot the teal on the water, but I rise up to scare them into flight so that we can take a shot. We miss.

The next birds are mallards and we shoot a hen. She falls into the water and flaps around, dipping her head in and out of the water, slapping her wings. Then she sits up, confused and frightened, and paddles toward the reeds. We know that if she gets into the reeds we will never find her again, that she will go in there and die, probably be eaten by a fox or a weasel, or, eventually, by the marsh itself. But I will still see our shooting her as a waste. My heart cramps up as we follow this bird in our canoe, paddling fast, trying to mark where she entered the reeds. We look for her for nearly an hour, straining our eyes for curls of soft breast feathers on the water among the reed stems. I engage in this search with a kind of desperation. But she is gone.

"If it's still alive, it'll come out," Craig says. He is impatient to get back to our blind. While we have been looking, another flock flew over and flared off, seeing us plainly in the water.

I feel defeated and sad. We paddle back to our spot in the reeds, drive our canoe into the grass, pull the long reeds over us to hide again and wait. Half an hour passes. The sun is out now and I am sweating in all the wool and cotton underneath my canvas hunting jacket. I doze off. I am bored. I take my duck call out of my pocket and practice making quacking noises.

Quack Quack Quack

Craig rolls his eyes. "Stop it. You might scare them away."

I throw the call to him at the other end of the canoe. "You do it then," I say, stuffing my hands back in the deep pockets of my coat.

The next birds to come over are bluebills, and I shoot one as it is flying away over my right shoulder. The momentum of its flight carries it into the reeds behind me. Again we spend forty-five minutes looking for the bird. We don't find the bluebill either. I want to keep looking. I insist we try again. Craig says, "We'll never find it. Give it up."

The next birds to come in are wood ducks, mostly males. We shoot at them just as they have set their wings and two fall in a mess of feathers and shot, the pellets dropping like hail on the water. We paddle out to pick them up. One is breast-down in the water and when I reach down with my bare hand and pull it up by the neck, I gasp. Its breast has been shot away. I shot away its breast. The white feathers are laid wide open, dark red breast meat split open, gaping, the heart smashed, the beak smashed, the head crushed. I swallow down something nasty rising in my throat. We pick up the other wood duck and head back into the reeds. I hold the broken wood duck on my lap. What is left of its blood is soaking through my tan pants onto my long underwear. The warm heavy body lies across my knee. I am stroking the bird's elaborate, feathery purple and orange and white crest, letting tears come up to the surface and roll down my wind-chapped face.

Craig says, "Let's get the camouflage back on the boat, and then you can play."

"Play?" I ask him. At this moment I hate him fiercely. I vow that I will never hunt with him again. I wonder why I ever did. Why I married him, stayed with him. Why I hunt at all. "I'm not playing," I whisper hoarsely. Later, after we have been quiet for a time, I say to him, "Maybe you want to hunt with a man, someone who doesn't cry." He doesn't answer me.

Still later, when we are cleaning the ducks onshore and I reach my hand into the cavity of the ravaged wood duck, scraping my hand on the broken bones such that I bleed, I ask him, "What would a man hunter do about this bird? Would he cry?"

Craig says, "No, he would throw it away." And there is a hardness in what he has said, so that I barely recognize his voice.

After the ducks are emptied of their hearts and livers and green, reeking, grass-filled crops, we line them up as before on the banks of the marsh and sprinkle cornmeal on them, in front of them, beside them, behind them. This time I complete the ritual with a sick resignation, as if there is nothing now that I can say or do that will make amends for this—for this hunting gone all wrong, for this hunting when the love between us has gone all wrong.

There is nothing I can do for this now, except take this wood duck home, save its skin, and give the lovely feathers to my father, who will make beautiful dry flies out of them to catch trout with in Montana. I will salvage what breast meat I can from this wreckage and make a soup or a stew; something good to eat, something hot and rich to share with my friends, or to eat alone.

Hunting with Craig has never been like this. My heart aches and I am afraid. I hate what we have done this year. It feels like murder. In the beginning, when Craig and I were first in love, everything was different. I wonder if I will ever hunt again. I wonder if I can make sense of what has happened here. I think now that hunting for us has everything to do with love; with the way we feel about ourselves and each other. The heaviness or lightness of our hearts, our smallness or our generosity, shows in the way we hunt; in the way we treat the bluebills and mallards and teal that we shoot and eat; in the way we treat each other. I want to correct this imbalance between Craig and me and inside myself. I want to go on hunting, but not this way.

Part of what hunting meant for us, when we were together, was feasting. It wasn't the shooting that ever mattered, but what we did with this food we gathered: how we prepared the ducks to eat, how we shared them with friends, how we raised our glasses before we ate, at a long table lit by candles, covered with a lacy white cloth, and thanked the ducks for their lives. Several times a year, at Easter, at Thanksgiving and at Christmas, Craig and I prepared banquets for our friends. Nearly everything we cooked for our feasts was from our garden, or collected from the woods, or killed by us. This, I think now, was why I hunted and why I still want to. Because I want this kind of intimate relationship with the food I eat.

There were some things—flour, sugar, oranges, walnuts, chutney—that Craig and I served at our feasts that we could not grow or collect ourselves. For these items I would shop at our local grocery store. To get to the checkout counter in the store, I usually walked down the meat aisle. There was hardly ever a whole animal for sale, only parts. There were double-breasted cut-up fryers with giblets. Three-legged fryers and the budget packs—two split breasts with backs, two wings, two legs, two giblets, and two necks. There were boneless, skinless thighs; packages of only drumsticks; plastic containers of livers. There were breaded, skinless, boneless breasts in a thin box—microwavable, nintey-five percent fat free, shrink wrapped, "all natural" and farm fresh. The meat cases were cool, so cool I could hardly smell the meat, only a sanitary wateryness. The smell was different from the smell of wet ducks and blood in the bottom of our canoe. The smell was different from the smell of the warm gut-filled cavity I reached my hand into when I cleaned a bird. The smell was different from the smell of the kitchen when we pulled out all the ducks' feathers, piling them up in a soft mound on the kitchen table; different from the smell when we dipped the birds in warm wax, wax that we then let harden and pulled off in thick flakes along with the ducks' pinfeathers.

The birds in the store were pared down and down and down so that what was left had no relationship to what these animals were alive. They were birds pared down and down and down, cut and sliced until all that was left were grotesque combinations of named parts. It always felt obscene to me. What were these birds like whole? It was hard, standing amid the dry coolness rising up from the meat cases, to imagine any life; hard to construct a picture of

these birds flying, walking, making morning noise, pecking for insects in the grass, fighting over corn, laying eggs. Hard to imagine
them in any way but stacked in their airless cages.

The Russian philosopher and critic Mikhail Bakhtin tells us that the
ritual of feasting serves as a way to bridge humans' most basic fear—
fear of what Bakhtin calls "the other," fear of that which is not subject to human control, fear of nature. In his writing about banquets
and feasting in the novels of sixteenth-century French author Fran-
çois Rabelais, Bakhtin says that in the act of eating, as in the act
of drinking, of making love, of giving birth, the beginning and the
end of life are linked and interwoven. In Rabelais's novels, eating
celebrates these joyful crossings or joinings, at the same time that it
celebrates the destruction of the powerful other. In feasting, the
mysterious unknown is taken into the human body, it is consumed.

One year, two weeks before Christmas, Craig and I invited twelve of
our friends to our house for a feast. We spent all day preparing for
this meal. I sliced through the dense brilliant layers of three red cab-
bages and set the purple shreds to simmer in a pot with honey. I
stuffed our ducks with apples, oranges, onions, and rasins, spread the
slippery pale breasts with butter and garlic, sprinkling on thyme and
rosemary. We took handfuls of dried morel mushrooms from a coffee can above the refrigerator, plumped them again with white wine,
sautéed them in butter.

Craig scooped out the insides of a pumpkin from the garden for
a pie. He walked to the freezer on the porch and brought back a jar
of frozen blueberries. Another pie. He took from the same freezer a
jar of cut-up frozen rhubarb. Another pie. The squash from the garden was piled in a cardboard box in the basement. I walked down the
stairs into the dark cool, collected four acorn squash, carried them
upstairs into the steamy kitchen, peeled off their tough green and orange skins, chopped them, added butter and onions and carrots,
cooked the mixture, and puréed it for soup.

We were drinking wine and dancing as we cooked. We were full of joy. We felt generous. To feed all of these people, our friends, with food that we knew in some intimate way, food we had grown or animals we had killed ourselves, was a kind of miracle. The meal we conconcted was nearly perverse in its abundance.

Appetizer: venison liver paté and hot spiced wine.

First course: acorn squash soup sprinkled with fresh ground nutmeg.

Second course: spinach and beet green salad with chutney dressing.

Third course: barbecued venison steaks, wild rice, morel mushrooms, buttered beets, and honeyed carrots.

Fourth course: roast duck with plum gravy, new potatoes in butter and parsley sauce and sweet-and-sour red cabbage with honey, vinegar, and caraway seeds.

Dessert: rhubarb pie, blueberry pie, pumpkin pie. Ice cream.

Then brandy. Coffee. Tea. As we sat and talked, we ate tart, green and red, thinly sliced apples, slivers of pear, and cheese and grapes.

In eating these foods—these ducks that we shot out of the sky, that fell, tumbling wing over head, with loud splashes into the cold pond beside our canoe; pumpkin pie that came from a pumpkin that grew all summer long in our backyard garden, surviving three weeks of me cutting open its stalk, scraping out squash borers with the tip of a paring knife; these mushrooms, collected over April and May in the just-leafing-out Minnesota woods full of cardinals, scarlet tanagers, bloodroot, new violets, nesting grouse, and baby rabbits; this venison, from a big-shouldered, spreading-antlered, randy buck Craig killed in November, which we tracked by following the bloody trail it left on bushes and dried grass and leaves—in eating these foods, in this passing of lives into ours, this passing of other blood and muscle into our own blood and muscle, into our own tongues and hearts; in this bridging we were taking up not only food for our bodies, but something that is wild that we wanted for ourselves. Perhaps it was our own power we were eating. Perhaps it was our own ability to grow, to shoot, to find food for ourselves, that we were eating; our ability to engage creatively with the world. We were eating what we wanted so much. We were eating life.

Audre Lorde has written about the erotic and its potential to help us redefine our relationships with ourselves, with each other, and with the world. Lorde, who died from cancer in 1992, wrote about the erotic as a way of knowing the world, as a source of power that is unlike any other source of power.

We live in a racist, patriarchal, and antierotic society, Lorde wrote in "Uses of the Erotic: The Erotic as Power." We live in a pornographic society that insists on the separation of so many inseparable things; that insists on ways of thinking that separate the body from the world, the body from the mind, nature from culture, men from women, black from white; a society that insists on bounded categories of difference.

But we can use erotic power to resist those splitting forces. The erotic is the sensual bridge that connects the spiritual and the political. It has to do with love. The word itself comes from the Greek word *eros*, the personification of love in all its aspects—born of chaos and personifying creative power and harmony. *Eros* is a nonrational power. *Eros* is awareness. *Eros* is not about what we do but about how acutely and fully we can feel in the doing, says Lorde. Its opposite, the pornographic, emphasizes sensation without feeling. Pornographic relationships are those that are born not of human erotic feeling and desire, not of a love of life and a love of the body, but those relationships, those ideas, born of a fear of bodily knowledge and a desire to silence the erotic.

Everything we have ever learned in our lives tells us to suspect feeling. To doubt feeling. To doubt the power of the erotic and to confuse it, conflate it with the pornographic. But the two are at opposite ends of the world. One is about parts, not wholes. One numbs us to the irrationality, the comedy, of eating animals that are strangers to us, who come to us as perverse combinations of wings and breasts.

I understand the horror among some people I know over my shooting and eating a duck. But while I have become accustomed to hunting and eating wild duck, they are accustomed to buying and eating chicken from the store. Our actions are somehow similar yet also fundamentally different. Buying and eating a shrink-wrapped fryer feels to me like eating reduced to the necessities of time, convenience, and cleanliness.

Lorde asks when we will be able, in our relationships with one another and with the world, to risk sharing the erotic's electric charge without having to look away, and without distorting the enormously powerful and creative nature of that exchange. Embracing the erotic means accepting our own mortality, our own bodiedness. Embracing the erotic means not looking away from our relationship with what we eat. And that can turn hunting into a relationship of love; at least not something brutal.

One spring I was walking around Lake of the Isles in Minneapolis with a friend. We were walking fast, dressed in sweatpants and tennis shoes. She would rather have run, but because I was recovering from knee surgery, I could only walk. We took long strides and when I stretched out my leg I could feel the scars there, the manufacturing of new tissue that gave me a strong knee.

We were talking about nothing in particular. About her job as an editor with an agricultural magazine, about running, about lifting weights, about books we had read. Suddenly I shouted, interrupting her. "Look at that."

She looked to where I was pointing and turned back to me to see what it was I was so excited about.

"Look at the ducks," I said. "All those ducks." As we came upon a gaggle of mallards, we stopped to stare. I was fascinated by the greenheads, how when they moved their heads turned violet and emerald in the light. How there was one duck there with a broken bill and a goose with only one foot. There was one female among the group of males. Two of the males were chasing her. It was mating season.

My friend and I moved on. She talked to me about her lover who teaches writing and literature at a local college. We stopped again because I'd seen a wake in the water, a silvery "V" streaming out behind a fast-moving muskrat. "Where?" She squinted.

"There," I said, pointing.

"What is it?"

"A muskrat," I said, watching it as it moved toward a small island, its whiskered nose in the air.

I hear geese honking outside my window in the middle of the city. I used to track the garter snake in our garden from its sunny place in the bean bed to its home under the house, its entryway a piece of bent-up siding. I watch squirrels in the trash cans at the university. I pay attention to spider webs.

Can I call this love? Can I say that I love the swimming greenheads in Lake of the Isles, when every fall I make an adventure out of killing them? Does killing have anything to do with love? What kind of language allows this paradox? This tragic conflation of violence and love is part of what I try to resist in the world, yet here I am, in the midst of it. How is my love for the greenheads, the swimming muskrat, the Canada goose different from the feelings other hunters have for the animals they kill? Can I have a relationship with these animals alive? Or is the killing, the eating, that magical bridging, a crucial part of my love, part of my relationship with these animals, with the world? What does it mean, that in my body, helping to keep me alive, to make me joyful, to share joy with people I love, is the breast of a greenhead mallard that I shot down on a cool autumn day and scooped from the cold water with my hand?

John Hildebrand

Fences

from *Mapping the Farm: The Chronicle of a Family*

I spent an afternoon tearing down a fence, three strands of rusty barbed wire strung between oak posts to keep cattle out of the orchard. I wore heavy leather gloves to coil the wire, which was brittle and kept breaking. One strand disappeared into a pine bole that had healed over it like an old wound, so I snipped the ends with a wire cutter and started a new roll. Dismantling the fence, like lowering a flag, signaled a shift in the land's meaning, namely that these ten acres were no longer an orchard but part of the lower pasture, a fact the cattle have known for some time.

Even without the fence, a border of pines remains to show that the hillside had been set aside for something special. Only a few apple trees are left, mostly wind-bent Greenings, to cast circles of shade in the afternoon heat. Now it's open ground covered by ox eye daisies, patches of white clover, and sunbaked cow pies. The orchard is my favorite place on the farm, maybe anywhere, because it's one of those half-wild places where the intentions of people and nature overlap, like an overgrown lilac hedge that marks a farmstead gone to woods. The land falls away to the west to overlook Sheehan's cows grazing on the opposite hillside, their black-and-white hides patterned like Mercator maps of the world. To the east, along the section of fence I took down, there's a sunken lane running between the orchard and Night Pasture that Ed's cows walked down every morning after being milked and then walked up again every evening.

Apple trees were the blaze marks of civilization. Government surveyors laying out Jefferson's grid upon the prairie often planted apple seeds to mark the section lines, knowing the settlers to follow could distinguish an apple tree from a wild plum or a thorn apple. It wasn't the settlers themselves but the next generation who planted orchards and ornamental shrubs around the farmhouse to show that the break with wilderness was complete.

I can guess the varieties John O'Neill planted from a map of the orchard that he sketched across two pages of a ledger sometime around 1906, each tree marked by a pen scratch in columns as even as figures on a balance sheet. The trees were a long-term investment, an act of faith that he and his descendants would be around for some time to harvest the fruit of his labors. He favored Russian varieties like Duchess of Oldenburg, Tetofsky, and Hibernal that could survive a short growing season, but he also planted the Iowa Beauty and the Wealthy, a variety developed by a Minnesotan who crossed a cherry crab with the common apple. The orchard held a dozen varieties in all to provide apples at different times of the year and for different purposes. There were Duchesses and Patten Greenings for cooking and pies, sweet Anisms for sauce, Whitney Crabs and Longfields—a yellow apple with red stipples—for pickling, Strawberry Crabs, which threshers called a harvest apple because it ripened early during threshing season, and finally the tart, hard-skinned Wealthy to close out the season. Whether John O'Neill drew his map after he finished planting or sketched it as a blueprint of things to come I'm not sure, but the orchard was his small-scale Eden, his clearest proof of order upon the land. When it was done, he pressed a lady's slipper between the ledger's pages as if to remind himself of what had been replaced.

"Some of those old Patten Greening trees were twenty-five to thirty feet high. Ma always wanted perfect apples, so I'd climb the tree and throw them down to her through the branches. She'd catch them in her apron."

Ed and I are pulling fence posts. I slip a chain around the post, hooking it to the bucket on the Bobcat. Then Ed raises it up until the fence post dangles like a hanged man. The oldest are white oak, furry with lichen, cut from the surrounding land as it was cleared for the plow. We stack them by the salt block for firewood.

"We had an apple shed out here that was like an outhouse with bins. Ma would come down and sit and sort apples. Some night when it was going to get good and cold we'd haul apples into the basement. We had a hard red apple that wasn't any good till winter. About February they were damn good apples."

A farm with a lot of fences is one that recognizes different kinds of land and different possibilities for them. A fence announces our designs upon the landscape; it imposes limits. Before fence laws were enacted in the last century, farmers fenced their crops to keep them from being trampled by horses and cows and hogs. Cowboys may have sung "Don't Fence Me In," but certainly not anybody who had corn or wheat in the ground. The first fence laws coincided with the development of cheap barbed wire, so that livestock could be fenced in rather than out, and owners were liable for any damage their animals incurred while running at large. The state's current fence law defines "at large" as "to stroll, wander, rove, or ramble at will." Before that, it was every swine for itself.

The fence lines on this farm were laid out by an agent of the Soil Conservation Service during the thirties, when much of the northern plains was blowing away in dust storms. Civilian Conservation Corps crews in blue denim outfits and floppy hats fenced off the hollow, put marginal land in permanent pasture, and divided big, square fields into long, contour strips to follow the slope of the land. The field pattern was designed when the farm was more diversified and horses still did much of the labor. As machinery continues to get bigger, many farmers tear out fences to enlarge their fields until they resemble vast seas of soybeans or corn, undoing the conservation measures of an earlier generation. Ed has maintained most of his fence lines because they allow him to see the land in segments, to fine-tune it accordingly, even though the layout can seem daunting.

One day a man from the grain elevator in Stewartville came to spray the corn with herbicide. The sprayer was mounted on the back of his pickup with a fifty-foot boom that folded up like the wings of planes on aircraft carriers. He had never been here before and studied Ed's crop map as if it were a jigsaw puzzle. "I think we got enough to do her, but you never know. Depends on how the fields are laid out. Yesterday I sprayed for this woman down in Predmore. She had a lot of fields like this." He made a triangle with his hands. "I ran out six rows short of finishing."

A Depression-era attitude about money lingers on the farm, nothing being purchased new if something can be reused, so fence building often starts with a salvage operation. When the corral needed replacing, we began by tearing down an old sheep shed that anchored one corner of it. The shed was of indeterminate age, having been skidded to the site from a neighboring farm in the twenties. It had housed sheep, then hogs, and more recently a transient population of raccoons, along with lumber salvaged from St. Bridget's church hall. Built in the 1870s to house a local chapter of Father Mathew's Catholic Total Abstinence Union, the hall had waited thirty years for us to resurrect it as a corral. Some of the rough-sawn boards of yellow elm were thirty inches wide with no knots. Nails melted when we tried to hammer them into the boards, so we used spikes instead. When the new corral was finished we chainsawed the palings to a uniform height and burned the ends in a bonfire in the middle of the cow yard. Cows are immune to history and could care less if their corral once sheltered temperance meetings and church socials, but for us the fence is a reminder that nothing is lost forever. A tree becomes a shed, becomes a fence, becomes black smoke rising through tree branches into an everlasting sky.

Sometimes the farm is so cluttered with the past that a bonfire of old things seems refreshing. But if the past is inescapable, the future remains a distant cloudland of possibilities. Sharon spends a lot of time imagining different scenarios for the farm in the event it stops being one. Some days she favors a pick-your-own strawberry patch, other days a hardwood tree farm, a bed-and-breakfast, storage for boats and RVs, a riding stable—any ruse she can think of to keep it intact. All this seems so much pie in the sky. You only have to look at the houses being built across Highway 52 to see the future.

One miserably humid afternoon a car with Iowa plates rolls up the driveway and parks in the shade. The driver, a soft-spoken man wearing yellow-tinted shooting glasses, gets out to introduce himself. He's a businessman scouting locations for new Sporting Clays courses and likes the farm, he explains, because it's close enough to Rochester for members to get in a round of shooting after work. He's brought his wife and daughter along for the ride, but they remain in the car, immured against the heat.

Sporting Clays is the sport of simulated hunting, the man explains, something like golf with a shotgun. Shooters walk through a course laid out with different stations, where they shoot at clay pigeons thrown to duplicate the flight of a particular game animal. The sport originated in England but is gaining popularity in this country, combining as it does the American affection for firearms with our propensity for turning anything elemental into a competition.

"Do you know the first thing General Schwarzkopf did when he returned from the Gulf war?"

I did not.

"He shot a round of Sporting Clays."

A championship shooter himself, the man asks to look around, so Sharon agrees to give him a tour, beginning at the south end of the farm on an old township road that dead-ends in a canopy of oak trees. Leaving the car, we hike through the woods and over a cattle gate to the narrow end of the hollow. No cattle have been pastured here this summer, and the hollow is waist-deep in tall grass, black-berry brambles, and stinging nettles. The man bounds ahead, point-ing out potential shooting stations, while his wife carries their little girl on her hip and swats deer flies tangling in her hair. The air is ge-latinous and thrums with insects.

"It's not like trap or skeet," the man says, "because every station is different."

The shooting stations are often elevated like backyard gazebos and named for the quarry they are meant to suggest. For instance, at Springing Teal the clay targets are launched almost vertically to match the flight of teal off a pond; at Bolting Rabbit, the targets bounce along the ground like scared bunnies; and at Fenceline Quail, they snap up like a wild covey. All the shooter needs is a shotgun and a vivid imagination.

Near the spring, the ground turns squishy and sends up clouds of gnats. We hike up a cow path out of the hollow and into a cornfield, which the man announces would make a good site for the clubhouse and parking lot. He's still laying out stations, but I stop listening once I figure out that the course would sound like a small war. (Maybe that's what Schwarzkopf missed—the rattle of gunfire.) I had dreamed up any number of scenarios for what the farm might be-come, but here was an unimagined future—a happy hunting ground where shooters ride golf carts through the fields after work and blast away at imaginary creatures.

As we walk along the edge of the cornfield I nearly step on a tiger salamander. Striped yellow and black, the salamander is hunting earthworms in the exposed soil. The tip of its tail is missing, as if the salamander had been hunted recently itself. Despite this, it doesn't spring or bolt or run away, but just lies there, a Stationary Salaman-der, and no sport at all.

What wildlife exists on the farm thrives, for the most part, on the edge of things, along the borders between fields and woods, between the cultivated and the wild. Fences bridge the gap between one world and the other. Leave a fence long enough, and a line of trees will grow along it. Like an ocean reef, a fence provides a foothold for plants and animals that would not otherwise survive the monoculture of cropland. The trees and bushes growing along it furnish nesting and food for songbirds, cover for rabbits and woodchucks, and a corridor for deer traveling from woods to cornfields. Ed tolerates the trees until their branches shade his crops or threaten to knock him off his tractor; then he gets out the chainsaw and cuts them back, because if he doesn't they'll eventually take over. Cultivation is not a permanent state. A cornfield will revert to a meadow, but it never works the other way around.

When I rolled up the barbed wire that had enclosed the orchard, I uncovered a linear prairie of weeds: gooseberries, purple vetch, milkweed, Canadian thistle, wild mustard, catnip, Queen Anne's lace, and wild grape—its twists and coils approximating the barbed wire it had replaced. Some of these species are native but many are not, such as cocklebur, which Ed never noticed until he combined a neighbor's oats during the sixties and the seeds hitched a ride back in the hopper. Eventually the cattle will graze or trample these plants to get at the grass, but for a moment I had a glimpse of what the land might have looked like before it was a farm and how it might look again if we just walked away.

Pioneers were too busy plowing the prairie into furrows to take inventory of what their moldboard plows turned over. If they noted anything, it was usually the bowl of blue sky or how the wind rippled the grass into sea waves. One of the most evocative and detailed accounts of the tallgrass prairie before it was plowed was written by Henry David Thoreau, who traveled to Minnesota in 1861 on the longest and last journey of his life.

Thoreau was forty-three at the time, and slowly dying of tuberculosis, when a doctor advised him to "clear out" to a more salubrious climate and recommended the West Indies. But Thoreau decided to try the air out West. Then, as now, easterners came to Minnesota for their health; the new state had been shamelessly promoted as a health resort for consumptives. Thoreau left Concord in early May with a seventeen-year-old companion, Horace Mann, Jr., and traveled by train to Niagara Falls, Detroit, Chicago, and East Dubuque, Illinois, where they boarded the steamboat *Itasca* for the trip upriver. Because he was obliged to stop and rest frequently, the journey progressed more slowly and in greater comfort than Thoreau was accustomed to. As they steamed up the Mississippi River, he coughed incessantly and wrote in his journal, along with descriptions of bluffs and Indian wigwams, how the *Itasca* always whistled its approach to a town before striking its bell six times "funereally."

Disembarking at St. Paul, Thoreau and Mann carried their carpetbags, coats, and an umbrella to the American House, where they ate breakfast, then traveled nine miles by stage over the prairie in the rain. They settled into a hotel within sight of St. Anthony Falls and made daily excursions into the countryside to botanize. Thoreau's method with wildflowers was to stoop and pluck the blossom, vigorously inhaling its fragrance before pressing it into his plant book. He also carried a compass, a notebook, Gray's botanical guide, insect boxes, twine and cards, a dipper and water bottle, and several handkerchiefs. He made extensive lists of birds and flora, freely mixing common names with the Latin and sometimes guessing outright: "Here on the prairie I see the plantain, shepherd's purse, strawberry, violet sorrel (?), common red sorrel, *Ranunculus rhomboideus*, *Geum triflorum* (handsome), phlox (as on Nicollet Island), *Druba nemorosa*, with black pods, a scouring rush by a slough, low grass and sedge. But here the prairie is fed over by horses, cows, and pigs."

Two weeks later Thoreau and Mann took a small steamboat up the snaggy Minnesota River to the Lower Sioux Agency at Redwood Falls to witness the annual treaty payment to the tribe. They watched as "half-naked Indians performed a dance at the request of the Governor, for our amusement and their benefit," and Thoreau noted that buffalo were said to be twenty-five miles away. In an earlier journal, Thoreau copied down what the Swiss naturalist Edouard Desor had told him about the Indians' lack of names for wildflowers, "that they had a particular name for each species of tree (as the maple), but they had but one word for flowers. They did not distinguish the species of the last." In fact, the Sioux had many names for individual flowers, such as the pasque flower, which they called *hoksicekpa* and used for medicine, as opposed to flowers in general, or *wahca*. (On the trip, Mann gathered quantities of pasque flowers to send to his uncle, Nathaniel Hawthorne.) Through interpreters, Thoreau listened to speeches by the Sioux chiefs, including Little Crow, the most prominent, who, a year later, would lead his tribe in a bloody uprising that resulted in the death of four hundred settlers and the total negation of the Sioux's claim to the land. But by then Thoreau himself would be dead of tuberculosis.

What conversations Thoreau might have had with settlers in Minnesota can only be imagined, because he wrote so little about them except that their houses were set half a mile apart on the prairie and their fences were built of sawn boards. But in *Walden* there is a memorable scene in which Thoreau, off on a fishing trip, escapes a rain shower by taking shelter with an Irish farmer, his wife, several children, and assorted chickens. While rain drips through the roof, the Irishman explains how he makes a living "bogging" for a neighboring farmer, turning meadow with a spade for $10 an acre and the use of the land and manure for a year. When Thoreau, transcendentalist and Yankee bachelor, regales the family with his own experiments in thrift, telling the poor bog-trotters that if they only worked less they wouldn't be inclined to eat so much, he sounds like a college kid home from the commune. "If he and his family would live simply, they might all go a-huckleberrying in the summer for their amusement." The Irishman heaves a sigh, and when the shower moves on so does Thoreau.

We've all gone a-huckleberrying of late, though our lives are hardly simple. Every schoolboy knows that the worst way to make a living is by physical labor. Leisure has been turned into an industry that even Thoreau would find unrecognizable, and the places we hold in highest regard are the scenes of our vacations, not our workaday lives. This public affection for wilderness often seems a way of pretending not to notice the wholesale destruction of our cities and countryside. If *Walden* remains a disturbing book, it is because the author advocates preserving the wild not by setting aside a few roadless parcels of land but by incorporating it into one's own life.

So I was interested when I heard that a pair of doctors who had bought an old farmstead between St. Charles and Chatfield were restoring part of it to tallgrass prairie. True prairie is made up of three-hundred-plus plant species, some of which have been lost forever, so a restored prairie is essentially a landscape of imagination. Re-creating a prairie ecosystem on a few acres of unmowed pasture may be no more possible than bringing back the herds of buffalo, but it's a landscape I wanted to see, and imagination didn't seem a bad place to start. "To make a prairie," wrote Emily Dickinson, a stay-at-home who certainly never saw one, "it takes a clover and one bee."

> One clover, and a bee,
> And revery.
> The revery alone will do,
> If bees are few.

Steve Henke and Nancy Peltola are family physicians who work in St. Charles and Chatfield, respectively, and bought their farm ten years ago because it lay equidistant from their separate practices. Henke gave me directions over the phone, explaining that if I passed the Amish school I'd gone too far. The Amish farms are easy to spot. There are always workhorses in the field, and no satellite dish. On the porch of one farmhouse I passed, an old woman was laying out quilts, her chalky face framed inside a black bonnet like water at the bottom of a well.

Overshooting my turn, I circle around at the one-room schoolhouse and backtrack to find the doctors' farmhouse at the end of an unmarked gravel road—and nobody at home. I hike up a grassy ridge past a windmill and a ruined cistern. The ridge is bright and windblown as it curves above the valley and the white road I came in on. At the end of the ridge, in the heat-wavering distance, two people stand in a swarm of horses.

Nancy Peltola sits in the spring seat of an ancient Farmall-M while her husband unrolls a spool of fence wire from a wagon hitched to the back of the tractor. They are stringing a new paddock for their horses, who drift around us like smoke. A fawn-colored foal keeps inserting her muzzle between us, and the mare doesn't mind; but when a sorrel gelding gets too close, she kicks him in the ribs.

Of the hundred acres the doctors own, roughly half are tillable and have been rented to a neighboring farmer; the rest is ridgetop and impossible slopes, a kingdom of sunlight and wind. The farmhouse had stood empty for years when the doctors moved into it. Friends suggested they bulldoze and start fresh, but they gutted the walls and rebuilt the house along its original lines. Not long after the renovation, a man came to the door and announced that he had been born in the back bedroom in 1927. His grandfather had built the house, and the man was surprised to find it still standing. Walking past freshly painted walls, he followed his memory to the scene of his birth and found, instead, a music room. Now the doctors are restoring the landscape along its original lines, burning hillsides in springtime and sowing the seeds of prairie forbs and grasses so that at least some of the land will remember its past.

"Before we came here we didn't know anything about prairies," says Steve Henke. "We were mostly interested in woods. If you asked Nancy or me ten years ago if we'd want to live in a place with few trees, we'd have said no."

Trees are the death of prairie, the climactic stage in a biological succession that in the wild was circumvented by drought and fire. True prairie has only one tree per acre. The only prominent trees in view here are a stand of Norway pines, the remnants of a windbreak behind the farmhouse. The doctors had planted maples along the south end of the ridge to provide cover for wildlife, but the saplings succumbed to last summer's drought and now poke leafless and wandlike from the grass.

While Nancy walks back to the house to fix lunch, Steve gives me a tour of the back side of the ridge. The terrain is dry and rolling, covered with only a thin layer of sandy topsoil, a good place for a prairie remnant to have escaped the plow. Steve stoops beside a fern-like clump of silvery green leaves. "These are leadplants. And when you see leadplant, it's a pretty good indication the land has never been tilled. Once its seedbed is disturbed, leadplant doesn't do very well."

It's hard to tell the native plants from the aliens, and the most pristine meadow of wildflowers may prove to be a gathering of immigrants. Steve points out the lupinelike blossoms of a prairie turnip, which is native, and yellow goatsbeard, or prairie dandelion, which isn't but performs the neat trick of closing its petals at midday like a long wink. He finds a pasque flower past its bloom. This was the first prairie forb he learned by sight and name, and it sparked his interest in the restoration project. One morning during their first spring in the farmhouse, Steve and Nancy looked out of a window and saw scraps of white paper littering their hillside. Taking a break from remodeling, they climbed the ridge slope to discover that the pale scraps were hundreds of pasque flowers in bloom. Last year they harvested one-third of a pound of pasque flower seeds to trade at Prairie Moon Nursery outside Winona for prairie seeds they didn't have. The mixture of wildflower and grass seed had been gathered from virgin prairie farther north, near the town of Fertile.

Steve wears sandals, white running shorts, and a big straw hat. When the wind ruffles the brim of his hat, it reveals a red bandanna knotted pirate style around a receding hairline. Wandering through the tall grass along the ridge, he tosses names over his shoulder as if introducing guests at a dinner party. "This is pussy toes . . . buffalo pea . . . harebell . . . wild rose. . . . Here's one of my favorites, prairie smoke. It looks like a puff of smoke. . . . This is . . . nope. That's wrong. We'll have to look that up in the book at home. . . . You know what this is, don't you?" He gestures toward a particularly lush, three-leafed plant growing by a sandstone outcropping. "Poison ivy."

Certainly the first act of restoration must be memorizing the individual names of flowers and grasses that would otherwise blur under the general heading of "weed." In Genesis, naming is Adam's only task in creation, and it seems a measly chore, the one we give children when we bring home a pet; except that without names there can be no personal connection, and there is no love in the abstract. The common names for plants—like "prairie smoke" for *Geum triflorum*, for instance—are memorable precisely because they're metaphoric, nicknames based upon prior associations rather than the cold logic of Linnaean taxonomy. They are terms of familiarity, and walking through a meadow calling the plants by name is like entering a room of friends instead of strangers.

When he comes across a spiny-leafed plant bowing under the weight of a purple flower head, Steve hacks off the stem with the heel of his sandal. He does the same thing to the next one, and the next. "If you don't control them, they'll take over a field. There's an Amish man down the road, and half his pasture is thistles. Even a goat won't eat them."

The Canadian thistle is an ornamental accidentally introduced from Europe when it was mixed with crop seed and quickly got a foothold in overgrazed fields. Like many native prairie plants, it's a perennial that can propagate not only by seeds from its purple flower head but also by its creeping root stock, or rhizomes, so that new shoots will soon replace the ones Steve has hacked off.

"The true management of thistles is pasture management. They like disturbed soil, so if you don't let your animals crop the pasture too low, they can't get a start."

In May, Steve and Nancy bought six bred Holstein heifers, which they plan to sell in September. The cows are summer guests and represent a paradigm shift in the doctors' original notion that the prairie could simply restore itself. The cattle are stand-ins for the wild herds that once grazed here.

"When this was tallgrass prairie, it didn't sit idle. There were animals and burns. We learned that for the health of the land it has to be grazed. There was a man down in Iowa trying to rejuvenate prai-

rie, and he wasn't having much luck until he borrowed a neighbor's
herd of cattle. It sure speeded up the process."

Buffalo kept the prairie grasses green by feeding on their com-
petitors, by fertilizing the soil with their manure, and by preparing
a seedbed as they tore up the thatch with their hooves. Domestic
cattle do all those things, but they do them to excess. Buffalo herds
ranged across the open landscape like the weather itself, but the livestock that replaced them were confined by fences into smaller and
smaller quarters and eventually grazed the prairie to death. The doctors' solution to that problem is more fencing. Using lightweight Po-
lywire, they strung a grid of eight paddocks across their pasture and
moved their Holsteins to a different paddock every three or four
days. Rotational grazing imitates the effects of migratory herds without the complications of loosing buffalo among the cornfields.

We climb a barbed-wire fence into a grassy swale that looks like
a neglected meadow except for the intense, pointillistic green blades
rising among the brown tangle of weeds. This is a mesic prairie, midway between dry and wet, better suited to native grasses than wild
forbs, so there is less phlox and bergamot but more porcupine grass
and clumps of little and big bluestem. We watch wind currents moving through the grassheads on the far hillside like waves of light. A
bobolink flutters overhead, singing like a hysterical music box.

"This is the area we burned last summer. We did roughly twelve
acres. Two weeks later you couldn't tell it had ever been burned."

Prairie restorationists use controlled burns to set back the cool-
season grasses introduced by Europeans—timothy, bromegrass, and
orchard grass—so there's less competition for native hot-season
grasses like big and little bluestem. Unless it is disturbed by periodic
fires or grazing, the accumulated thatch grows so thick that the prairie eventually suffocates much of its variety or is invaded by forest.
Fire does no permanent damage to the prairie plants, whose underground root systems resemble the tributaries of a great river system
and allow the plants to conserve moisture, making them virtually
immune to drought or fire. It was the constant growth and decay of

these roots that formed the rich, chernozem soils of what would eventually become the corn belt. The thickly woven mat of roots was so interlaced that it broke the pioneers' wooden plows and awaited the development of John Deere's steel moldboard plow.

Indians set the prairie afire for a variety of reasons. A wall of flames was useful for driving game, eluding enemies, greening up horse pastures, or just cutting down on summer insects. The fires were great natural spectacles. A Methodist circuit rider described one such encounter in 1835: "The last twelve miles we traveled after sundown & by firelight over the Prairie, it being on fire. This was the grandest scene I ever saw, the wind blew a gale all day, the grass was dry . . . In *high* grass, it sometimes burns 30 feet high, if driven by fierce winds. By light of this fire, we could read fine print for ½ a mile or more." Of course, the spectacle could prove fatal if the observer was caught without a swift horse. One writer advised settlers to light a backfire to delay the inferno's advance, then "ride madly before the wind." If that failed, the settler could always disembowel his horse and climb into the cavity until the flames passed.

Maybe what the countryside needs is a good conflagration now and then to cleanse it, an annual rite of purification by which we torch the old growth and then "ride madly before the wind." Afterward we'd return to find the land uncluttered again, and could sustain for a little longer our belief in its endless possibilities. Not a bad idea. We'd get to see the landscape as the Sioux or Thoreau did, its wide-open horizons the perfect screen on which to project our daydreams. The only catch is that we'd have to be willing to travel light, nothing more than could fit onto a travois or a prairie schooner. Not long ago, one of the immense new houses south of Highway 52 caught fire when a rag soaked in paint thinner ignited spontaneously in the garage. The blaze spread quickly and the house burned to the ground; but it must have had tough rhizomes, or good insurance, because a few months later it had grown back, bigger than ever, squatting on the hillside and ugly as a toad.

When Steve and Nancy burned their twelve-acre swale, they could have jumped over the flames. The Minnesota Department of

Natural Resources, which issued the permit, stipulated that the winds on the day of the fire should not exceed five to ten miles an hour, or the humidity be less than 50 percent. The permit was issued for the first Saturday of the month—May Day, as it turned out. A crew of friends used torches dipped in a mixture of gasoline and diesel fuel to ignite the north end of the swale so the fire would burn against the slight breeze. The flames may have been small, but the green prairie grasses sent up a billowing screen of smoke. Sparrows and meadowlarks shot ahead of the blaze. The crew, carrying five-gallon piss packs, contained the fire except when sparks from an old cedar fence post ignited the edge of a nearby field and the flames had to be swatted out with rakes and brooms. A neighboring farmer, drawn by the smoke, came up to watch the doctors burning their prairie. "Oh," he said dryly, "I see you're making a clearing for thistles."

When sons-in-law get itchy to drive your tractors, you put them to work repairing fences because it's nearly impossible to wreck a post-hole digger. I spend the morning straightening metal T-posts on a section of fence over east, staggering them with pressure-treated wooden posts that the frost can't heave. Unless I feel like chipping through limestone, it's necessary to find the old post holes. The digging is tolerable where the fence line dips into shade, but in open ground the sun beats down like a hammer. I roll barbed wire off a spool in the bed of the pickup and, after it's secured at one end, use a fence tightener to pull it taut. A good fence is horse-high, hog-tight, and bull-strong. It's also a way of keeping faith that the land will remain a working farm.

Driving past the old orchard, I stop to pick a prairie bouquet for Sharon: bergamot, ox eye daisies, wild phlox, Queen Anne's lace. The cows haven't cropped the grass along the fence line yet, and I wonder what her grandfather would think of his bare hillside now or how he'd feel if it was diced into view lots or restored to tallgrass prairie. Either way, a kind of betrayal.

Sherry Simpson

The Book of Being Lost

from *Sierra*

When I was ten, my great-aunt sent me a blank book of joined pages, an accordion of whiteness squeezed between green covers. The book clearly was meant to be filled in one long, unfolding crescendo of words. So I began my first and only book. The plot of this adventure tale featured me, my siblings, and various friends, all flying from Juneau to somewhere along the coast of Southeast Alaska when suddenly, our plane crashed. There we were, stranded on a remote island on the turbulent edge of the Pacific Ocean.

The pilot had to die. It was too bad, but this was to be an adult-free tale, so we could spend our days being plucky and clever as we struggled for survival in the wilderness. The story emerged from a plagiarized mishmash of plucky-children-lost-in-the-wilderness books that I adored. In one, a boy with nothing but a pocketknife and a dog wandered through the wilds, eating raw fish and navigating by the stars. In another, several boys spent a week lost in the desert; by the time they were rescued, they had created an underground heating-and-plumbing system based on Roman engineering techniques. All of these tales revolved around boys, but I didn't care, because it never occurred to me that wilderness was not a place for girls. Still, I cast as my boyfriend my neighbor, John, a darkly handsome boy who was the indifferent object of my affection. Together, our lost and innocent band would somehow overcome the perils of the wild.

A common-enough fantasy, I suppose. Alaska is full of romantics like me, people who understand the impossibility of surviving in the wilderness and yet who can't help wishing for that very thing their whole lives. But now I see there was another story I didn't write, a story in which the forest was not a haven, not a refuge for rebellious preteens, but an impenetrable mystery, an old, dark symbol of longing and fear. At ten, though, I wrote the only tale I could, neatly marching the words in blue ballpoint pen across the snowy unlined paper. It was hard to keep the lines straight. Eventually they sagged across the pages, the line endings pulled down as if dowsing toward some heavy truth.

The airplane crash was a plot device necessary to remove us from familiar territory. I spent so much time playing in the rain forest near our house that I did not fear being lost. Unlike Hansel and Gretel, who had not read the survival manuals I studied, I minded my way with mental constellations formed by the alignment of trees and boulders and streams. I puzzled over the bread crumbs in the fairy tale, wondering why the children marked their paths by what disappears. Twenty-five years later, I could sketch the paths and trails I roamed through the Mendenhall Valley, though now most have been erased by tract homes, roads, and malls. It seems I can, after all, navigate by what no longer exists.

I recall the sensation of crossing a border every time I slipped between trees or through the claw of alder brush into the woods. Years later, I learned a word that describes the texture of dusky green light in the rain forest: gloaming. Few people use this word anymore, except possibly the Scots, but it is the right word to describe the dreamy density of air, the constant sheen of rain, the way spruce and hemlock trees rise from the earth, their corrugated trunks weeping sap, their crowns meshing so tightly that sky splinters into vagueness. In the gloaming, it is not day, it is not night. Shafts of pearly light penetrate where downed trees sheared the canopy. A kind of vegetative hush cushions the air. The raven's thick dialect, the chime of a thrush, the red squirrel's curses resonate like a ritual response to the litugy, familiar yet always meaningful.

Biologists call the rim where dense forest meets open ground an "edge." A deer, for example, might forage in a meadow and take shelter among the adjoining trees. In Southeast Alaska, the forest harbors many internal edges, where one kind of habitat or vegetation eases into another. Animals and birds shift back and forth through these places, seeking what they need from different kinds of landscape.

Edges rim human history, too, creating borders where event and myth and legend rub together, where people move from one kind of story into another. It is humanity's pride and haunting that we tamed ourselves by striking down frightening forests, flushing out wild animals, baring the horizons. But in the oldest part of our minds, a thick forest stands, inhabited by talking beasts, changelings, and lost children; by nightmares, reveries, and profound silences; by tricks of shadow and light; by everything we once were, and never will be again. Along this boundary between wilderness and society dwell all the wild men and wild women, sinners and noble savages, saints and exiles.

The book I wrote as a child extended a life I already knew along this edge. My family lived in one of the first subdivisions in Juneau, an orderly crop of small frame houses individual only in color. The blue face of Mendenhall Glacier bulged above the trees three miles to the north. Beyond this pioneering swatch of suburbia, the forest washed along the flanks of the costal range for hundreds of miles. The score of children along my street roamed these woods as if they were captured territory. In the dim, green light we became different children than we were in the open, where anybody could see us.

With scavenged lumber and bent nails, we cobbled together rough forts, reenacting the rise of civilization in our own playful, vicious way. Instinctively, we sought safety against dangerous creatures—not wild animals, but the mean teenage boys who skulked in the trees, smoking and cursing and reading *Playboy*. We abandoned trails, slipped through the understory of devil's club and blueberry bushes, pressed against old trees that were three children wide. I wore a ratty pair of moccasins everywhere because I did not want to be tracked and found. Sometimes I hid by climbing high into a spruce tree, where I listened to the thin, distant sounds of kids playing, mothers yelling, lawn mowers droning—all part of someone else's painfully ordinary life. At night I slept with hands tarred by spruce pitch. Bits of spidery lichens and dry needles tangled in my hair. I smelled clean, like a tree.

But the edge was not far enough when I was a child. And so I wrote the book of being lost. Life was not easy on our wild island. Until we fashioned rough dwellings from downed timber, brush, and spruce boughs, southeasterly storms engulfed us in miseries of wind and rain. The surf dragged the airplane wreckage down to the bottom of the sea, taking our supplies with it. We scraped a grave for the pilot in the forest floor and piled it with rocks hauled from the beach. Among us we had only a couple of pocketknives, some string, a book of matches, a few pieces of gum.

I became the band's leader because of my extensive knowledge of wilderness lore. I had prepared for exactly this kind of situation, and I longed to use everything I knew about surviving in the wilderness: Moss grows on the north side of trees. Chewing on willow bark relieves headaches. Ward off scurvy by eating beach lettuce. Build your shelter on top of a rise to prevent runoff from pooling on the floor. Dry leaves and needles make good insulation. I memorized poisonous and edible mushrooms, though at home I refused to eat mushrooms at all. I couldn't wait to make pemmican from berries and venison.

Once I grew up, I realized that people disappear into the woods all the time, lost, stranded, or looking for themselves. Sometimes we never know they've gone. And when they return, if they return, they often have changed. It does not take much to rub away the gilt of society and order. Living alone among trees, where the mind strains to make sense of every breeze, every bird call, every rustle and whisper, unravels that fine tautness we require to live together.

That wilderness can undo us is a fear that has long inhabited folklore, religion, and literature. The Middle English meaning of "mad" was "wood," a pun that Shakespeare could not resist in *A Midsummer Night's Dream*: "And here am I wood within this wood?" The Puritans' stern vision colored the wilderness long before they arrived in America and confronted what poet Michael Wigglesworth called "a waste and howling wilderness" that echoed the inner and untamed darkness of the ungodly. And ungodly beings did inhabit the forest—mysterious wild people who have always lingered on the outskirts of societies urban or indigenous. I don't mean the pallid figures of pop psychology—the male who paints himself up and beats on drums at weekend gatherings of men with too much money and not enough imagination, the overanalyzed female seeking secondhand empowerment from fairy tales. I mean the hairy, frightening figures of folklore who know too much about us, who inhabit both the real world and the mythical. Scholars describe them as figures of anticivilization, godless beings who seek only to satisfy animal appetites. In Alaska, the Athabascans and the Inupiat know that wild ones lurk out there. It's better not to speak their names. But for all their slovenly, frightening ways, the wild people also remember secrets of nature most people have forgotten. This makes them dangerously attractive, the objects of loathing and longing because they remind us of who we used to be. The ambivalent way people regarded wild people—as repulsive and romantic—echoes the way many cultures have responded to wilderness itself.

It's not so hard to find wild people even now. It's not so hard to become one, either. Those who venture beyond the forest's edge risk assuming a wildness, or madness, that they cannot recover from. Occasionally, solitary people seek this fate by entering the wilds deliberately. That they would purposefully drift away from society to become mountain men, or hermits, or self-exiles only seems like madness to those of us left behind. More often this fate mysteriously finds people who have somehow lost themselves.

" 'Wild Man' Seen At Pt. Retreat," says the *Daily Alaska Empire* on May 25, 1937. The account describes how a ragged figure emerged from the woods that surround the Point Retreat Lighthouse on Admiralty Island, not far from Juneau. But at the lightkeeper's approach, the man fled back into the forest. This happened several times. The town marshal sent a rescue party after him, believing him to be a missing trapper named Bud May. Somehow capturing or coaxing the man into their midst, the rescuers discovered he actually was Albert Niles, a sixty-five-year-old prospector marooned on the island two weeks before when his skiff's motor broke. Then his camp caught on fire, leaving him only a rifle. Niles had since lived unsheltered, eating game and fish as he wandered through the trees. After his return to Juneau, the newspaper wrote, "The pioneer declares reports of his being a 'wild man' are erroneous. The only thing he was wild about was the loss of his boat and equipment, he pointed out."

But something happened to Albert Niles as he roamed the forest. No explanation emerged for why he repeatedly fled help. Back in Juneau, the marshal put him aboard a steamship bound for a veterans' hospital in the States, but Niles created such a fuss—over what, the newspaper doesn't say—that authorities jailed him and charged him with insanity after all. Evidently the old prospector had lost some ability to play by the rules. Perhaps his sojourn tainted him; perhaps people could only see him as mad after his return. Bud May, the missing trapper, never did reappear. His bones have long since melted away in the rain forest.

"End-of-the-roader" is the Alaskan name for those people who abandon the known world and venture north seeking peace or oblivion in the wilds. They have always come here. In the summer of 1945, Juneau residents grew afraid at reports of a man named Tony "running wild" in the woods just south of town. Tony, a man in his fifties who spoke broken English, had come from Seattle to work in a cannery, but something drove him into the forest. Occasionally he ventured out to beg food or clothing from people who lived on the town's outskirts. The last time anybody saw him, he wore only underwear. "Wildman's Body Found on Beach South of Thane," the headline read three weeks later. Judging from what remained of his decomposing body, authorities believed he died of exposure. In the forest they found his lair, where he had been sleeping under a rock overhang.

Sometimes, when I am alone in the woods, I think of Tony and Albert as the hours passed in solitude. Surely they tested their voices in that mossy stillness, perhaps calling out uncertainly "Who's there?" Imagine how hungry they felt among the green extravagances of forest. If Albert shot a deer, he ripped at it with his teeth, devouring hunks of bloody meat still hot and raw. Tony must have foraged along the beach, sucking briny, living mussels from their indigo shells, prying limpets from rocks. They shivered as they slept, tormented by cold and wet. Toward the end they sought others, and yet they hid when confronted by those who had once been their own kind. Neither ever found his way back. They were wood within wood.

Does madness call people into wilderness, or does wilderness drive people mad? When I was in sixth grade, a classmate discovered a human skeleton lying in a cave on Thunder Mountain, the broad-shouldered ridge that shadows Mendenhall Valley. We begged him for details: The bones—what did they look like? Did animals chew on him? Why did he go there? Why didn't he come back? Not long ago in Juneau, a tourist wandered away from a visiting cruise ship and disappeared. Two years later hikers found his scattered bones part way up Heintzleman Ridge, several miles south of town. His death bothers people less than his disappearance. We have no way to explain why a 72-year-old retired business executive would abandon his wife and his expensive vacation to roam a steep, forested mountain.

I lost myself once, deliberately. My high school biology teacher wanted us to learn some of the lessons that had emerged from the recent shipwrecking of a Sitka teenager who had spent days and days alone in a forest, barely surviving the cruelties of November. The following spring, the teacher sent us into the woods for a solitary day, to teach us something about mental self-sufficiency. He had a point. People hardly ever enter the woods alone and without purpose. We're raised on the buddy system. We know where we're going and when we're coming back. We make trails and follow them faithfully.

On the designated morning, I stood alone at the end of the road on north Douglas Island, studying the blunt wall of trees. Dark gaps suggested openings, and I twisted through blueberry bushes and devil's club to find a way in. In a few moments, I could no longer see the way out.

Sometime during that dreamlike day, I sat stunned into stillness, huddled against the knotted roots of a spruce tree, listening, listening. Something was there. I could feel it. Every motion, every noise, attracted me: the slow wave of ferns, the clatter of a blue jay, the sly trickle of water.

Remembering my childhood, I tried to move slowly, easily, but this talent seemed lost to me. At times I forgot what I was doing and dissolved into long, vacant contemplations of the way trees thrust skyward. Other times I thrashed through the brush. Clambering over rotting logs, my hands shrank from clammy moss and fleshy mushrooms. I grasped at the wrong things. Devil's club spines prickled under my skin; they wouldn't emerge from my hands for a month. Black stinking mud sucked at my boots. Brambles ripped at my hair and jacket. I felt submerged under the tangled, moist heaviness that clotted the air. I inched along an alder fallen across the amber waters of a creek, and the sodden bark peeled away under my grip, baring yellowish wood that made me think of cartilage and bones. I didn't know why I was crossing the creek. Hours later, I fell out of the forest into the open, healing air, never having glimpsed what I was hiding from, or what I was looking for.

Not everyone who enters wilderness returns mad, of course. A border exists that most people will not cross. Many vow to find places free of footprints, and when they do, declare themselves new citizens of a wild nation. Yet always people shield themselves against wilderness with whatever devices lend survival and solace: large guns, neon-colored tents, guidebooks, expensive boots, freeze-dried food, tools of every sort. They file return plans, or arrange to be picked up. Some carry handheld beacons that can signal an orbiting satellite and pinpoint their position on the globe within a few hundred yards. Nobody ever has to be lost again.

I do not fool myself. I know the forest does not welcome me, does not care about me, will not nurture me. Alone and bereft of bits of string, scraps of wool, leather for my feet, I would not survive long. I suspect a night's sojourn alone in the heart of the rain forest would drive me mad. I would emerge babbling about things I had seen, things I had done. They might find me on my hands and knees gnawing roots. Perhaps I would prefer eating small animals raw. Ravens might tell me jokes I would understand. I could invent a new religion. I might discover fire all over again. Insanity brought on by too many trees might be something I would enjoy.

Knowing this, I return to the shadow of forests and always will. Who doesn't want to go mad sometimes, to be swallowed up by something greater than ourselves? And yet, we can never truly be lost without somehow relinquishing the one thing we can never escape from—ourselves. All else is pretense.

Still, I remain a romantic. I believe I've earned it by learning that the same wilderness that can undo us can also heal us. Disillusionment and reconciliation share an edge.

A year or two after I wrote my book, I returned from the neighborhood fort with John, the boy whom I had idealized in the story. A bit older than I, he had black hair, blue eyes and fine brown hands that somehow made up for his natural arrogance. Our mothers were best friends, so we spent a lot of time together. His bedroom window paralleled mine, and some nights I turned off the lights in my room and peered through my window, watching his shadow move against the shade. On this summer evening, as we walked through the woods, John suddenly pushed me down and straddled me, trying to shove his hands into my jeans. I writhed beneath him, pummeling him as hard as I could with closed fists. My long hair caught in my mouth as I struggled. He worked his hand down past my belly, and then, as I twisted to evade him, drew it out and released me. He pulled me to my feet.

We walked out of the woods then, without saying anything. I pulled bits of moss from my hair. He brushed off my back and said, "See ya," and I said, "Yeah," and we went into our houses. Whatever had happened, we didn't want to reveal it to any adult. But after that, I stopped goofing around and wearing those silly moccasins. I had learned self-consciousness. I had learned there was something to fear in the forest.

My first lover and I went into the woods when I was seventeen. We stripped off our clothes, lay against the forest floor, and made love in the slow shadows of trees. Sometimes rain veiled us, sifting through the fronds of hemlock and spruce. He covered me against it, cupping me against the fragrant duff, the feathery mosses. The wet earth yielded beneath me, and I beneath him. Above us the trees were always rising.

In the forest, with my lover, I opened myself to the world. A madwoman, a lost woman, could be no less astounded, no less shaken by the longing and loss that suffused me, lying there in the forest with a man. When I returned home and undressed in the summer twilight of my bedroom, I found twigs and needles scattered in my clothing, and tiny green plants clinging to my flesh.

My life, from the first time I went into the forest alone as a child, is one long craving for that moment when the self is lost and found, all at once. If that kind of wildness means the way we loosen ourselves from the human world and its requirements, it must also mean the way we bind ourselves to the natural world, the way we surrender to the oldest provinces of brains and bellies. We bare ourselves to the world. We become most completely ourselves. That is the frightening, delicious, nature of madness.

I miss my childhood in the woods. I wish I could unfold that book again and follow the uneven lines as they trailed from page to page. Now I live in a small, plain house without plumbing on the outskirts of Fairbanks, surrounded by white birch and black spruce trees, my only discontent the nearness of neighbors. At night I lie in bed, warmed by my husband, and through undraped windows we watch the stars scraping away darkness as the earth spins. Once in a while I take out my maps and pinpoint where we live. Then I draw an imaginary line from our doorstep north, as if one day I might set out and walk all the way to the Arctic Coast. At dusk I've stood among the trees and studied the distant yellow light swelling from the windows of my house, trying to imagine who lives there on the edge of the forest.

The book I wrote, a book I no longer have, was not really about being lost so much as wishing for what is lost to us. The point was not to be rescued at all. Yes, we were cold and often miserable. Rain proved to be our worst enemy. We fought over small things, and the boys sometimes challenged my authority. But how happy we became as we learned to spear salmon, snare deer, dig up roots that tasted like earth, feast on berries and bitter leaves. We wove spruce boughs into fragrant beds. We set elaborate traps to warn us when brown bears came around. Every day, we drank deeply from the nearby stream, chewing on strips of smoked salmon and venison, tidied our camp, and then, carrying pemmican to sustain us, set out on exploratory hikes. We mapped our island by engraving the terrain on the tender inner layer of spruce bark.

At night, we squatted around the fire and told stories, the flames illuminating our solemn faces, darkness washing around us like a high tide that would ease by morning. We twisted cedar twigs and blue clay in our hair. We said we missed our parents, but soon their faces blurred and disappeared from memory. When search planes droned overhead, we hid in the understory. Sometimes I still feel the old fierce needs that thrummed in our hearts: to kill animals with our hands, drench ourselves in blood, invent songs against the night, pray as if we meant it.

Stephen Trimble

Sing Me Down
the Mountain

from *The Geography of Childhood:
Why Children Need Wild Places*

I.

At twenty-six, I married a woman, adopted a dog, and, with the risks of responsibility, began to lose my innocence. I may have ceased being a child, but I had not yet reached adulthood.

The marriage was brief, but the dog lived with me for more than eleven years. As my companion in the wilds, he taught me how to share my life. Before fathering a child, I was father to a dog—and it helped.

We first saw him on the concrete floor of a cubicle at the Tucson Humane Society, waiting with equanimity for someone to rescue him—his nose resting between his paws, his brown eyes watchful under furrowed brows. He was two, and had been left behind by a military family assigned overseas. The card on his cage said: "Name: Jack. Breed: wolf/shepherd." I always believed the shepherd was Australian shepherd but never knew for sure about the wolf. One-syllable Anglo-Saxon "Jack" did not seem to suit this gentle, intelligent being. Since we lived in the Hispanic Southwest, we named him Carlos.

Carlos stayed with me when the marriage ended, since my life of fieldwork and writing suited his needs. At home, Carlos slept on the floor under my desk by day and, at night, next to my bed. Camping, he had the luxury of nestling close to my sleeping bag. Carlos learned to be a photographer's dog, curling up by my camera bag or digging himself a cool patch of fresh dirt to lie on while he waited for me to exhaust my ideas with a photo subject.

Carlos was good company. I teased him and talked to him—when I needed to talk but might have felt too self-conscious to talk to myself. I could amble along, watching for the small events that would become journal notes, and Carlos would not distract me from my reveries. He added another's life to my experience and connected me to the wild world in a way only a nonhuman life can.

I came close to taking him for granted. Twice, when I forgot he was out of the truck and drove off without him, I realized how much I would miss him if he were gone.

The first time, I had pulled over to sleep for a couple of hours one moonlit night near the mouth of Tsegi Canyon on the Navajo Indian Reservation in Arizona. I let Carlos out to empty his bladder, went to sleep, and woke up to a few spitting snowflakes. Nervous about traveling in the storm, I cranked the truck to life and drove off.

Some fifty miles later, in the middle of Monument Valley, I addressed something to the back of the truck, and realized no one was listening (you could sense Carlos listening even when he didn't answer). Frantic—picturing Carlos dead on the highway—I spun around, raced back, got a speeding ticket in Kayenta, and at 2:00 A.M. reached a spot near where I had left him. I began to stop every quarter mile and call into the darkness. Many Navajo dogs answered me from their owners' hogans. Finally, Carlos came trotting out of the night, back from his adventures, grinning.

The second time, I had been talking with Hualapai Indian people one summer evening, telling Coyote stories—or rather, talking around the edges of Coyote stories, since, in summer, one avoids telling stories that arouse the ire of what one Hualapai elder carefully referred to as "crawling long things." These were stories not just of any coyote, but of Coyote, the trickster-hero of Native America.

I left George Rocha's house in Peach Springs, Arizona, and drove a set of branching dirt roads headed for Madwita Canyon overlook, above the sacred place where the Hualapai lived with their gods in the Grand Canyon before emerging into this world. I stopped at a junction to hop out and peer at a fading sign, returned to the truck, and took the dimmer of the two forks. A few minutes later, a coyote (or was it Coyote himself?) trotted across the track through my headlight beams.

Some miles later, I reached the overlook, stepped out, and called Carlos. He was not there, and I realized he had jumped out when I checked the sign. I sensed Coyote laughing at me from somewhere off in the piñons. I drove back to find Carlos panting along the road trying to catch up, reminding me to pay more attention to him, to animals, to life.

Carlos's best time came in the early 1980s, when I spent months hiking with him in the Great Basin Desert, researching a book. Few human companions joined me on these trips. When I think of the Great Basin, I do not think of being alone, though some observers would say that I was. I think of being there with Carlos.

Carlos and I climbed peaks in isolated Nevada and Utah mountain ranges and walked frosted sand dunes on winter mornings. He curled into the roots of a four-thousand-year-old bristlecone pine while I photographed its branches. I watched him sniff at the view— as I looked at it—when we stopped at the end of a long switchback climbing into the Jarbidge Wilderness.

Carlos was known to chase squirrels, bark at deer, and keep pikas and marmots at a distance. He also provided counterpoint to my solitary perspective. His concreteness, his vitality, his simple affection, made the abstractions of the universe less ponderous. When I lay down in my sleeping bag on the enormous expanse of cracked mud polygons that forms the level floor of the Black Rock Desert playa and looked into a bowl of sky filled with stars, his warm back pushed against mine and his paws trembling in dreams of chasing jackrabbits helped me to comprehend my relationship with the Milky Way. He was another life, in a land so vast that I needed such grounding.

Tumult in other parts of my life seemed very far away at these times. Now, when I read the ramblings in my journals, the miles of walking come back, vivid. Sunsets watched between sips of scotch from an enameled metal cup flare again. Though each way of traveling in a landscape has its advantages, remembering the places I shared with this dog always cheers me.

II.

When I was thirty-six, I married again. This one will last. My wife came West after college and swore ever after she actually had been born a westerner in the wrong place. As we walk and run rivers and camp together in these great spaces, another way of relating to the land becomes real for me.

My wife, Joanne, both enhances and distracts from what I see in nature alone. She asks questions and enthuses; we talk. In striving to articulate what we feel, how each of us reacts to the land, we use language earlier than I would alone to recreate the feel of light on sandstone or the smell of cliffrose. In some ways, I use up the words by sharing the experience; alone, I hoard them, secreting them away in my journal. Talking with the woman I love about the places we pass through makes the experiences warmer, simpler. The landscape becomes a part of everyday life, and I have trouble separating from it sufficiently to describe it as a writer.

At the same time, Joanne sees what I do not. She points out details I would miss. She questions things I take for granted; interested though untrained in natural history, she asks about birds and behavior and ecological patterns in an observant way that demands clarity and understanding in order to answer. She makes me think beyond where I might have stopped.

On the Black Rock Desert, we once took turns leaving each other. One of us would step out of the vehicle with no gear—no pack, no camera, no water bottle—and simply stand there in T-shirt, shorts, and thongs, with the silence ringing in our ears, while the other drove out of sight. Each of us had a few minutes alone, turning in circles, trying to orient ourselves in the endless miles of barren clay—a near-impossible task. The disorientation was stunning; it was delightful.

When Joanne drove back, the distinction between aloneness and sharing overwhelmed me. The difference was palpable, although both can bring joy.

By 1988, we had a daughter. When we began to hike with Dory, she rode in my backpack with her gurgles and small, singing sounds of wonder a few inches from my ears. She tugged at my hat, grabbed for my glasses, trickled graham cracker crumbs into the neck of my shirt, and craned her head to look around when I stopped.

With Dory, I forged yet another relationship with the land. I walked up mountains, and she slept on my back. I carried through the landscape the feeling of *family* that other generations of parents carried while migrating into North America along the ice sheets, or crossing savanna in Africa, looking for new country.

Parenthood demands everything I have to keep up with its challenges. Hiking with my daughter on my back gave me a sense of fragility and mortality I never had in the days when I always hiked alone. I walked more carefully, both when I carried her and when by myself, for there suddenly was so much to lose to a misstep. I felt vulnerable in a new way.

My sense of time changed forever when Dory was born. People on the trail asked, "How old is she?" Up to about ten weeks, I changed my answer every few days. After the answer could be calculated in months, I could let two weeks go by without marking the passage. But, oh, how different the passage of these weeks and months felt with this living clock in our lives. Wilderness time—the kind that slows when you hike for several days, the past and the future fading, until you live exclusively in the present—will never slow quite as much again.

Her birth transformed my parents and Joanne's mother from parents to grandparents in the moment she slipped from Joanne into my hands. Our only surviving grandparent, Joanne's Grandma Rose, died just four months after Dory's birth. The generations all bumped up a notch. We all moved a little closer toward death.

When Dory was about six months old—and I was more aware of life and death than ever before—Carlos began to fail. Organ after organ slowed until his liver gave out, and he stopped eating. I talked with the vet, who gave him only a couple of days on his own. Carlos maintained his dignity throughout his life, and I felt he should die with dignity. I made an appointment; the vet's secretary entered in her book, "Carlos: euthanasia." I took Carlos home for one last night curled at the foot of our bed.

The next morning, I looked into the brown eyes of my dog, said goodbye, and carried him in from the truck to the vet, to his death. He was weak and old, barely able to walk out the back door that morning to turn the snow yellow one last time. As rickety as he was, in my arms he still felt like Carlos, still my familiar friend of so many years.

The doctor injected him with the jolt of barbiturates that relaxed him so fast neither Carlos nor I had much time to think about it. One moment he lay on the table, alive. The next moment he sprawled on the table, dead. We wrapped him in a green plastic garbage bag, and I carried him back out to my truck. He felt warm and limp inside the plastic. He was not the same dog; I understood the meaning of dead weight.

I sobbed as I began the drive out to the desert to find a place to bury him. I was taking him to the Great Basin, the place where we had shared those fine days of solitude. It was the only place I considered. I would not mind being taken out there myself some faraway day.

I drove seventy miles. On the tape deck I played the first Bach cello suite and the choral finale to Beethoven's Ninth Symphony, music that suited Carlos—the first deceptively simple, the second intense but joyful. As I climbed between the Stansbury and Onaqui mountains, I pulled into a turnout near a line of hills overlooking Rush Valley, its sloping basin full of rough, aromatic sagebrush. The East Tintic Mountains, another small gray-blue range, rolled along the southeastern horizon under a high overcast. A front was headed in from the Pacific. I curled Carlos in his garbage bag into the main compartment of my backpack, shouldered it, and walked off into the piñon and juniper trees through calf-deep snow.

Carlos inside my pack? What an odd thought. I climbed a ridge, using my shovel as a walking stick, found an anonymous clearing between the little conifers, laid the royal blue pack on the white snow, and began digging a hole. The soil was rocky, full of cobbles eroded from the mountains in winter, washed down in summer flash floods to skirt the Stansburys with alluvium. I moved rocks, cut through roots, but did not dig deep.

At the bottom of the hole I put a small photo of Carlos with me and our old truck, a Zuni bear fetish carved with a heartline, and a chocolate chip cookie from a batch my mother had sent at Christmas—Carlos's favorite treat. Then I opened the pack and poured Carlos in a limp curl from his garbage bag. He was still warm. I tucked his teeth under his lips and moved his paws to a comfortable position. I stood back from the grave and leaned on the shovel.

I looked up at the horizon. I had done my crying. Carlos had a good life. This was the end of a time in my own life that had included more time alone, more time shared with my dog, than I ever would have again. Family had ended my solitude; Dory was growing; time was ticking away.

I covered Carlos with stones, then shoveled earth back over his grave. It was deep enough to cover him but not deep enough to keep Coyote away.

My pack felt unnaturally light when I walked back to the truck. I was drained. I drove home. Joanne was out of town. I picked Dory up from the babysitter; I could feel my life ceaselessly pushing ahead, curving into the future.

That night, the front blew through northern Utah, softening the mountains, the silent basins, and Carlos's grave with a foot of fresh snow. I awoke the next morning to a sky scoured by the storm, crisp with cold, clean and crystalline, blazing with restorative sunlight.

Many weekends during the summer after Carlos died, Joanne and Dory and I hiked in the Wasatch Range above our home in Salt Lake City. When fall came, closing in on the equinox, I could feel the seasons turn, the earth spin, time wheel by. On a day of special radiance, I walked down from a glacial basin through aspen forest, warm sun, cool air. Joanne was ahead, with friends. I walked along aware of the absence of my dog trotting beside me, occasionally pushing against my legs in affectionate reassurance. I was alone—except for a small, banana-smeared hand on my shoulder giving me a pat. And a coo in my ear, singing me down the mountain.

III.

Jacob was born in 1991. Dory, like any strong-willed three-year-old displaced by her new brother from her father's backpack, ceased singing me down the mountain and took to whining me up the trail.

The birth of our second child changed the dynamics of our household. With our daughter, we remained two adults—with a child. Once we had two children, we truly became a family. That fact has enormous consequences on both our lives together and on the contrasting experiences with nature of our first- and secondborn.

For three years, Joanne and I planned our family travels primarily to meet our own needs, keeping Dory in mind. On our journeys, however, Dory received the undivided attention that an only, or oldest, child enjoys. When we walked in the desert or the woods, I looked for burrows and beetles, leaves and feathers to point out. Soon she began to notice these things herself, showing them to me, noticing what I had not. Dory became my guide, if I slowed enough to listen.

For Joanne and me, camping had always seemed an athletic experience, involving hiking and climbing and the exultation of ending a day with a satisfying sense of tiredness, having used one's body efficiently to *walk* through the landscape. Good food and going to bed under the stars ended the day, our senses filled to the brim in the best way. With one child, our activity level remained high, for Dory simply came along in the backpack. With the addition of Jacob, even our non–goal-oriented hiking ground to a dead halt.

Now our family lives—and camps—in an intertwining flux of four personalities. Going to the land as a family is a social experience. We all sleep in the family tent. The two children interact with each other. Jacob's need for an afternoon nap meshes with Dory's need to explore around camp and to have our undivided attention for a reasonable interval; we stay put. I trade my solitary intimacy with the earth for the chance to share in my children's small discoveries. Doing what we must to end each day with everyone happy in our temporary home replaces seeing miles of new country as the measure of a successful trip.

Parent and child mutually reinforce each other's enthusiasms, right from the beginning. As a newborn, Jacob calmed down whenever we took him outside in his carriage. When he is fussy at a year-and-a-half, I still take him for walks. Another couple's newborn girl quieted when carried out to watch the evergreen trees waving against the sky at the family's cabin in the Wyoming woods. Babies and parents are learning and teaching: the outside—"nature"—is a soothing place of refuge, filled with interesting things.

As the months progress, infants make more sophisticated choices, fixing on their favorite objects. Jacob looks for birds at the backyard feeder the first thing each morning and the last thing each night. When he was fifteen months old, I joined Jacob and Joanne at a window, and he enthusiastically pronounced his first sentence: "Daa— birr!" A few months later he woke us one spring morning at first light, calling intently—and repeatedly—from his room to announce what he could hear now that the storm windows had been removed: "Bird wake up!" We reinforce his enthusiasm, carrying Jacob to the window every night to say goodnight to his bird friends—and he learns something about what we value.

I love photographing the moon. Dory liked helping to watch for the moonrise, even at two years. Most faraway objects, however, cannot compete with small objects or organisms close at hand. In a child's landscape, everything reduces in scale. If we can be sufficiently patient, we adults can partake a little in our children's journey.

My children encounter various creatures outside our family, too. Dory returns home from a day at the babysitter's asserting that "Vampires are real; Michael says so." She plays with smiling plastic dinosaurs and My Little Ponies, watches Bambi, Benji, and Barney on video, and reads Dr. Seuss books—entering a sanitized world of happy anthropomorphs. Dory seems to distinguish between these play animals and real ones. She tells endless stories about her small realistic plastic figures. She asks to look at the bird book in the truck, leafs through *The Field Guide to Insects* in camp, and concludes that "Insects don't know anything about love." She listens to fairy tailes one night, National Geographic wildlife books the next, and then asks, not surprisingly: "Are wolves bad?"

Joanne and I take our children to the land in part because it simply feels good. Camping gives us a chance to be together without distractions, a place to play together. We also hope that a fundamental connection is growing from these experiences, that the earth will become a source of strength and sustenance for our children, a dependable spiritual bedrock. That feeling grows slowly; how can we nurture it? Experience, positive experience anywhere in the out-of-doors, seems the answer.

When Pueblo Indian potters speak of their work, and of passing on their knowledge to their children, over and over they speak of simply letting their children play with clay. The children learn by watching and doing, not by rote. Bernice Suazo-Naranjo, Taos Pueblo potter, learned potterymaking from her grandmother: "You've got to be there and do it; they are not going to explain, step by step."

As a child, potterymaking was simply part of what happened in Nora Naranjo-Morse's Santa Clara Pueblo home, along with cooking, eating, sleeping, and speaking the Tewa language. Now, she and her sisters and nieces make pottery, but, says Naranjo-Morse: "I rarely talk to my mother about pottery; that connection is instinctively there." Mother of twins on the verge of adolescence, Naranjo-Morse expressed her concern to me that: "A lot of Pueblo kids see this culture in a completely different perspective than our generation; they are more in touch with different worlds. That's why it's so important for me to keep talking to my kids. They don't understand the [Tewa] language; they just accept. And so we instill things in our kids that go beyond the language."

Pueblo Indian children learn about connections to the earth through virtually every experience in their culture. Beginning at about three years of age, Pueblo boys dance in their village plazas as animals, transforming themselves into the spirits of antelope and deer. They wear gray fox skins, deer-hoof and tortoise-shell rattles, parrot feathers, antler and horn headdresses, and skunk-fur gaiters. A little later, the girls may dance as parrots or buffalo mothers. The words of the songs, the symbols painted on costumes, and the choreographed gestures all connect the dancers with the earth: corn, clouds, the sun, rain, lightning, thunder, rainbows, evergreen trees. Life, growth, harvest.

Though I have watched Pueblo dances for many years, I can never share completely in Pueblo faith, even if that were my hope. I remain an outsider. But I feel reassured and renewed by these acts of ritual attention to the earth—to seasonal cycles and sacred mountains and nourishing rains. Pueblo dances remind me to pay more attention to my home landscape, to remember its power and the equality of all life.

And now I take my children to see the plaza dances. Through these occasional visits, I hope that they will come to respect the traditional Native American understanding of the earth and our relationship with its creatures. Pueblo Indian people generously share these ceremonies with anyone who comes to watch. By being there, respectfully, every spectator shares in the power of the dance, every person subtly increases the resonance of the connections celebrated by the dance.

I wonder how my children will remember these times. Dory's strongest memories so far include the snow cone given her by a corn dancer at San Felipe Pueblo and Nora Naranjo-Morse's family dogs, Snickers and Hamburger. Beyond these beginnings, what will my children's need for answers to mysteries lead them to believe? How will the land figure in our communal life?

They will come to know the canyons and mountains, and together we will watch for full moons and rainbows and mark each equinox and solstice. They will have a home landscape. They will not dance as animals or pray for rain to come to their clan's cornfield. They will likely learn more about other creatures from living with dogs and cats than from hunting deer or buffalo.

They will take in all we experience together and combine that with unique genetic destinies. These two forces together will carry them on their personal journeys. As parents, our job is to pay attention, to create possibilities—to be careful matchmakers between our children and the Earth.

Susan J. Tweit

Weeds

from *Barren, Wild, and Worthless:*
Living in the Chihuahuan Desert

Weed—Any plant or vegetation, . . . interfering with the objectives or
requirements of people.
 European Weed Research Society, statutes, article III, 1975

No human being is illegal. Elie Wiesel

On the afternoon of Wednesday, July 1, 1992, the Doña Ana County
Sheriff's Office responded to the report of a body in the desert near
War Road on the Texas–New Mexico border some thirty miles
southeast of Las Cruces. Sheriff's officers arriving at the scene found
the body of an older, dark-skinned Latino man, about 5 foot 2 inches
tall with salt-and-pepper, shoulder-length hair. He was lying face
down in the dirt near the signs marking the state boundary, just eighteen inches over the line in New Mexico. Despite the hundred-plus-
degree heat of that summer afternoon, he was dressed in several
layers of clothing: a blue sweater patterned with stylized birds and
colorful stripes on top, another sweater under that, faded blue
button-fly Levi's and a pair of gold corduroy jeans underneath, black
socks, and black leather tennis shoes tied with baling wire.

He had been there a while. Employees driving War Road to work at White Sands Missile Range had first spotted the man nearby five days before on Friday, June 26. He was carrying a gallon jug of water, a white straw cowboy hat protecting his head from the merciless sun. According to one witness, he was last seen alive sitting on the ground, propped up against the state boundary signposts "looking sick," still wearing the cowboy hat, still carrying the plastic jug, on Monday, June 29. By Wednesday afternoon, he was dead, his sun-blackened body bloated and stinking, his discarded water jug empty. He had died of thrist.

War Road, so called because it links northeast El Paso with the sprawling army facilities of Fort Bliss and White Sands Missile Range, runs through the desolate creosote bush desert across the Franklin and Organ mountains from my house in Las Cruces. It is the main route to and from work for hundreds of El Paso–area commuters bound for the Missile Range. Near where the man died is the main entrance to a cattle ranch. As they zipped by in their air-conditioned vehicles, passers-by could not have missed seeing the man as he stood just a few yards from the road, growing increasingly delirious from hunger and thirst. Yet only a handful of people responded to the pleas of the sheriff's office for witnesses who had seen or talked to the unidentified man. Several reported seeing him; one couple said that they'd seen another driver stop and motion to him as if to offer a ride. But, according to Investigator Ed Miranda of the Doña Ana County Sheriff's Office, not one of the hundreds who must have driven by ever admitted to stopping to talk to or help him. If anyone played Good Samaritan, they didn't admit it.

Fear is a powerful barrier. The dead man was an illegal immigrant, a Mexican national who had crossed the border without papers to come north. Title 8, section 1324 of the U.S. Code makes it a felony to "willfully or knowingly . . . transport . . . conceal, harbor, or shield from detection . . . any alien." For years, federal law forbade giving a ride to a migrant who had crossed the border without papers but not to pay that same person to mow your yard, clean your house, pick your orchard, or weed your chile field. Then came the Immigration Reform and Control Act of 1986, Public Law 99-603, which added "employ" to the list of ways you cannot assist an undocumented immigrant. Today's legal code imposes stiff penalties for "aiding and abetting" illegal immigrants: up to three thousand dollars and five years in jail for each migrant that you give a ride to, allow to sleep in your basement, or pay to work. It is probably not illegal to give a drink of water to a dehydrated and delirious illegal immigrant, but the law is unclear. Better to pretend that you didn't see him. Better to not get involved, even to save his life. Even if some Good Samaritan had overcome her or his own fear and had stopped to offer the now-dead man a ride, he might not have accepted the offer, paralyzed by his own barrier of fear: fear of the Border Patrol, which would arrest him and send him back across *La Frontera;* fear of gang members, thugs, and others who beat up, rob, and generally prey on illegal immigrants; fear of the unknown in this strange country.

We treated the man by the side of War Road as a human weed. He was in the way, unwanted. *Webster's New Universal Unabridged Dictionary* defines *weed* as "any undesired, uncultivated plant that grows in profusion so as to crowd out a desired crop, disfigure a lawn, etc.," or "something useless." An agricultural definition calls a weed "any plant or vegetation, . . . interfering with the objectives or requirements of people." Clearly, a weed is something that we consider an obstacle. *Weed* is a subjective label, not a scientific truth. One person's weed is another's wildflower.

The definition of weed is also clearly flexible. Whether something is a weed or not depends on one's personal viewpoint; how we see things changes as conditions change, and varies over time. One thing remains constant: *Weed* is always derogatory. It designates "other," something or someone that we consider an obstacle to our own success. A weed is ineligible for compassion. A weed is less a reflection of our knowledge than of our prejudices and fears.

In 1894, E. O. Wooton, the first botanist at the New Mexico College of Agriculture and Mechanic Arts (now New Mexico State University) in Las Cruces, wrote a treatise on New Mexico's weeds. His "List of Several of the Worst Weeds of the Southern Part of the Territory with Notes on Each" details nineteen plants, all but one of which are native to the area. Time, new technology, and changing cultural values have radically changed the status of Wooton's worst weeds. Many are no longer problems; some are even valued for their beauty or utility. For example, the common sunflower or *mira sol*, described by Wooton as taking "complete possession of fence corners, roadsides, and ditches and . . . ever encroaching on the cultivated fields," is no longer so common. Herbicides have nearly eliminated it here in the Mesilla Valley. Indeed, a variety of the common sunflower has been completely absolved of weed status and is now grown as a profitable crop.

We treat some human beings like weeds. Just as we may decide that a particular plant is in our way, we sometimes deem whole groups of human beings in the way, threats to our livelihood, security, or prosperity. When we refused asylum to boatloads of Haitian refugees, and sent them home to slow starvation or death squads, we were treating them as weeds. When we seized Native American lands in trade for reservations much like the impoverished black "homelands" of South Africa, we treated them as weeds. When we allow our police forces to harass young blacks or Latinos just because of their skin color and dress, we are treating them as weeds.

The dead man's name was Ramón Vásquez Ramírez. After extensive inquiries in México and the United States, Investigator Miranda finally learned his name from old fingerprint records maintained by the Federal Bureau of Investigation in Quantico, Virginia. Besides his name, the FBI record simply says that he was born in 1923, in Atotonilco, Jalisco, in the tropical highlands of México some fifteen hundred miles south of where he died. Beyond that, the records are silent. Nor did his body say much more. His pockets held neither identification nor family pictures. He died with just six dollars, a cigarette lighter, and a book of matches. With so few details, it is impossible to be certain of Vásquez Ramírez's story. But some things can be inferred. The style of his ivory-colored straw cowboy hat, stiffly creased with an unturned brim, suggests that he was a country-dweller. His short stature, dark mahogany skin, and the broad cheekbones of his face say that he was probably more Indian than Spanish. Bad teeth tell of a life of poverty with no dental care. His plastic water jug says that he was planning to travel through the desert.

Vásquez Ramírez died just outside of Chaparral, New Mexico, the outer edge of the El Paso–Juárez metropolitan area. How did he end up in the desert alongside War Road some twenty miles north of the border? Perhaps he had been dropped at the state line by a *coyote,* a smuggler, who, for a stiff fee in cash, transports human beings across the United States–Mexican border. Maybe the smuggler demanded more money than Vásquez Ramírez possessed and when he couldn't pay enough, the coyote abandoned him there. Or perhaps thugs robbed him and then dropped him off in the desert. Maybe he was waiting for a ride further north, a ride that never came. Or perhaps, too poor to even afford a coyote, Vásquez Ramírez was headed north on foot, alone.

If so, he faced a perilous journey. Ahead of him lay a hundred miles of desert, blazing in the summer heat. Twenty-five miles north —a very long day's walk in hundred-degree temperatures—sprouts the small cluster of buildings that make up the headquarters of White Sands Missile Range. The next human habitation, some thirty-five miles across the open desert, is Holloman Air Force Base, and fifteen miles beyond it is Alamogordo, a military town not known for its friendliness to Mejicanos. Beyond Alamogordo stretches the desert offering neither shade to soften the scorching midday sun nor shelter from the bone-chilling night air, peopled by four-footed coyotes, by rattlesnakes and scorpions, studded by all manner of spiny plants and unexploded army weapons, and marked only by the army's gravel roads, barbed wire fences, tank tracks, and bomb craters. But to an illegal immigrant, the desert might seem safer than the occasional towns, where he is more like to meet *La Migra,* the Border Patrol, or *cholos.*

If possible, most illegal immigrants bypass the desert entirely. Those with enough money buy counterfeit papers and travel north on a flight high above the desert on a commercial airplane. For the many who cannot afford plane fares, the next best and considerably cheaper way is to watch the desolate landscape roll by from an air-conditioned bus. Those without papers may pay coyotes to smuggle them north. These people—called *pollos,* chickens, in México, a term indicating clearly the prey-predator relationship with those who smuggle them—make the journey like so many sacks of con-traband, sometimes stuffed into suffocatingly small compartments in trunks, trailers, or under the floors of a coyote's vans, or even herded into empty cars on freight trains. The coyotes may not bother to fig-ure out where the train is going. The pollos may die from suffocation or heat exhaustion if the train cars end up parked on a siding in the desert and the frightened occupants are unable to open the airtight doors, or may freeze if the train goes north into winter weather they are not prepared for. The poorest undocumented immigrants, un-able to afford coyotes, may hitch their own rides on freight trains, risking heatstroke by clinging to car roofs, or decapitation by hook-ing themselves onto the framework underneath the cars, inches from the track rushing by. Or they may band together and hike across the desert in groups, moving at night. But to cross the desert alone, on foot, is rare. A very poor, very desperate person might attempt it in order to find a job and secure for himself a slice of the good life in *El Norte* or in order to join a family already safely merged into the Latino neighborhoods of Albuquerque, Denver, Los Angeles, or Chi-cago.

Vásquez Ramírez's swollen and sun-blackened body cannot tell us where he was headed and what happened. It says only that he had probably crossed the border before at least once; his fingerprints in that old FBI file date to an arrest in 1951, most likely for illegal entry into the United States. But this last time, Ramón Vásquez Ramírez was not successful. Instead of finding a job and his small piece of prosperity, he died a slow, horrible death.

Investigator Miranda's photographs bear mute witness to Vásquez Ramírez's lonely agony: His plastic water jug, a gallon size that once held Price's Lowfat Milk, lies empty and abandoned on the dusty ground across the road from his body. A cluster of round, green, softball-sized wild buffalo gourds, the kind called *chichicoyotas*, trickster breasts, in México for their stomach-wrenching bitterness, lie nearby, their green surfaces scoured by human teeth marks, like the frantic nibbling of a starving mouse. (Despite the gourds' succulent appearance, few desert animals eat buffalo gourd. The poisons that cause their bitter taste produce nausea, cramps, and vomiting or diarrhea in humans.) Another photo shows only a blackened stain on the ground, the remains of a bloody pool of vomit or diarrhea perhaps caused by the buffalo gourd that Vásquez Ramírez nibbled in desperate thirst. Other photos show scuff marks in the dry, tan soil around his body; his empty right shoe lies kicked away from his black-stockinged right foot, a record of a man thrashing around in delirium before succumbing to the merciful oblivion of unconsciousness. The death of Ramón Vásquez Ramírez, in full view of a well-traveled road, is not a pretty story.

In the late 1870s, Ukrainian farmers in Bon Homme County, South Dakota, inadvertently sowed the seeds of the West's worst weed epidemic when they broke the tough prairie sod to plant flax seed brought from their homes in Russia's arid shrub steppes. Unbeknownst to the farmers, another Russian immigrant, tumbleweed, had hitchhiked a ride along with the flax. Within less than two decades, aided by the wholesale plowing of the prairies, tumbleweed had bounced its way across the Great Plains and was sprouting throughout the West.

The spiny weed, also called Russian thistle, popped up quickly wherever the soil was bare, crowding out crops in fields, clogging irrigation ditches, and spoiling pastures. Its strong spines tore at the flesh of threshing crews and their horses; its seeds fouled grain harvests. Highly flammable, tumbleweed spread prairie fires by rolling and leaping across fire lines to set houses and crops ablaze. Panic-stricken farmers in some places began abandoning their farms.

Drastic eradication measures were proposed. Edward T. Kearney, a North Dakota legislator, imagined building a wire fence around his state to keep tumbleweed out. The Wisconsin Experiment Station suggested that a tumbleweed plant be placed in every schoolhouse and the children be taught to kill it "as they would kill a rattlesnake." New Mexico's E. O. Wooton urged: "Kill it all and now. . . . Never let a single plant bear seed."

Eradication proved impossible. Given a home by poor farming and ranching practices and transport by railroads and irrigation ditches, tumbleweed, the weed that the Hopi call "white man's plant," spread like wildfire across disturbed ground in the West. By the time the Sons of the Pioneers recorded their hit song "Tumbling Tumbleweeds" in 1934, this invader had become such an integral part of its adopted land that it symbolized the West.

There is a heart-wrenching irony here. Tumbleweed, a plant that has come to stand for the West in popular American culture, is truly alien. But the human "weeds" migrating north from México and Latin America belong here. Descended in part from the Maya, Quechua, Aztec, and other ancient cultures of Latin America, these people have more claim to the term *native* than pale-skinned *norteñas* like me. My roots in this American soil are not nearly as deep. My grandfather, my father's father, Olav Tweit, emigrated from Norway in 1917; his wife, my grandmother Christine Farquharson, was the youngest daughter of a Scottish immigrant. Although my mother's family traces some of its roots in America back to the 1700s, most of her Swedish and English forbearers are much more recent arrivals. Yet our political system gives me a citizenship right denied Vásquez Ramírez and his kind; no matter that the cultural right, the right of long-term tenancy, of roots in this American landscape, is clearly theirs. If anyone is an "alien" here, it is newcomers like me.

Even supposing that we could—or should—draw the line between who belongs here and who doesn't, it is no more possible to
stop the tide of illegal immigrants like Ramón Vásquez Ramírez than
it was to stop the spread of tumbleweed. Between three hundred
thousand and half-a-million people enter the United States illegally
each year according to a 1993 report by the federal Commission on
Agricultural Workers. The number of illegal immigrants in this
country is tough to figure, since people afraid of being deported are
understandably reluctant to fill out questionnaires. Still, experts estimate that at least 3.5 million such "undocumented" people live
amongst us. Some eighty-five to ninety percent of them, like Vásquez Ramírez, come from México.

The United States' border with México stretches two thousand
miles from the Gulf of Mexico to the Pacific Ocean. Beginning at
Brownsville, Texas–Matamoros, México, on the Gulf Coast, it runs
up the Río Grande River for twelve hundred miles to where the river
turns north into New Mexico. There the border cuts west across the
arid grasslands and deserts of southern New Mexico, Arizona, and
southern California. It ends where the southern California chaparral
meets the Pacific Ocean between San Diego, California, and Tijuana,
México. Most of this immense sweep of landscape is "unpopulated,"
that is, home to many times more jackrabbits and harvester ants than
people. Tiny towns like Antelope Wells, New Mexico, too small to
be noted by my Rand McNally Road Atlas, home to just a handful of
people and a border station, dot the lonely miles.

The United States' side of this immense stretch of landscape is
patrolled by some thirty-five hundred agents of the Border Patrol
(the agency will not reveal the exact number), the police agency
of the Immigration and Naturalization Service. These one-and-a-
half agents per linear border mile are assisted by local police, state
police and county sheriff's officers. The humans of the Border Patrol
depend on billions of dollars of advanced technology: electronic
ground sensors that detect and report the motion of passing humans to monitors at Border Patrol stations, land-based and airborne

infrared imaging equipment, low-light-level television systems on posts along frequently traveled sections of the border, and helicopters equipped with "Nite Sun" searchlights and infrared radar with heat-sensing capabilities. Still, at its own estimate, the Border Patrol intercepts only one of every three people who enter the country illegally each year. We are asking them to do an impossible job.

The numbers are on the migrants' side. The 625 Border Patrol agents based in the El Paso sector are responsible for patrolling 289 miles of the international boundary, plus 125,000 square miles of landscape—the whole of New Mexico and that portion of west Texas including El Paso. In fiscal year 1992, they picked up 252,066 deportable immigrants, an average of 600 to 900 people per *day,* most of those along the border between El Paso and Juárez, where illegal migrants can simply dash across the political line and blend into crowds of resident Latinos on the United States' side. Ninety-eight percent of the migrants caught by the Border Patrol come from México. Since most Mexican immigrants without papers are simply deported voluntarily—unless they have a criminal record—it is impossible to tell how many of these arrests represent repeaters. Sometimes a deportee will be picked up crossing the border again within an hour after processing.

On a tour of the El Paso–Juárez-area border with Doug Mosier, public affairs officer with the Border Patrol's El Paso sector, I watched dozens of people cross the narrow, concrete-lined waterway of the Río Grande, going from Juárez to El Paso—from legal to illegal, from native to weed—by simply crossing a muddy river. These commuters bypassed official entrance stations on the bridges by riding the informal system of commuter "ferries" across the river itself. Most were simple affairs: a truck tire inner tube with a piece of plywood serving as a deck, towed across by a ferryman who wades or swims depending on the depth of the river. Men and women, some holding a child tightly by the arm, lined up on the Juárez bank of the river waiting for each ferry. Just across the river from the Border Patrol processing station in downtown El Paso itself was an actual ferry boat, a small aluminum skiff bearing the neatly painted name *Río Bravo Trabajo Social,* "Río Grande Social Work." Its musta-chioed captain did a brisk trade carrying customers across the river. Those too poor to afford ferry fare simply undressed and waded or swam across, holding their clothes out of the water. (Wet clothes mark one as distinctly déclassé in El Paso.) It was all part of the morning commute.

Once across the river, the commuters scrambled up the cement embankment on the United States side and collected in small groups just outside of holes torn in the eight-foot-high chain-link fence, waiting until no pale green Border Patrol vans were in sight. When the coast was clear, they would dash across the levy road and cross an adjacent railroad yard, and disappear in downtown El Paso. Bor-der Patrol policy, said Doug Mosier, forbids arresting migrants near the river because of the danger of drownings. Patrol agents therefore wait until the illegal immigrants are away from the river before at-tempting to nab them.

Since I toured the border, the patrol has begun "Operation Hold-the-Line," stationing 400 of its agents within sight of each other in a twenty-four-hour watch along a twenty-mile-long stretch of the Juárez–El Paso border. Operation Hold-the-Line has slowed the flow of illegal crossers in that area to a trickle: apprehensions of undoc-umented immigrants are down to around two hundred per day. But the police line is horrifically expensive, costing U.S. taxpayers $250,000 in overtime for its first two weeks alone, and has also strained relations between the two cities. Further, it seems to have only deflected the flow, other border towns are reporting up to two hundred percent increases in illegal crossings. More people are crossing the desert, and more are dying as they try. Crime in El Paso is down some, according to a recent study by professors at the Uni-versity of Texas at El Paso, but, by concentrating agents on the bor-der, Operation Hold-the-Line has made it easier for those who do make it across to work illegally in El Paso. Once border-crossers are in El Paso, they need not fear La Migra will pick them up.

As we drove along in the air-conditioned Border Patrol sedan, isolated behind tinted windows, I felt profoundly uneasy. I do not visit La Frontera often; I have traveled to Juárez only twice since we moved here. The discontinuity of the Border—relative wealth on one side of La Frontera, poverty on the other—rubs my conscience raw. The ugly, eight-foot-high chain-link fences and uniformed police patrolling this artifical line make the boundary between peoples seem as cruel as the now-torn-down Berlin Wall. Besides good fortune—largely a matter of luck—and pale skin, what separates me from the neatly dressed people who cross the river to work in El Paso each day? Not much. I wanted to get out and talk to the groups of people on the other side of the fence, but I did not know what to say. Instead, I took the coward's way out and waved at the people that we passed, feeling very much like the rich American. To my surprise, since I was riding in a Migra patrol car, many smiled and waved back.

When the Ukrainian farmers of Bon Homme County, South Dakota, stripped the thick prairie sod from atop the black soil to plant their crops, they had no idea that, once they bared the soil, devastating weed infestations were inevitable. Before they plowed the prairies, the dense thatch of grasses left no space for weed seeds to germinate. But once thousands of acres of rich soil were bare, nothing prevented weeds from taking over this new, fertile habitat. Tumbleweed's lickety-split spread across the West was made possible by the farming practices of the day.

So, too, with humans. Today's human migrants are drawn by opportunity, by the promise of jobs, the chance to earn money and live a comfortable life very different from that of the impoverished and crowded conditions of their home places. Per-family income in Latin America averages around twenty-three hundred dollars per year; in the United States, per-family income averages nearly ten times that, or over twenty thousand per year. Unemployment rates are stuck at around forty percent in México, nearly one of every two people cannot find work. In rural México and the Central American–refugee-

clogged south, unemployment rises to eighty or even ninety percent. Just as the plowing of the prairies gave tumbleweed and other
adventitious plants the opportunity to spread, so, too, does the
promise of economic opportunity, real or not, lure today's human
migrants north. We all seek an environment where we can flourish.
If to find that, we must cross La Frontera despite the laws and risks,
so be it. Dreams and aspirations are powerful motivators.

No one knows how many who cross the border surreptitiously
survive the trip. Ramón Vásquez Ramírez's fate is not uncommon,
except for the public aspect. From the hoods who hang out on the
United States' bank of the Río Grande and extort money or sexual
favors from those who swim, wade, or ride across, to the gangs and
banditos on the Mexican side who congregate near popular border
crossing spots to rob, rape, and sometimes kill helpless migrants, to
the coyotes who rob their pollos before abandoning them, the border is a dangerous place. Accurate statistics are hard to come by,
since illegal immigrants are understandably reluctant to report
crimes to the police, who might deport them. But the scattering of
information available is sobering. Between 1984 and 1989, fifteen
hundred people are known to have died along the busiest section of
the line, the California–México border. In 1989 alone, 117 bodies of
drowning victims were recovered just from the Lower Río Grande
Valley in south Texas. Fifty-three of those were never identified, and
no one knows how many more bodies were never found. The total
in 1992 was closer to two hundred; bodies are so commonly pulled
from the river now that some authorities refer to the dead people
casually as "floaters." A year spent reading border newspapers is en-
lightening, and numbing. Stories of accidents to border crossers are
routine. Besides the floaters, people die or are injured when trying
to board or leave moving freight trains; they are raped, beaten, and
shot by thieves, gangs, or American hate groups; they suffocate in
coyotes' vans, trailers or in locked train cars; they are hit and killed
while trying to run across highways; or, like Ramón Vásquez Ramírez, they die of exposure in the inhospitable desert.

Then there is official violence. In México, immigrants must slip past the national and local police without being caught or be subject to beatings, torture, and extortion of money and/or sexual favors. (At the 1989 meeting of the Border Commission on Human Rights, Mexican participants reported 826 "disappeared" persons along the border in México.) In 1992, then–Mexican president Carlos Salinas de Gortari raised the salaries of federal police and border inspectors, vowing to root out corruption. So far, the effect on the largely poor, powerless, and uneducated migrants is not clear. Mexican officials are reluctant to discuss migrants; their continuing flight across the border is an embarrassment to that country.

Nor is this side of the border the promised land. Once safely inside the United States, immigrants like Ramón Vásquez Ramírez often face discrimination, harassment, and worse. Roberto Martínez of the Immigration Law Enforcement Monitoring Project in San Diego keeps tabs on La Migra and other immigration law enforcement agencies in the United States. A recent report from his group, covering the two years from May of 1989 to May of 1991, tallies 1,273 instances of abuses ranging from sexual and physical abuse, including 7 deaths, to denial of due process. The deaths are especially poignant, a record of extreme frustration or hatred erupting into violence. For example, seventeen-year-old Ismael Ramírez died of a brain hemorrhage after a Border Patrol agent lifted him up and threw him down on the street while questioning him in Madera, California. Attorneys for Ramírez's family say this was at least the fifth incident of serious misconduct in the agent's career; the others included a death by vehicle rundown and the beatings of legal immigrants. Eleven months later, the agent was promoted. In another case, a Border Patrol van ran down and killed Luis Eduardo Hernández as he was trying to slip back through the border fence into México. His family sued the Border Patrol and was awarded fifty thousand dollars in damages.

I asked Roberto Martínez if the violence had abated since the 1991 report. "Yes, and no," he said. There had been just one killing in the most recent two-year period, he explained, perhaps because of the publicity brought on by the Immigration Law Enforcement Monitoring Project. But physical and sexual abuse, he thought, were on the rise. Just the previous week, Martínez said, he had taken half a dozen victims of physical abuse that week alone to hearings. One twenty-year-old Mexican national was kicked so badly by Border Patrol agents that he nearly died from injuries to his pancreas. Martínez told of a Border Patrol agent recently sentenced to prison for kidnapping and raping a sixteen-year-old Mexican girl from a migrant labor camp in the United States. After raping her, Martínez said, the agent deported the girl to keep her from testifying against him.

Beatings and harassment are not confined to illegal immigrants; all Latinos, legal residents and citizens alike, and people who look Latino are subject to abuse. In El Paso, students and faculty of Bowie High School, a predominantly Latino high school in a neighborhood next to the border, filed a class action lawsuit against the Border Patrol for continuing harassment. They allege that Border Patrol agents routinely swept the school grounds, picking up all present and taking them to the border for questioning on the presumption that they look like illegal immigrants. On July 15, 1989, Border Patrol agents picked up Pedro Garcia, a nineteen-year-old Bowie High School student and a legal resident, handcuffed him, and drove him to the Paso del Norte Bridge (the border station) to question him because he was not carrying his Green Card, proof of legal residency. "Questioning" in this case involved banging his face against the wall and kicking him.

The Border Patrol dismisses these cases as rarities, problems with "a few bad apples," inevitable in trying to do an impossible job. In El Paso, faced with the Bowie High School suit and other lawsuits, the Border Patrol has begun a pilot sensitivity training project for its agents, has recently set up a twenty-four-hour phone line to receive complaints and comments, and has established a community relations board.

Even if immigrants to El Norte manage to successfully settle and find work, they still face extreme prejudice. Like Ramón Vásquez Ramírez, many are the poorest of the rural poor, with little or no formal education. Many Latinos (and non-Latinos) in the United States despise these *paisanos* as the underclass. Segregated by their lack of English, their lack of education, and their low social status, they keep to their own Spanish-speaking communities. Although they may be highly skilled, their skills as storytellers, *curanderos,* carvers, weavers, potters, and small farmers do not count for much in our society. I was surprised to discover how rigid is the social stratification, how bitter the prejudice against *mojados,* wetbacks, the derisive term for newly arrived illegals.

Take my friend Cruz and her husband, Adrian. Cruz, one of eleven brothers and sisters, was sent north from Guadalajara by her family about four years ago. Determined to finish her education—her dream is to graduate from beauty school and become a hairdresser—she lied about her age in order to enroll in junior high school. After graduating, she married Adrian, born in Torreón, Chihuahua, but now a resident of the United States. They both work hard to make ends meet. Adrian cleans a store at night and bags groceries by day; Cruz struggles to learn English and finish her G.E.D., cleans houses, does ironing, and looks after their two children. It is Cruz's determination that pushes their family towards a better life. Adrian became a United States citizen at her urging; recently, she parlayed their income tax refund into the down payment on a tiny piece of land for their house trailer. Ironically, Adrian's family, immigrants who arrived here just fifteen years before Cruz, treats Cruz like dirt. Some days she despairs. If she could, Cruz says, she would return home to Guadalajara and her family. But there is no work there; economics keeps Cruz here in the strange, hard world of the United States. It is a bitter necessity. "Here," she said to me one day, fierce pride mixing with tears, "I am a nobody, just a *mojada.*"

Despite all, people continue to come north. As I wrote this essay, twenty-nine-year-old Oscar Cardenas said goodbye to his wife and children in Palomas, México, a border town in northern Chihuahua about sixty miles southwest of Las Cruces, and set out on foot across the desert with his twenty-year-old cousin, Chumel Cardenas Castillo, and his cousin's friend, Lalo. They intended to walk to a ranch near Albuquerque, New Mexico, some two hundred fifty miles north, to work. A day later, while crossing a ranch outside the town of Deming, New Mexico, about thirty miles north of Palomas, they ran out of water and became separated. Chumel Cardenas Castillo and his friend turned around and headed home. Oscar Cardenas, chased by wild animals—probably peccaries, boarlike creatures with sharp tusks—fell out of a tree and broke his leg. He crawled to a nearby cattle watering tank and lay there for five days without food, drinking the water from the cattle tank. Cardenas was lucky. The ranch owners found him, close to death, and took him to the hospital. Oscar Cardenas recovered and was sent home to Palomas two weeks after he and his cousin and friend left to walk north. Later that summer, the desert claimed the lives of a Salvadoran woman and a Guatamalan man.

When E. O. Wooton, the botanist at the New Mexico College of Agriculture in Las Cruces, wrote his treatise on New Mexico's weeds in 1894, it was a group of natives, including globemallow, blueweed, and common sunflower, that he considered most vexing. Wooton could not have imagined how time would change his list of worst weeds. As farming practices changed, especially with the chemical herbicides developed after World War II, the perennial natives that Wooton worried about became less and less troublesome. Most are no longer considered problems today. Some, like globemallow, have changed status completely and are now valued as wildflowers; others, like common sunflower, are grown as crops. Wooton's 1894 list didn't mention tumbleweed, that opportunistic alien. Yet within a decade, tumbleweed had swept across the region, taking over cultivated fields, overgrazed rangelands, abandoned farms, and other disturbed ground all across the West. It and other annuals, most introduced, are today's "worst weeds." Tumbleweed not only flourishes still, but this introduced foreigner is so firmly rooted here that it has come to symbolize the West in popular culture.

When does a weed become a problem, something that we root out, spray with herbicides, destroy? Why do we tolerate or ignore some people and then suddenly focus our fear and hatred on them? A few tumbleweeds were no cause for panic. It was only when the invader spread like fire across the bared soils of the West that farmers, legislators, and others began calling for drastic measures to halt the "scourge of the West." When weeds multiply, we see them as a threat to our existence. But it is not that simple. Sometimes weeds are the fall guy, taking the rap for conditions caused by a complicated array of problems.

At the time that grain farmers of the northern Great Plains were panicking and abandoning their tumbleweed-infested farms in the 1890s, a national financial panic was causing widespread farm and bank failures. Easier to blame the foreigners, like invading tumbleweed, than to confront the more complex reality of economics, politics, and culture. These days are similarly uneasy times: The number of low-skill, high-paying industrial jobs continues to decline. In the past decade, major corporations have laid off hundreds of thousands of employees. A college degree no longer guarantees a job. We are frightened for our futures. Rather than tackling the difficult issues involved in today's conditions, we look for a simple solution—someone to blame. Someone who is not "us." "Aha!" we say when we see the hundreds, or thousands, of Vásquez Ramírezes crossing the border. It is "their" fault. "They" are taking our jobs, swelling the welfare rolls, filling our schools with Spanish-speakers, draining our state and federal treasuries dry. So we slam the gates shut, circle the wagons, put up the "No Vacancy" signs.

In 1989, we cheered as the Berlin Wall came down. Half a decade later, we are building our own Berlin Wall along the United States–Mexican border. Between San Diego and Tijuana, the most heavily traveled section of La Frontera, a wall of ten-foot-tall steel planks now replaces the chain-link fence. ("The Tortilla Curtain Goes Steel," reported one newspaper headline.) Steel walls are scheduled to go up along other sections of the border, including one just south of where I live. Edward T. Kearney, the North Dakota legislator who proposed building a wire fence around his state to keep tumbleweed out, would be proud. California, the state that is home to the most illegal immigrants, recently passed Proposition 187, a law that would bar resident illegal immigrants and their children—even if legal residents—from receiving any government services, including public education, all but emergency medical care, and welfare or disaster assistance. The message is loud and clear: "We don't want you. Go home."

In fact, whose "home" is this? We Americans are newcomers, having wrested this northern Chihuahuan Desert country from Vásquez Ramírez's country in the Mexican-American War between 1846 and 1848. The current United States–México border is a political line imposed across a people, artificially dividing the residents into "Mexicans" and "Americans." Many still have family on both sides of the line, another echo of the Berlin Wall. Who, then, are the "natives" and who are the "weeds"?

In the early 1800s, before the United States acquired by force, by purchase, and by treaty what is now the Southwest, a stream of American citizens was already encroaching illegally onto this foreign territory, looking for profits to be made trading, trapping, mining, and farming. During that period, the fledgling government of México, worried about securing what is now Texas against the French, invited Americans to apply for land and, if accepted, colonize the area and become Mexican citizens. Many did. But others avoided the official process and moved in on their own as "illegal aliens." The private land agents set up to process American settlers complained bitterly about the illegals, whom they considered to be "wanderers" and "ne'er-do-wells" harmful to the well-being of the territory. Sound familiar?

Many Mejicanos are newcomers too, descendants of the Spaniards who wrenched this Chihuahuan Desert country from the resident Native Americans in the 1500s and 1600s. Even Native Americans came from somewhere else: the Apaches, Athapaskan speakers most closely related to Aleuts, moved down from the North as recently as the 1400s, encroaching on the resident Manso, Jano, Suma, Jumano, Piro, and Tewa peoples. These cultures, descendants of the Mogollon and Anasazi, are themselves descended from "illegal aliens," migrants who probably arrived in what is now the Chihuahuan Desert from the steppes of Siberia as recently as fifteen thousand years ago. The history of "illegal immigration" to the Southwest is thus a long one.

Immigrants from México were not always seen as weeds. When the United States first began to restrict immigration in the late 1800s, Americans were not concerned about migrants from south of the border at all. The first exclusion acts aimed to stop the flow of people from across the Pacific. In the Go-West-Young-Man boom days after the Civil War, thousands of Chinese, mostly from Kwangtung Province around Canton, came east to the West as contract laborers. They built our railroads, dug our mines, and tilled our farm fields. In his book *Border,* a history of the United States–México boundary, historian Leon Metz calls the Chinese the "economic precursors to the Mexicans." Willing to work cheaply in conditions intolerable to others, many Chinese came, stayed long enough to satisfy their contract and accumulate what in China was a fortune, and returned home.

As the West's boom years were punctured by economic hard times, public feeling turned against the Chinese. Trade unions and newspaper editorials excoriated the "yellow peril" for taking jobs from American laborers. Fueled by the growing climate of hatred, mobs of toughs beat up or lynched anyone who looked Oriental, looted their stores and restaurants, and burned Chinese neighborhoods. But just as immigrants continue to come to El Norte today, neither violence nor prejudice nor laws stemmed the flow of Chinese. Plenty of Chinese needed the work; plenty of American employers wanted cheap, hard-working laborers. After Canada banned their passage, the Chinese slipped across the border from México. Coyotes of the day guided them across the border to Chinatowns in western cities, a situation eerily similar to today's Latino migrants.

In those years, Mexicans were welcome. They took the place of the now-banned Chinese in railroad construction and in working the huge areas of agricultural land created by new federal water projects in the Southwest. In fact, when Congress appropriated 1 million dollars in 1924 to create the Border Patrol, its mission was to prevent illegal European and Chinese immigration along the Mexican border, not to stop Mejicanos.

Then came the crash of 1929 and the Great Depression. Suddenly Mexican laborers were in the way; they were seen as taking American jobs: weeds. In an echo of the "yellow peril" of the late 1800s, prejudice against Mexicans and Mexican Americans rose dramatically. People looking or sounding Mejicano were the target of harassment and violence. Between November 1929 and the end of 1931, over 350,000 Mexican nationals—and some Mexican Americans—left the United States for México, most voluntarily, taking advantage of free transportation, food for the journey, and even cash inducements offered by government agencies.

Not until World War II were Mexicans welcome across the border again, and then only under certain conditions. The Armed Forces, wartime industry, and internment camps absorbed the low-wage labor force, leaving western farmers literally helpless. Hence the "Bracero" agreement, a regulated program of contract labor that allowed American farmers (and railroads) during the war to import Mexican workers. As long as they came under the Bracero Program, Mexicans were welcome again.

In 1964, the door slammed shut again when the Bracero Program was terminated. Nowadays, unless they are family members of permanent residents or of U.S. citizens, ordinary Mexicans like Oscar Cardenas or Ramón Vásquez Ramírez have almost no chance to come here legally. We do not want them. They are weeds.

When my grandfather Olav came to the United States as an immigrant in 1917, he was seeking just what the migrants from México and Central America seek today: economic opportunity. He worked his way across the ocean from Norway doing hard, dangerous, low-paying work, shoveling coal into the blazing fires of ships' engines. The car factories of Detroit attracted this farm boy; he dreamed of becoming a design engineer. With just a high school education and no English, Olav started at the bottom, guiding freshly painted wooden wheel rims off of the assembly line at the Maxwell auto plant for thirty-one cents a day. By the time he married my grandmother Chris, the youngest daughter of a Scottish immigrant, he had learned English and had moved up to draftsman. Eventually, he achieved his dream and designed coke ovens for steel plants. But in 1917, newly arrived from impoverished Hardanger Fjord in rural Norway, what was then the "Third World," my grandfather Olav was surely just as much a weed as those who cross the border today. How many among us are the children and grandchildren of just such immigrants?

It seems to me that the only sin of immigrants like Oscar Cardenas and Ramón Vásquez Ramírez—or my grandfather Olav—is poverty. And poverty is no sin—it is something that we relatively well-off Americans fear. If we let too many of "them" in, "they" will take "our" jobs, bankrupt "our" schools, hospitals, and welfare systems; we will all be poor. Indeed. The greatest and only poverty that we need fear is the spiritual and moral poverty resulting from our own lack of generosity.

We cannot draw arbitrary political lines in the desert and declare that one side is "ours" and the other "theirs." Such boundaries are imaginary. Poverty and crime cross them every day. So do air and water pollution, disease, and prejudice and fear. "They" are, in reality, "us." None of us—Anglos, Latinos, Native Americans—has a superior claim to belong here. In one way or another, we are all weeds. Our challenge is not to draw lines but to erase them. If we see immigrants like Cardenas and Ramírez as weeds, perhaps it is our vision that is at fault. As Ralph Waldo Emerson said, "A weed is a plant whose virtues have not yet been discovered."

What haunts me about Ramón Vásquez Ramírez is that we, who have plenty to share, allowed him to die. No, worse—we *watched* him die a horrible, prolonged death in the desert. If I had been speeding along War Road in my air-conditioned car to work at White Sands, would I have stopped? Would I have gone out of my way to help this slight, brown-skinned man? I wish that I could answer with an unswerving "yes." But I am not sure. It all depends, doesn't it, on whether we see the human being through our prejudices and fears. Would I see only his dirty sweater, his stained jeans, his bad teeth, and his obvious poverty and illegal status? Or would I see someone's well-loved brother, uncle, father, *abuelo?*

Investigator Ed Miranda of the Doña Ana County Sheriff's Office reports that, although he informed Mexican authorities about Ramón Vásquez Ramírez's death as soon as he identified Ramírez, no one ever claimed the body. In the end, Ramírez was given an indigent's burial by Crestview Mortuary in Albuquerque. Next time I go to Albuquerque, I think I'll visit him and put flowers on his grave.

Weeds. Who are they anyway?

Scott Russell Sanders

Buckeye

from *Orion*

Years after my father's heart quit, I keep in a wooden box on my desk the two buckeyes that were in his pocket when he died. Once the size of plums, the brown seeds are shriveled now, hollow, hard as pebbles, yet they still gleam from the polish of his hands. He used to reach for them in his overalls or suit pants and click them together, or he would draw them out, cupped in his palm, and twirl them with his blunt carpenter's fingers, all the while humming snatches of old tunes.

"Do you really believe buckeyes keep off arthritis?" I asked him more than once.

He would flex his hands and say, "I do so far."

My father never paid much heed to pain. Near the end, when his worn knee often slipped out of joint, he would pound it back in place with a rubber mallet. If a splinter worked into his flesh beyond the reach of tweezers, he would heat the blade of his knife over a cigarette lighter and slice through the skin. He sought to ward off arthritis not because he feared pain but because he lived through his hands, and he dreaded the swelling of knuckles, the stiffening of fingers. What use would he be if he could no longer hold a hammer or guide a plow? When he was a boy he had known farmers not yet forty years old whose hands had curled into claws, men so crippled up they could not tie their own shoes, could not sign their names.

"I mean to tickle my grandchildren when they come along," he told me, "and I mean to build doll houses and turn spindles for tiny chairs on my lathe."

So he fondled those buckeyes as if they were charms, carrying them with him when our family moved from Ohio at the end of my childhood, bearing them to new homes in Louisiana, then Oklahoma, Ontario, and Mississippi, carrying them still on his final day when pain a thousand times fiercer than arthritis gripped his heart.

The box where I keep the buckeyes also comes from Ohio, made by my father from a walnut plank he bought at a farm auction. I remember the auction, remember the sagging face of the widow whose home was being sold, remember my father telling her he would prize that walnut as if he had watched the tree grow from a sapling on his own land. He did not care for pewter or silver or gold, but he cherished wood. On the rare occasions when my mother coaxed him into a museum, he ignored the paintings or porcelain and studied the exhibit cases, the banisters, the moldings, the parquet floors.

I remember him planing that walnut board, sawing it, sanding it, joining piece to piece to make foot stools, picture frames, jewelry boxes. My own box, a bit larger than a soap dish, lined with red corduroy, was meant to hold earrings and pins, not buckeyes. The top is inlaid with pieces fitted so as to bring out the grain, four diagonal joints converging from the corners toward the center. If I stare long enough at those converging lines, they float free of the box and point to a center deeper than wood.

I learned to recognize buckeyes and beeches, sugar maples and shagbark hickories, wild cherries, walnuts, and dozens of other trees while tramping through the Ohio woods with my father. To his eyes, their shapes, their leaves, their bark, their winter buds were as distinctive as the set of a friend's shoulders. As with friends, he was partial to some, craving their company, so he would go out of his way to visit particular trees, walking in a circle around the splayed roots of a sycamore, laying his hand against the trunk of a white oak, ruffling the feathery green boughs of a cedar. "Trees breathe," he told me. "Listen."

I listened, and heard the stir of breath.

He was no botanist; the names and uses he taught me were those he had learned from country folks, not from books. Latin never crossed his lips. Only much later would I discover that the tree he called ironwood, its branches like muscular arms, good for ax handles, is known in books as hop hornbeam; what he called tuliptree or canoewood, ideal for log cabins, is officially the yellow poplar; what he called hoop ash, good for barrels and fence posts, appears in books as hackberry.

When he introduced me to the buckeye, he broke off a chunk of the gray bark and held it to my nose. I gagged.

"That's why the old-timers called it stinking buckeye," he told me. "They used it for cradles and feed troughs and peg legs."

"Why for peg legs?" I asked.

"Because it's light and hard to split, so it won't shatter when you're clumping around."

He showed me this tree in late summer, when the fruits had fallen and the ground was littered with prickly brown pods. He picked up one, as fat as a lemon, and peeled away the husk to reveal the shiny seed. He laid it in my palm and closed my fist around it so the seed peeped out from the circle formed by my index finger and thumb. "You see where it got the name?" he asked.

I saw: what gleamed in my hand was the bright eye of a deer. "It's beautiful," I said.

"It's beautiful," my father agreed, "but also poisonous. Nobody eats buckeyes, except maybe a fool squirrel."

I knew the gaze of deer from living in the Ravenna Arsenal, in Portage County, up in the northeastern corner of Ohio. After supper we often drove the Arsenal's gravel roads, past the munitions bunkers, past acres of rusting tanks and wrecked bombers, into the far fields where we counted deer. One June evening, while mist rose from the ponds, we counted 311, our family record. We found deer in herds, in bunches, in amorous pairs. We came upon lone bucks, their antlers lifted against the sky like the bare branches of dogwood. If you were quiet, if your hands were empty, if you moved slowly, you could leave the car and steal to within a few paces of a grazing deer, close enough to see the delicate lips, the twitching nostrils, the glossy, fathomless eyes.

The wooden box on my desk holds those grazing deer, as it holds the buckeyes and the walnut plank and the farm auction and the munitions bunkers and the breathing forests and my father's hands. I could lose the box, I could lose the polished seeds, but if I were to lose the memories I would become a bush without roots, and every new breeze would toss me about.

All those memories lead back to the northeastern corner of Ohio, where I learned to connect feelings with words. Much of the land I knew in that place as a child had been ravaged. The ponds in the Arsenal teemed with bluegill and beaver, but they were also laced with TNT from the making of bombs. Because the wolves and coyotes had long since been killed, some of the deer, so plump in the June grass, collapsed on the January snow, whittled by hunger to racks of bones. Outside the Arsenal's high barbed fences, many of the farms had failed, their barns caving in, their topsoil gone. Ravines were choked with swollen couches and junked washing machines and cars. Crossing fields, you had to be careful not to slice your feet on tin cans or shards of glass. Most of the rivers had been dammed, turning fertile valleys into scummy playgrounds for boats.

One free-flowing river, the Mahoning, ran past the small farm near the Arsenal where our family lived during my later years in Ohio. We owned just enough land to pasture three ponies and to grow vegetables for our table, but those few acres opened onto miles of woods and creeks and secret meadows. I walked that land in every season, every weather, following animal trails. But then the Mahoning, too, was doomed by a government decision; we were forced to sell our land, and a dam began to rise across the river.

If enough people had spoken for the river, we might have saved it. If enough people had believed that our scarred country was worth defending, we might have dug in our heels and fought. Our attachments to the land were all private. We had no shared lore, no literature, no art to root us there, to give us courage, to help us stand our ground. The only maps we had were those issued by the state, showing a maze of numbered lines stretched over emptiness. The Ohio landscape never showed up on postcards or posters, never unfurled like tapestry in films, rarely filled even a paragraph in books. There were no mountains in that place, no waterfalls, no rocky gorges, no vistas. It was a country of low hills, cutover woods, scoured fields, villages that had lost their purpose, roads that had lost their way.

"Let us love the country of here below," Simone Weil urged. "It is real; it offers resistance to love. It is this country that God has given us to love. He has willed that it should be difficult yet possible to love it." Which is the deeper truth about buckeyes, their poison or their beauty? I hold with the beauty; or rather, I am held by the beauty, without forgetting the poison. In my corner of Ohio the gullies were choked with trash, yet cedars flickered up like green flames from cracks in stone; in the evening bombs exploded at the ammunition dump, yet from the darkness came the mating cries of owls. I was saved from despair by knowing a few men and women who cared enough about the land to clean up trash, who planted walnuts and oaks that would long outlive them, who imagined a world that would have no call for bombs.

How could our hearts be large enough for heaven if they are not large enough for earth? The only country I am certain of is the one here below. The only paradise I know is the one lit by our everyday sun, this land of difficult love, shot through with shadow. The place where we learn this love, if we learn it at all, shimmers behind every new place we inhabit.

———

A family move carried me away from Ohio thirty years ago; my schooling and marriage and job have kept me away ever since, except for occasional visits. I returned to the site of our farm one cold November day, when the trees were skeletons and the ground shone with the yellow of fallen leaves. From a previous trip I knew that our house had been bulldozed, our yard and pasture had grown up in thickets, and the reservoir had flooded the woods. On my earlier visit I had merely gazed from the car, too numb with loss to climb out. But on this November day, I parked the car, drew on my hat and gloves, opened the door, and walked.

I was looking for some sign that we had lived there, some token of our affection for the place. All that I recognized, aside from the contours of the land, were two weeping willows that my father and I had planted near the road. They had been slips the length of my forearm when we set them out, and now their crowns rose higher than the telephone poles. When I touched them last, their trunks had been smooth and supple, as thin as my wrist, and now they were furrowed and stout. I took off my gloves and laid my hands against the rough bark. Immediately I felt the wince of tears. "Hello, Father," I said, quietly at first, then louder and louder, as if only shouts could reach him through the bark and miles and years.

Surprised by sobs, I turned from the willows and stumbled away toward the drowned woods, calling to my father. I sensed that he was nearby. Even as I called, I was wary of grief's deceptions. I had never seen his body after he died. By the time I reached the place of his death, a furnace had reduced him to ashes. The need to see him, to let go of him, to let go of this land and time, was powerful enough to summon mirages; I knew that. But I also knew, stumbling toward the woods, that my father was here.

At the bottom of a slope where the creek used to run, I came to an expanse of gray stumps and withered grass. It was a bay of the reservoir from which the water had retreated, the level drawn down by engineers or drought. I stood at the edge of this desolate ground, willing it back to life, trying to recall the woods where my father had taught me the names of trees. No green shoots rose. I walked out among the stumps. The grass crackled under my boots, breath rasped in my throat, but otherwise the world was silent.

Then a cry broke overhead and I looked up to see a red-tailed hawk launching out from the top of an oak—a band of dark feathers across the creamy breast and the tail splayed like rosy fingers against the sun. It was a red-tailed hawk for sure; and it was also my father. Not a symbol of my father, not a reminder, not a ghost, but the man himself, right there, circling in the air above me. I knew this as clearly as I knew the sun burned in the sky. A calm poured through me. My chest quit heaving. My eyes dried.

Hawk and father wheeled above me, circle upon circle, wings barely moving, head still. My own head was still, looking up, knowing and being known. Time scattered like fog. At length, father and hawk stroked the air with those powerful wings, three beats, then vanished over a ridge.

The voice of my education told me then and tells me now that I did not meet my father, that I merely projected my longing onto a bird. My education may well be right; yet nothing I heard in school, nothing I've ever read, no lesson reached by logic has ever convinced me as utterly or stirred me as deeply as did that red-tailed hawk. Nothing in my education prepared me to love a piece of the earth, least of all a humble, battered country like northeastern Ohio; I learned from the land itself.

Before leaving the drowned woods, I looked around at the ashen stumps, the wilted grass, and for the first time since moving from this place I was able to let it go. This ground was lost; the flood would reclaim it. But other ground could be saved, must be saved, in every watershed, every neighborhood. For each home ground we need new maps, living maps, stories and poems, photographs and paintings, essays and songs. We need to know where we are, so that we may dwell in our place with a full heart.

Adrienne Ross

Homecoming

First publication

One day, seven years after coming to Seattle, I looked up at the fiery red leaves of a vine maple and thought not of the brilliant fall colors of my old home in upstate New York, but rather that the leaves were changing, that it was almost the Jewish New Year of Rosh Hashanah, and that soon the salmon would be back. I no longer expected bitter winds and snowstorms as fall crept into winter. I had integrated my life into the more subtle changes of the seasons that occur in my new home, cyclic shifts marked by rain and the salmon, or what remained of them, coming back to take possession of their once undisputed waterways.

When I first came to Seattle, I found it hard to live again in a city after three years in a country cottage where a boulder-strewn creek flowed through my backyard and the green hillsides of the Catskill Mountains surrounded me wherever I looked. I longed for nature, and the more I tried to find it in my new home in the Pacific Northwest, the more curious I became about the salmon. They seemed to be everywhere yet nowhere; appearing suddenly and then disappearing like an old family ghost, spoken of often but usually in the past tense. People talked of the fish once seen in creeks now long gone to strip malls and parking lots; they spoke of how many salmon they could once catch and how big the sockeye or chinook or chum used to be. And like ghosts fading from human memory, the salmon's return to their ancestral home seemed to become more tenuous with each passing year.

Once I started to search for the salmon, I never imagined they were here with me in the city. Last fall, some 5,000 wild sockeye salmon journeyed up a small creek as it flowed alongside housing developments and highways in the suburban community of Redmond, home to the Microsoft Corporation and only a half-hour from Seattle. The sockeye's journey up Cottage Creek was part of an ancient, now tattered but once great annual homecoming of salmon returning from the ocean to mate, lay their eggs, and then die in the same creeks where they were born. Salmon, having long bridged river to sea, were now linking the urban to the wild.

I first discovered Cottage Creek during mid-October, never expecting to find a suburban stream filled with sockeye crimson and gleaming in the swift, clear water. An unmarked blacktop footpath, easily mistaken for a driveway, went from a two-lane road to the creek. Behind the neatly cut lawns and two-car garages, flowing through a wild riot of sword ferns, lichen-encrusted alders, and the ubiquitous tangled thorn bushes of Himalayan blackberries, Cottage Creek was thick with pairs of mating sockeye darting back and forth, nipping the tails and fins of intruders to keep them from the precious redds, the sites for their egg nests.

The males were humpbacked and their snouts were descended into fangs. I watched as sockeye gathered in the circular redds dug into the streambed, their bodies pressed close to their mates, their tails quivering in rapid, intense bursts. It seemed almost absurd to hear cutting through the Sunday suburban sounds of barking dogs and pounding hammers, the sharp, almost frantic slapping noises of a female salmon lying flat against the creekbed, her crimson body arching out of the shallow water, tail thumping in determined flaps to carve a redd into the gravel and loose soils of the streambed. The fins and dorsal spines of most of the sockeye were pale, and their bodies were abraded with a white fungus heralding their incipient deaths.

Salmon are the great gift of life. Their death and decay restore nutrients that have drained off the land during the winter rains and washed out to sea. These nutrients are eaten by plankton that are in turn eaten by larger organisms. Eventually these once landlocked nutrients travel through the food chain until they return to the forests in the form of spawning salmon. This great, circling dance of death and resurrection has made salmon a staple in the diets of human and nonhuman denizens of the Pacific Northwest. Dozens of species rely on the annual return and subsequent death of the five species of Pacific salmon (and two species of trout) that occur every August through January. Shrews and coyotes feed on them, as do many other birds and animals; even black-tailed deer have been known to daintily nibble their streamside carcasses for nutrients. Like many cities, Redmond has a rich and secret wildlife. Even in this affluent neighborhood of cedar-shingled homes, raccoons, river otters, eagles, and herons will come to eat the salmon and scavenge their carcasses. Black bears have been spotted in the area in the past, and undoubtedly the stream is visited by city coyotes.

As a girl growing up in the New York City suburbs, the only salmon I ever saw was the neon-pink lox eaten with bagels and cream cheese each Saturday after Temple Zion's Sabbath services. Yet I knew, even then, that this fish not only came from the Northwest but was somehow identified with it. Even on the other side of a continent, I had heard the stories of rivers so thick with salmon that a person could walk across their backs from one shore to the other. When the earliest white settlers and fur traders came to the region, they first used salmon as a subsistence food source. By the mid-nineteenth century, however, salmon had become a commodity that could make or break personal fortunes. Entire industries built up around the annual return of the fish; even today, salmon continues to shape the economic growth of the Pacific Northwest.

To indigenous cultures on both sides of the Pacific, though, salmon have been both food *and* spirit. A common theme in Pacific Coast mythology is that returning salmon are actually the Salmon People, supernatural beings who go about in human form in their undersea villages. Every year, the Salmon People don fish disguises and make a great sacrifice of themselves so that their land-brethren can have food for the year. Many Pacific Coast cultures treated the first salmon caught as an honored guest, greeting it with sacramental songs and processions, a special feast of its flesh and, in many areas, a ritual return of its bones to the sea. If the first salmon were given its due, it would tell the rest of the Salmon People who would then return out of appreciation for the respect and courtesy shown them.

Twisting weakly in the thick mud, half out of the shallow water, a male sockeye struggled to make his way back to Cottage Creek. The fish had swum underneath the partially raised roots of a huge old cedar, and wound up not in a part of the creek thick with females, but in a tiny mud puddle. He had lost the genetic race. None of the sockeye had eaten since they left the ocean weeks ago to make their way upstream to where they were born. Their sole drive was to breed, and this male was stuck in the mud.

A Sierra Club field trip was at the creek that day, and one of the men waded into the black mud, grabbed the struggling sockeye, and tossed it back into Cottage Creek. Immediately, the fish continued on his way upstream. A brief and heated discussion on the ethics of interfering with natural selection ensued, but it ended quickly enough when someone said, "We can't afford to lose a single one."

Bear Creek, of which Cottage Creek is a tributary, saw a record 40,000 sockeye swim up it last fall, making it one of the most successful wild salmon runs in western Washington. King County's new Waterways 2000 program has made habitat protection for Bear Creek and a handful of other local waterways a priority. Yet sockeye and other salmon are steadily losing ground in other areas of the Pacific Northwest. Sockeye, which were once found in over 3 million acres across the Pacific Northwest, are now extinct in 60 percent of their original range.

Though their numbers are dwindling, salmon still possess their eerie ancestral genetic determination to return. Only now, wild salmon fight their way past estuaries clogged with factories and industrial ports. They swim up polluted rivers, past dams and hydroelectric plants, trying to ascend streams and creeks that often have run dry from clearcutting, grazing, mining, or urban sprawl. The wild salmon must compete with the genetically less fit yet far more aggressive hatchery-reared salmon for food and what little habitat remains. Since the turn of the century, hatcheries have been the technological fix promoted to replace wild runs destroyed whenever a dam was built, a stream was siphoned off for irrigation, or fishing limits were raised. Yet hatchery fish released into regional waterways have the same need for habitat as wild fish.

Cottage Creek's wild salmon function as canaries in an aquatic mine in a way that hatchery fish cannot. Keeping hatchery numbers high can be done by raising production so that the survival odds for any given generation are increased. Wild runs—even those found in a stream that flows partway under culverts or alongside country clubs—reflect centuries of careful evolutionary adaptation to local waterways. When spawning time comes, hatchery fish return to the hatcheries while wild fish return to their natal streams. This makes wild salmon a sensitive indicator of the health of local waterways. Since salmon, whether wild or hatchery raised, require healthy streams and river systems, productive and unpolluted estuaries, and an ocean environment that is not overfished, they span the economy and ecosystems of the Pacific Northwest in a way that is unmatched by virtually any other species.

I came back often to Cottage Creek, snatching a few hours away from weekend chores to see the salmon. Their presence was somehow in keeping with the season. Fall was always my favorite time of year, poised as it is between summer's joyous fertility and winter's long, dark gestation. Fall also brought the Jewish High Holy Days of Rosh Hashanah (the New Year) and Yom Kippur (the Day of Atonement), a time set apart from the rest of the year. It was during the High Holy Days that the deeds of the last year were carefully scrutinized, sins acknowledged, and hopeful prayers said for the new year. Salmon, with their own peculiar joining of past, present, and future, fit the character of the season.

One Sunday afternoon, I watched as a blonde girl of seven or eight ran up the paved trail to Cottage Creek's footbridge. She was pulling her older sister and grandmother in her wake. At the sound of footsteps, several sockeye quickly hid in the shadows under the bridge.

"Pew! Stinky!" she squealed, holding her nose at the smell of the carcasses that, even early in the run, were beginning to line the muddy streambanks. That rotting smell was the sign of a healthy Northwest stream, one still clean and free-flowing enough to support salmon. It is a smell that has become all too rare.

"What are those?" The girl pointed to two enormous salmon, easily twice the size of the sockeye, which suddenly swam into view. Thrashing the water with strong bodies specked with black dots, the fish displaced a sockeye from a shallow pool.

The girl's grandmother, a plump dark-haired woman in an embroidered pink running suit, sighed and looked away, saying, "I eat them, but I don't know what they are."

I pointed out the fish to the older girl and asked her if she knew what it was. The girl hesitated, her dark hair falling across a face tight with concentration. She chose her words carefully, with a scientist's instinct for exactness. "Our teacher said two kinds of salmon come here. These are the sockeye," she said, pointing to a female holding still in the shade of an alder tree. At last she confessed, with a disappointed shrug, "I'm sorry. I can't remember the other kind."

"They're *tyee,*" I said. "Chinook salmon."

Throughout western Washington, there are hotels named *tyee,* boats named *tyee,* even restaurants and convention centers named for these fish. Yet how many people still know that *tyee* is Chinook jargon for "chief, the big fish," the giant that reached record sizes of over 100 pounds and once swam thick up Northwest rivers such as the Elwha? Wild fish adapt to match their home streams, so a basic axiom in salmon biology is that the size of the fish indicates the size of the river where it spawns. A fierce river such as the Elwha acts as a mechanism of natural selection favoring chinook of impressive size and strength. The chinook in Cottage Creek, on the other hand, share ancestors that spawned in medium-size rivers and tributaries, producing salmon of noticeable but nowhere near legendary size. *Tyee* were particularly hard-hit by dam building on their native rivers, making them now among the least abundant and most highly prized of all Northwest salmon species. Yet what is in danger of becoming extinct is both the fish and the meaning of the word. Each species lost, and each name of a species forgotten, is a loss not only of a unique life form. It is a loss of how we relate to the rest of the world. Whether we realize it or not, each extinction of an animal means an extinction of human wisdom and culture.

"Here comes another family!" the blonde girl squealed, interrupting her older sister's explanation of how far the salmon travel to finally reach the creek. Quickly I looked at the water, expecting to see two sockeye working their way upstream. Instead, another human family, fuzzy in their blue Polartec jackets, joined us at the footbridge. The father stood near his son, both wearing matching Mariners' baseball caps, and pointed out the humpbacked males from the females.

"Those are the daddies! Where are the girls?" cried his young son, interrupting his father to point to a carcass in the mud. "It's covered with ice!"

"It's not ice, it's mold. The fish are decomposing," the father said patiently, slowly and carefully stressing each syllable as he gave his son a new word. "De-com-po-sing. The fish are dead. Their bodies are rotting away."

"Look, Grandma, there's one with its eyes poked out," the blonde girl yelled, again interrupting her older sister's careful, if halting, explanation of how the eggs get laid. The younger girl clenched her fists and pressed them tightly against her bright blue eyes.

Most people see salmon only at the end of a long and complicated life cycle. The sockeye that hatched out the following spring stayed in Cottage Creek for only a short while, spending their juvenile years feeding and pooling in nearby Lake Washington or Lake Sammamish. After staying there for anywhere from one to three years, the juvenile sockeye will make their way downstream. Once at sea, Pacific Northwest sockeye swim in a great spiral dance northward along the Pacific Coast, up to Alaska, veering west toward the Aleutians. From there the sockeye will turn again, this time south and east toward a home they barely know. This maritime waltz can last as long as four years and carry the Pacific Northwest sockeye thousands of miles from where they began.

Despite their brief sojourn in Cottage Creek, these sockeye know this area better than I do. The map I used to get here showed streets and intersections, highway entrances and city limits, not watersheds and drainages, nesting sites or rookeries. Another terrain is present underneath the industrial overlay, another set of haunts and routes, hidden yet coexisting with roads leading to soccer fields and Pizza Huts, or concrete trails bisecting suburban housing developments. Habitat, after all, is never simply destroyed. It is recreated in ways that express our current values and the limits of our imagination.

When I returned to the creek several weeks later, a light rain was falling with the twilight. Walking down the slick blacktop path, I jumped as a muffled boom greeted my footsteps. A great blue heron emerged from tree cover and wheeled its sinuous body over the creek, its huge blue-gray wings slapping the darkening sky. The heron flew into a brisk evening air rich with smells raised by the afternoon rains. Cutting through the thick aroma of fertile earth was a sharp smell of sweetness gone too far, lost and turning past ripeness into something bitter, pungent, and decaying.

I counted seventeen sockeye salmon carcasses belly up, twisted, some a fading pink; others silver; still others with the skins pulled back to expose cream-colored flesh and fragile vertebrae. Their bodies seemed to bubble with algae, and their mouths gaped open, filled with fallen leaves.

A chinook was in the creekbed, so still that I thought it was recently dead until I saw the faint movement of its jaw. A humpbacked male sockeye undulated slowly through this maze of death. I couldn't help but wonder what, if anything, it made of the dead bodies of its brethren.

Yet Cottage Creek was filled with living fish; unseen, tiny eggs gestating amid the oxygen-rich gravel of the streambed; forming, waiting in the creek's dark, rain-swollen waters. By the following spring, when they hatched from their eggs as alevin, their yolk sacs swollen with nourishment, there would be no sign of their parents, not even a skeleton picked clean and abandoned in the black mud where the creek meets the shore. Yet their unknown parents bequeathed them a vast inheritance of genetic wisdom that will guide them to hide in riffles and logjams, to follow the creek to a lake and then out to sea, to school past the waiting jaws of orcas and fur seals, and then one day to start their way home.

We have shared a common home with the salmon since the last retreat of the glaciers some 10,000 years ago, when salmon permanently colonized the rivers and coasts of the Pacific Northwest. No other animal has done more to shape the natural history and culture, native and white, of the Pacific Northwest. Standing in the deepening twilight, surrounded by Cottage Creek's fragile wildness, I realized that salmon, with their characteristic insistence, blurred that firm line humans like to draw between nature and the city. Now the city is their home and keeping them here will mean learning from their persistence, their dedication to their ancestral lands and rivers, and their unswerving commitment to the next generation.

Fish are strange creatures, always submerged from view, slimy and quick, living in depths I cannot see. I had never before concerned myself with the coming and going, the lives of fish. Yet watching the few remaining sockeye in the creek, I had a greater appreciation, even awe, for the complex instinct and drives that had kept them alive for so long, and brought them to a habitat we share. Their presence created an enclave of wildness in the city. It was a peculiar kind of wildness, though, one found only in the Pacific Northwest. We live in a time when contemporary culture encourages a mass market's homogeneity, so that a McDonald's in Cle Elum will serve the same fish sandwiches as one in Moscow. Yet here in this tiny creek, the sockeye were bringing the Pacific Northwest's history and special nature back home to a region increasingly at risk of looking just like any place else.

Where a few weekends ago the creek was filled with sockeye, tense and protective of their redds, there was now only one solitary pair. Their crimson bodies shone in the darkening light. They sidled next to one another, quivering, undulating over each other's bodies. The female snapped the creekbed with her tail as she dug the redd. They continued with their courtship and nest building, oblivious to the deaths around them, unconcerned with their own fate.

David Petersen

What the Animals Know

First publication

I'm day-hiking through a wildly beautiful Colorado mountain meadow a thousand feet below the Continental Divide when the sky suddenly goes dark. My day, I fear, is about to hit the proverbial fan. Sure enough, within minutes I'm under assault by lightning, thunder, rain like a carwash, and swirling fog—your standard surprise September storm here in the high San Juans. And par for my course, my high-dollar, high-tech rain suit is back in camp (where it won't get wet). When hail like shrapnel joins the attack I flee like some panicked animal for the iffy shelter of the nearest finger of forest.

As I enter the dripping woods, something huge and vaguely ominous materializes a few yards ahead, then melts away into the gloom. This is dead-center the only place in Colorado that might still hide a last few ghostly grizzlies, and my pulse quickens with the possibility. But in the same instant a brief thudding of hooves cancels my paranoia: Bears don't have hooves. I hurry over to where the mysterious animal had been bedded and there, at the leeward base of an umbrella-limbed old-growth spruce, I find a bathtub-sized oval of earth scraped clean of ground litter. And dry as Noah's socks. A pungent barnyard stench confirms it: wapiti. I gratefully claim the evicted elk's nest for my own and settle in for the duration of the storm.

Amazing, the elk's ability to locate such efficacious refuge as this, albeit mere mindless instinct, I suppose, like a dog circling before it lies down. An innate inclination hard-wired into the beast's cerebral circuits through countless millennia of selective reinforcement. Or, perhaps, nest selection is a learned skill in elk, passed down from cow to calf, generation to generation. The wapiti aren't saying.

My curiosity stirred by circumstance and with time on my hands, perhaps all night if the storm says so, I'm soon lost in the maze of an old favorite conundrum: What do the animals know?

Certainly, animals know more than people about wilderness comfort, navigation, survival, and other such basics—witness the ptarmigan, an alpine grouse that escapes killing blizzards by diving deep into powdery snow, where it finds shelter from screaming arctic winds and insulation against the subzero cold; thus did a humble bird invent the emergency snow cave. At the opposite extreme, desert animals know enough to take care of their strenuous business at night and along the cool edges of twilight, then siesta in shady hidey-holes during the frying hours, thus defeating dehydration, heat prostration, sunburn, cataracts, and scorched feet while demonstrating a commonsensical intelligence that's rare, sometimes fatally so, among human desert denizens.

And animals know enough to relax and enjoy life. The other day a hiking companion and I were sitting quietly in the shade of an aspen tree watching a family of mallards fool around in a beaver pond a few yards to our front. Suddenly one cow elk came bounding out of the woods nearby and leapt explosively into the pond, sending the ducks into panicked flight. For the next quarter-hour we spied as the big deer splashed, played submarine, blew bubbles, slapped the water with her hooves, and stared, mesmerized, as her wave-circles expanded outward.

Clearly, this was no example of the "training behavior" so often cited by biologists as the practical motivation for play in young animals. This was a quarter-ton adult. Nor did the elk's aquatic freak-out serve any apparent "practical" purpose, such as escaping

predators (weren't any) or drowning mosquitoes (the day was bug-
less). It was play for play's sake.

Yet what do such behaviors really say about whether or not animals possess conscious intellect—the ability to think, reason, plan,
and act from self-directed choice? Not much, says traditional biology, arguing that even such seemingly spontaneous and inventive behaviors as play can be chalked up to instinct rather than thoughtful
intent.

So, what *do* the animals know?

It's a lot to think about and I think about it a lot. Nor am I alone
in the pursuit of this beastly koan; people have been pondering the
nature and extent of animal consciousness since before the opening
of recorded history, with early students including such cerebral ce-
lebrities as Aristotle the Greek and Aesop the fable.

But serious consideration of animal intelligence didn't really get
up to speed until thirteenth-century Italy and the revelations of Saint
Thomas Aquinas. All living things, reasoned Aquinas, have "soul,"
with animals being more soulful than plants because they, we, are
equipped with sensory organs—eyes, nostrils, ears—through which
to gather information about our surroundings. These data subsequently are computed and used to act profitably upon the world. The
more soulful the animal, the more sophisticated its computation of
sensory data until, with humans, soul is sufficiently powerful to fa-
cilitate self-awareness, symbolic thought, language, art, science, religion, politics, and all the other "higher qualities" that have brought
humanity to its present state of arrogance, overpopulation, angst,
war, and woe.

Not such shabby logic, even by today's standards, so long as we
substitute some contemporary term—such as intellect, cognition,
consciousness—for Aquinas's mystical "soul," and doubly impressive considering the good saint lived during a time when the finest
minds debated whether the seat of the soul was the heart, brain,
liver, or some more obscure innard.

Aquinas's placement of the various species on an ascending intellectual scale, like the rungs of a ladder, remained more or less in vogue until the 1600s, when animals' souls were rudely repossessed by the French anthropocentrist René ("I think, therefore I am") Descartes, the so-called father of so-called modern philosophy. Toadying the religious dogma of his day, Descartes preached that animals were created expressly for human use and are, by Divine Design, devoid of soul—mere senseless automatons, flesh-and-bone machines, fur-covered robots lacking any shred of consciousness or feeling. In sum, from Descartes's *Discourse on Method:* "There is [no supposition] more powerful in leading feeble minds astray from the straight path of virtue than that the soul of brutes is of the same nature with our own." Even the agonized screams of beasts in pain, in Descartes's hard-hearted view, were nothing more than the screeches and groans of stressed machinery.

Handy, this "Cartesian dualism" worldview, with humans on the sentient side of creation and all the rest of nature over on the senseless side of the tracks (as it were), thus granting us moral license to use and abuse animals any way we wish, handily unburdened by conscience, empathy, or "humanity."

And abuse animals we did, and in many ways still do. Consider the assembly-line oppression of industrial animal-farming (by comparison, ethical hunting is a blessing). Consider every American neighborhood's examples of shameful neglect of *Canis familiaris,* "man's best friends," kept caged or chained in suburban backyards and neglected until they turn loud and mean from lonely frustration. And consider, please, the living nightmare of vivisection, that bloodsplattered circus of Nazi Dr. Doolittle laboratory tortures inflicted on hundreds of animals every day ("How smart does a chimp have to be before killing him constitutes murder?" asks celebrity scientist Carl Sagan), most often for blatantly commercial or scientifically redundant ends rather than to gain vital medical knowledge.

(Beyond the invisible walls of my sylvan shelter the tempest rages on. The lightning and thunder have jumped the Divide and are moving away, the hail has petered out but rain pours with redoubled vigor from a ruptured firmament. And here I squat, carefree as a Caliban.)

But all things pass, including René "Wise Use" Descartes, whose arrogant old soul, we can presume, now resides in a PC heaven where angels sing but hermit thrushes do not and no lowly deer or antelope are allowed to play. Sounds like hell to me, as it did also to most post-Cartesian thinkers, including one Percy Bysshe Shelley, an early nineteenth-century English poet of some renown who slam-dunked Cartesian dualism thus: "The monstrous sophism that beasts are pure unfeeling machines, and do not reason, scarcely requires a confutation."

Likewise, the Scottish philosopher David Hume attacked the Cartesian legacy by asserting, "No truth appears to me more evident than that beasts are endow'd with thought and reason as well as men." And in his turn, the German thinker Art Schopenhauer added yet more fuel to the funeral pyre of dualism by expressing the opinion that even though they lack language, animals nonetheless possess conscious understanding and can exert free will. And so on through a lengthy litany of philosophical opinion, more often than not coming down on the animals' side.

But philosophy, alas, *is* mere opinion and ultimately fails to answer the query at hand: What do the animals know?

In the twentieth century there finally arose a school of serious scientific investigation into animal intelligence, maybe too serious. Its name was, and remains, behaviorism, and its guru was psychologist B. F. Skinner. Intrigued by the work of that infamous Russian dog trainer "Drooling Ivan" Pavlov, Skinner specialized in tormenting animals with crowded cages, mazes, surgically implanted electrodes, and suchlike devices in hopes of demonstrating, among other things, that for every stimulus (say, cramming more and more rats into a cage), there follows a predictable response (more and more aggression, murder, incest, depression, and other familiar urban social problems). Behaviorism came to so dominate the study of animal intelligence that for decades researchers with conflicting ideas and data were reluctant to publish their views for fear of professional ridicule. Hardly an open-minded atmosphere conducive to doing good science.

Only in recent years has fundamentalist behaviorism finally begun to give way to a kinder and gentler school of inquiry called cognitive ethology. Cognition is just a fancy word for thought, while ethology is the study of animal behavior under natural (as opposed to clinical) conditions. Nor is it all so new. As early as the fifth century B.C. a Greek slave writing under the name of Aesop dabbled in cognitive ethology when he celebrated in fable a raven he'd seen dropping small stones into a narrow-necked jug half-full of water, gradually raising the level of the liquid in the container until it could be reached for a drink. More than two millennia later, in his *Advancement of Learning*, English historian and philosopher Sir Francis Bacon echoed Aesop when he asked rhetorically, "Who taught the raven in a drought to throw pebbles into a hollow tree, where she espied water, that the water might rise so as she could come to it?"

Recent experiments conducted by University of Vermont cognitive ethologist Bernd Heinrich validate the raven's far-flung historical reputation for ingenuity. After suspending a bit of food on a long string below a perch pole, Heinrich photographed one of his birds solving the problem by lifting a length of string with its beak then anchoring the coil with a foot, over and over again, until it had reeled in the bait. (Crows, on the other hand, never got past flying at the suspended morsel and having it jerked from their beaks.) Meanwhile, a second raven, watching the first, didn't merely ape what it saw but improved on the technique by grasping the string loosely in its beak and walking the length of the perch pole to bring home the bacon both faster and with considerably less effort.

Similarly, anthropologist Richard Nelson, in his award-winning natural history *The Island Within,* reports that ravens are believed by the Koyukon Indians of interior Alaska to lead respectful hunters to game. Having witnessed this fascinating behavior myself, I too have come to view the raven as a hunter's helper. At least on occasion.

Like so: I'm dressed in camouflage and either sitting or creeping quietly through the woods—hunting for my winter's meat, photographing wildlife, or just looking—when ravens, usually a pair, appear and circle low overhead, croaking grandly as if saying *Look! Look!* Our relationship thus established, the birds clam up and scram. Then, sooner more often than later, the same ravens sound off again, this time from a near distance and in harsher, more urgent tones, repeating a call that I've come to hear as *Elk! Elk!* (In the Koyukon language, says Nelson, it comes across as *Animal! Animal!*) Through conditioning I've learned to perk up at such times, for once in a while—not often, but often enough to astound—the birds are announcing the whereabouts of elk or deer.

I'm no dreamy-eyed nature mystic, and neither is Dr. Nelson. Nor are we suggesting that ravens are attempting to establish some mystical connection with humans. Rather, it seems obvious that they're displaying the utmost in practical intelligence by working for wages in the form of offal and meat scraps left behind by the hunters they help. The conscious intellect implied here—visualizing a profitable end, conceiving a strategy, recognizing and recruiting a potential ally, communication, persistence, and more—is food for one hell of a lot of thought.

On the other hand, as any cautious behaviorist will eagerly testify, innate behavior patterns can provide animals with an impressively broad choice of responses to apparently unique stimuli, leaving unsophisticated observers (like me) with the false impression that thinking has happened.

Certainly, that *can* be the case. But, I wonder, does it *have* to be either instinct or cognition with never the twain to meet? Not so in humans with our complex hodgepodge of both innate and intellectual behaviors. Why must it be so in animals? I find it easier to believe that the occasional Stephen Hawking of the raven realm has the ability to conceive the simple dynamics of volume displacement in liquids or purposely join forces with human hunters, than to accept that natural selection would bother to imprint such complex and in-dividualized behaviors in instinct.

For those interested in such matters there are bookfuls of scien-tifically documented near-human intellectual feats performed by an-imals of every stripe, from pigeons to primates. In summarizing a few of the highest such points, science writer James Shreeve, in his invigorating *The Neandertal Enigma,* reminds us that "Given a little training, chimps and gorillas can communicate by using symbols, teach each other sign language and, by some accounts, even discuss their emotions and ideas of death with their trainers. We now know that even in the wild, vervet monkeys utter different alarm cries de-pending upon what sort of danger is imminent—perhaps the begin-ning of language. . . . Lions hunt cooperatively, wolves share food, elephants regularly display an emotional depth more profound than, say, some modern human beings working on Wall Street."

Also like some modern human beings working on Wall Street, an-imals are not above deceiving one another for personal gain. Among the most famous of animal "liars" is the plover, which deftly decoys predators away from its ground nest by employing such deceits as flopping off with a faked wing injury or squeaking like a rodent while running away through tall grass, the style of pretense cleverly tai-lored to fit the nature of the threat. As long ago as 1833, John James Audubon wrote of the piping plover, "You may see the mother, with expanded tail and wings trailing on the ground, limping and flutter-ing before you, as if about to expire [but] when the bird has fairly got rid of her unwelcome visitor, and you see her start up on her legs, stretch forth her wings and fly away piping her soft note, you cannot but participate in the joy that she feels."

Similarly, I've had ground-nesting nighthawks, and even mule deer, boldly attempt to divert my attention to themselves when I've bumbled too close to their nurseries.

James Shreeve has noted the extensive predator-alarm vocabulary of vervet monkeys, but even more impressive is how these fiercely territorial primates employ their "beginning of language" to deceive one another. When a home-team clan of vervets is under attack by an invading clan and the battle seems all but lost, one or more of the defenders may suddenly start screaming the vervet equivalent of *Leopard! Run for your life!* It's the most urgent, frightening, and powerful phrase in the vervet repertoire, and it invariably sends the invaders packing. No mere monkey business, this, but cunning psychological warfare.

Yet such deceits as the vervet's and the plover's are "honorable" lies told not for greedy ends but to protect home and family. More self-serving, and thus more humanlike, are the screeching raptor imitations I've so often heard uttered by Steller's jays as they swoop toward my backyard feeder, effectively clearing the crowded perch of chickadees, nuthatches, juncos, and even other jays. Do "selfish" tricks such as this not suggest a thoughtful, creative, one could even say Machiavellian intelligence?

Deceit aside, a uniquely impressive example of what appears to be high-order animal intellect was related to me by Colorado's world-class black bear biologist Tom Beck. Your standard live-trap for bears consists of a section of large-diameter steel culvert pipe with one end capped shut and the other equipped with a heavy, guillotine-type door that slides up between parallel tracks and is held open with a substantial pin. When a bear enters the big baited barrel and tugs the T-bar trigger mechanism, the pin is pulled, allowing the door to slam shut and trap the bear within. Says Beck, "I've watched bears who've never seen a culvert trap before walk up to one, check it out from various angles then stand up, grab the steel door plate and with a powerful twisting motion wrench it sideways to bind it in the open position . . . then step inside, take the bait and walk away."

This same widely experienced field biologist also reports seeing bears toss rocks or sticks onto the triggers of spring-activated leg snares to fire them off before going for the goodies. "Bears," Tom

Beck will tell you, "appear to be capable of reasoning, planning and spontaneous problem solving."

Seconding Beck is grizzly guru Doug Peacock, who professes that grizzly bears are smart enough to know when they're being tracked, are aware of their own prints, and will sometimes take great pains— such as walking in water or on rocks while avoiding snow and mud—to throw hunters and hounds off their trail . . . occasionally even backtracking to lie in hiding and watch (and, we may presume, chuckle at) their confused pursuers.

And one more from Beck: In winter, in a shallow creek where the water was frozen solid, Tom found a place where a deer had pawed dirt onto the ice. Curious, he returned the next day and, lo and behold, saw that the deer had been there again to lap up the resulting meltwater. "I don't know that deer consciously employ the dynamics of solar heating," says Beck, "but I do know that a deer intentionally pawed dirt onto ice and returned later to drink from the little pool of water created by the heat absorbed by the dark dirt."

Even so, all these feats of apparent animal intelligence notwithstanding, it remains that without true language with which to share and expand whatever knowledge they possess, animals are doomed (or blessed) never to enjoy (or endure) the abstract cognitive abilities that define the human mind (just try thinking without words). Some theorists even venture that language *is* consciousness.

The most accomplished linguist of the animal kingdom is the parrot. Yet parrot "talking," we well know, is the mere mindless mimicking of human word sounds. What, then, to make of Alex, an African gray parrot in the care of Northern Arizona University ethologist Irene Peppenberg. When Alex became ill awhile back, Peppenberg took him to an animal clinic where the vet advised her to leave the old boy overnight for observation. As Peppenberg was departing, Alex became visibly distressed and called out: "*Come here. I love you. I'm sorry. Wanna go back.*"

How, short of *thinking in words,* to explain Alex's spontaneous, unrehearsed linking of those four distinct phrases (he knew them all beforehand, no doubt, along with others, but had never been taught to combine them) to compose such a complex, poignant, and emotional plea? And how to explain those "exclusively human" emotions—confusion, betrayal, affection, guilt, remorse?

What do the animals know?

The animals, above all else, know The Secret of Life, as evidenced by their ability to exist in perpetual balance (if not always harmony) with their fellow creatures and the environment that sustains us all. It's an essential quality of intelligence that we feeble-minded *Homo saps* seem destined never to acquire.

But ask now the beasts, and they shall teach thee; and the fowls of the air and they shall tell thee. Or speak to the earth, and it shall teach thee.

Fat chance, eh, Mr. Gingrich?

As suddenly as it came, the wind now flags. The rain fizzles and stops. And thanks to the practical intellect of a cud-chewing ungulate I've ridden out the storm sitting pretty—pretty dry, pretty warm, pretty comfortable, pretty grateful. "Intelligence," I reflect, is whatever works to satisfy a species' needs in the circumstance in which it finds itself. I mean—what would an elk do with a Ph.D. in philosophy?

It has been suggested that even if we could find some way to talk with the animals, what they had to say would be Greek to us, so different is their perception of the world from ours. If so, why then do we persist in trying to rank animal intelligence by human standards?

So many questions, so few answers.

I stand and stretch and stumble amongst the dark dripping woods and back out into the big montane meadow where my hike was so rudely interrupted by whimsical nature. Night has slammed down hard and black as obsidian, erasing all landmarks and shifting my mood from the philosophical to the paranoid: *Where the hell am I, and which way back to camp?*

Now, from somewhere out in the inky void, rises an eerie fluted wail followed by a series of five braying chuckles. My reluctant wapiti landlord, I suppose, enjoying the last laugh. In spite of my navigational fix, I have to smile . . . the bull elk's bugle is a language imbued with more mystery, magic, passion, and sustainable intelligence than we feeble-minded humans can ever hope to comprehend. That beast out there is already home, while I have yet to find my way.

Louise Wagenknecht

Dancing with Cows

First publication

In 1985, in midcareer, I went back to college. I wanted to be a range conservationist. At the time, I thought that I was the only student who wanted to study range management so I could later have an excuse to chase cows on government time. Silly me. Even at granola-crunching, holistically groovy Humboldt State in Arcata, California, the range kids were in love with horses and cows.

During one spring break I learned that this ambition knows no age limits, when I attended an annual National Forest range permittee meeting, in a banquet room with a spectacular view of Mount Shasta.

"I became a range conservationist because I really wanted to be a rancher, and since I couldn't buy into it or marry into it, this seemed like the next best thing." The keynote speaker, the man who administered the range program on the Forest's heaviest range District, grinned down at the weathered faces of his audience. The ranchers chuckled politely. I gaped at him over my steak. Well, I'll be dipped, I thought. He's a romantic, too.

A few years later, after my husband and I had moved to a small Idaho town, the local Ranger District welcomed a new District Ranger. I wasn't surprised to see him alight in full cowboy regalia from a pickup truck towing a horse trailer, with a degree in range management and quite a few years of range experience under his large silver buckle. I *was* a little startled to learn that he was not only a cattle rancher himself, but also held grazing permits on both National Forest and Bureau of Land Management lands. No one else in the Forest or community seemed conscious of any irony or possible conflict of interest. I mentioned it to the Forest Supervisor one day and was treated to the silent stare usually reserved for people who break wind in good restaurants. Well, of course, stupid, I rebuked myself. He *hired* the man, after all. He must have *known*.

Incestuous relationships between commodity interests and federal employees are nothing new, of course. It's almost inevitable in small western communities where members of logging and ranching families work for federal agencies. They measure the grass, mark the timber, grade the roads, maintain the trails, keep the trucks running, and fill out the forms. They know where the bodies are buried and who isn't speaking to whom, and why. But most of them aren't managers. They don't make the decisions.

The upper ranks of line officers, who do, are still dominated by foresters and range conservationists. And although private company foresters and Forest Service foresters may stand around at the Christmas party talking about timber sales, they don't go out and log together on weekends.

Range people have a harder time keeping their jobs separate from their hobbies; they like cows and pastimes involving cows. On summer evenings, some can be seen tossing a loop in the roping arena beside the same rancher whose cattle were in the wrong allotment yesterday. They buy and sell cattle and horses with the people they are assigned to regulate. They dress like cowboys, walk like cowboys, and talk like cowboys. They believe that the grasses of the West should be eaten by cows. (People whose sympathies are with the plants tend to become botanists.)

The first range management plan I wrote was for an allotment held by a permittee whom I had known for twenty years. He had worked with my father and I had gone to school with his kids. I flattered myself that the plan would improve conditions on some alpine meadows at the crest of the Siskiyou Mountains on California's northern border. But I had a definite sentimental interest in keeping alive his family's tradition of grazing cattle in the high country. Excluding cattle from even the most fragile portions of the allotment never crossed my mind. I ignored the concerns of the District's wildlife biologist about black bear habitat.

One day, I saw an anti-cow diatribe by Edward Abbey tacked to a bulletin board in the District office. I stopped to read it. Soon I was literally shaking with anger. Abbey would be content, it appeared, with nothing less than the removal of all cattle from the public lands.

Who the hell was Abbey to tell ranchers they shouldn't be doing what they had done for a hundred years? More to the point, who was Abbey to tell *me* that the greatest joy of my life—looking for cattle in the mountains on the back of a good horse—was wrong? I fumed for days, thinking up counterarguments to this fanatic.

Abbey seemed like a direct threat to my way of life. I had carved out a niche among a few of the small ranchers in the Siskiyous. I hadn't married it or inherited it: I had earned it. My time and the sweat, hide, and shoes of my horses spent rounding up cattle in mountain meadows had bought me entry into the cattle culture, the dream of my childhood. I could ride horseback and check allotments during the week, then spend the weekend rounding up or moving cattle. Who was Abbey to threaten something so harmless, so enjoyable?

I needn't have worried. It turns out that the 27,000 range permittees of the West have tremendous political power and the ability to wield it against all enemies, real or imagined.

As the range debate grew more heated, my search for full-time range work took me out of California to the Southwest and Great Basin, and I saw at last what Abbey meant. All the wishing in the world won't make eight inches of precipitation a year in these high, cold deserts equal the fifty inches that fall on the Siskiyous. Yet the

Great American Desert is more heavily stocked, its soils more trampled, its riparian species more threatened.

While I was slowly, painfully, learning this, one of my grandmother's sayings began replaying in my mind. "You dance with them what brung you," she used to say.

When the cow culture brings range conservationists into the field, they inevitably follow the culture's agenda, and not the agenda of the soil, or the water, or the wildlife. If you try to dance with a cow, the cow will lead, even when you no longer want to follow.

Louise Wagenknecht

Strangers in the Forest

First publication

From 1975 to 1987, I inspected tree planting in the Klamath National Forest on the Oregon–California border. I knew many of the planters were illegal aliens. So I had to laugh at a recent newspaper story about illegal aliens apprehended while planting trees in the Boise National Forest here in Idaho.

"The Forest Service does not knowingly hire contractors who break federal immigration and labor laws," the agency told a Boise newspaper.

I wondered if the writer had ever followed a planting crew, if he or she had any memories similar to mine. What I remember are dark and rainy February mornings, as two cranky forestry technicians dragged bags of trees out of the tree cooler, stacked them in the bed of the green pickup, and covered them with outdated fire shelters. We filled the two milk cans near the tailgate with water, stuffed a couple sacks of vermiculite beside them, and roared back up to the station. It was 5:30 A.M.

Beneath the sulfurous glow of the parking lot lights, two dark vans had appeared; faces peering at us from foggy windows. The vans followed us as we pulled onto the highway, then turned off onto a logging road, coffee splashing into our laps as we hit the first potholes.

An hour later, the muddy road ended. Between the clacking windshield wipers we saw a steep, steep slope of more than 60 percent, 1,000 feet from top to bottom. Here, a piece of pie had been sliced from the forest and every living stick removed or burned. At the clearcut's edge, the old growth reared abruptly, the slick orange trunks of madrone and black-gray ones of Douglas-fir just visible in the slight lessening of the soupy darkness.

The rig was swiftly surrounded by about 20 planters, as the foremen slit open tree bags to lift out bundles of 2-year-old conifers. Crew members seized the tiny trees, sloshed the roots in a slurry of water and vermiculite, then stuffed them into rubberized bags belted to their waists. Each bag held about 500 trees.

The planters were Mexican nationals; only the foremen spoke fluent English. You could always spot the new arrivals, clad in cheap tennis shoes, polyester trousers and loud cowboy shirts. Many of them had no gloves or hats. We and the foremen wore hard hats and good raingear.

Bags loaded, the crew dropped over the edge. Eight feet apart, they worked their way downhill, searching for planting spots among blackened debris left from burning slash. Each carried a hoedad, a flat steel blade about 18 inches long and 4 inches wide attached to an axe handle. Plunging it into the bare soil, then popping the handle up to break out a space for the roots, they deftly slipped seedlings into place, tamped the soil back in, then slid another 8 feet down the slope.

We watched the planters work. When they were far enough ahead, we abandoned our perches on 7-foot-wide stumps and "threw a plot" by tossing a spike over a shoulder to mark the center of a one-fiftieth acre plot. We counted the number of planted trees, then dug up several, carefully. If the tap root dove straight down, the tree was well planted. A good crew planted 95 percent or more of their trees correctly.

At lunchtime, the crew built an enormous fire on the roadbed to brown tortillas and fry meat and beans. Peppers, salsa, cans of soda, and cookies appeared and disappeared as the planters laughed and talked. Though their hands and whippety bodies testified to a lifetime of hard labor, they seemed far happier than we were at the prospect of three months' picnicking in a deluge. Most were under 21, some admitted they were only 14; a few were probably even younger.

We didn't ask their history, though sometimes strong clues surfaced, as when a Forest Service silviculturist paid an unannounced visit in his own truck. The crew dropped their tools as one and raced for the timber. The two foremen plodded up to the road. Realizing that the visitor was only another agency employee, they laughed in relief.

"Your truck," they chortled. "It's the same color as the Border Patrol trucks: you scared them pretty good!"

The silviculturist repeated this anecdote *ad nauseum* all over the office, just in case there were still line or staff officers who could yet claim ignorance of the status of the crew.

Real U.S. Immigration and Naturalization Service raids usually came at night, often when the crew had rented motel rooms in town. Raids could be a welcome break for inspectors, allowing us to catch up on paperwork, clean out the tree cooler, do our laundry and shop.

One morning after a raid, 80,000 seedlings arrived from a Forest Service nursery. We made room in the cooler, and there they sat for a month, until the 23 planters returned from their bus ride across the border.

Working 14-hour days, 7 days a week, they planted as many as 90 acres and 23,000 trees a day as April ended. A week of hot weather in May ended the planting season. We waved good-bye to the crew, hauled the leftover trees from the cooler, poured diesel on them, and set them afire.

By the early 1960s, the Forest Service believed that nursery technology had made artificial regeneration of large clearcuts possible. What they forgot was that planting, unlike logging, cannot be mechanized on the steep slopes of the Pacific Northwest. We had to plant as many as 1,500 acres of clearcuts every spring. This required large crews, a niche quickly filled by big contractors with access to the bottomless reservoir of Hispanic labor in the Sacramento–San Joaquin Valley. Local residents lacked the cash to compete for the huge contracts put up by the Klamath National Forest.

So, every winter after the contract bids had been awarded, Forest Service contracting officers in warm headquarters buildings solemnly told the successful bidders at prework meetings that the hiring of illegal aliens was, well, illegal. Contractors solemnly assured the contracting officers that all their workers had green cards. The contracting officers, paperwork in order, went back to their desks. And 70 miles away, in the freezing rain, a couple of GS-5 forestry technicians followed two dozen ill-clad teenagers across a scarred mountainside, and silently prayed that these cheerful and competent people would not be sent south until they had crawled out of the last clearcut and planted the last tree.

Barry Lopez

In the Garden of the Lords of War

from *Manoa*

One hundred and twelve years after the Universal Holocaust, in the natural deserts of what was once western China, the Dobrit practice of staying War had reached a plateau of refinement. The Four Lords, nameless men chosen by a council of women, moved from season to season in cycles regular as the Once migration of birds, and there attained a Lyric Passage, the harmonics of stability.

In countries I had walked through in the preceding six years—Beywan, Cruel, Muntouf, and tiny Begh on the Yellow Sea in old Manchuria—I found consistent agreement at all levels of society on the worth of the Four Lords and their Rule. It was my privilege as a Wenrit scribe and a Deformed to visit the Garden of the Lords of War. Now, I convey that story, another given me on a Witness Path to the Black Sea, along which, by every country, I have been given Safe Passage.

The Circle of Women for the Study, with whom I apprenticed for five months, numbered thirteen. The youngest was maturely fifteen, the eldest eighty-one. My apprenticeship occurred at irregular hours during the winter and spring moons. I occupied one chamber, alone, adjacent to a central meeting house. It was made clear I should always be available to listen when the women told stories or during the preparation of food. When the women convened to discuss the Cultures and Texts to be presented the Lords, I was sent out into the city. I memorized thirty-four of my tutors' stories in this apprentice time, good by their account. The women were always gentle in instructing, but strict that my accent and inflections should not interfere in the Music.

I will transcribe these stories into my Given Pattern when I one day arrive at the Black Sea, the fourth, now, of the books of my Sent Journey.

The Garden of the Lords of War is surrounded by a wall three times my height. It is woven of peacock feathers in such a way as not to impede the movement of air but to be opaque to passersby. The four walls do not meet squarely at corners but in round, enclosed spaces, roofless, inside each of which stands an attendant's small house. In the outer wall here, at each corner, is a Gate of Admission. Within, a Gate of Entry opens to stretches of wild grass, gardens of flowers and vegetables, the separate houses of the Four Lords, large pine and laurel trees, and small plots of maize, beans, and wheat. Of course, it is not permitted either to view or to speak with the Lords, so I can only offer an impression, based on the testimony of the Circle of Women for the Study.

Most often, men in their late twenties are chosen as Lords, and it is rare for one to serve past his middle forties. The unvarying criteria for selection are as follows: (1) a man must never have taken a human life, for any reason; (2) he must never have struck or in any way harmed a woman; (3) he must be Dobrit, though I was told this designation refers to spiritual and philosophic temperament, not ethnic origin; (4) he must have raised children not his own. Finally, he must read with perfect fluency in at least three languages. Added to these criteria are some requirements of a more general nature. To be considered at all, a man must be formally recommended by an aunt, and then an uncle must compose the Story of his life and recite it before the council of women and all the Dobrit. At this presentation, any person may object to his appointment. With cause, following deliberation, the candidate might no longer be considered.

After his selection, a man begins his time of service by becoming an attendant. It is his responsibility to prepare meals for the Lords, to see to the plots, orchards, and gardens in the interior, to the pathways and a wood lot, and to assist those people chosen to change the Texts. (These are always young women and men from among the Dobrit, chosen Word of Mouth, who study under the Circle of Women before performing their duties four times a year, at Change of Season.)

From the outside, the houses of the Lords resemble one another closely, though slight differences in construction, for instance in the mortise and tenon of framing, were apparent to me. Each house sits just off the ground on chestnut posts and is girt by a veranda. Sliding walls, inset with carved cypress panels, open all around onto the porch. The low-pitched shed roofs, composed of long, half-round tiles, slope outward. Inside, the four trapezoidal rooms converge on an open courtyard. These rooms are identical, each spacious enough to contain two or three large tables (upon which rest the Texts), a sleeping mat, or *futon,* and a small serving table. A flat chest for clothing, several wood chairs, and a washstand complete the furniture. A slate apron in the center of each floor surrounds a small firepit. Firewood is ricked on the porch outside, an ash bucket sits opposite on a tile. From one corner of the roof, a chain leads to a rain barrel.

The day I was admitted to the Garden of the Lords of War was in the fourth week of spring. Many of the trees were in blossom, vegetable gardens were budding with early onions and two types of lettuce, and the flower pots were effulgent with carmine, lavender, and sulfurous blooms. I walked with two of my hosts, an older woman named Kortathena and a girl about eighteen called Marika, and with the attendant at whose gate we had entered. It was a visit of only three hours but we walked leisurely through the grounds—time

enough for me to see well how closely tended they were, and to observe that though the design of the pathways and the placement of
the gardens suggested symmetry they were not so laid out. Some of
the pines were of such great size I felt the area must have been sacred
to others before the Dobrit arrived. Certainly nowhere have I ever
seen so many spiders or butterflies, or heard so many sorts of birdsong—five altogether.

The arrangement of the Prayer among the Lords of War is as follows: each Lord lives the whole of a season in a single room of the
house he occupies. At Change of Season he moves across the courtyard to another room, which has been prepared with a fresh set of
Texts and drawings and enhanced with artwork—textiles, sculpture,
and paintings. He remains there until the following seasonal change,
reading and studying. This practice and sequence permitted me to
view each type of room empty, though I was able to step into only
two houses. (The design of these rooms is similar from house to
house, though I was told the four styles of design found in each
house are not meant to correspond to the seasons. The rooms are
commonly called by the color of the glazed pottery on which meals
in that room are served: ocean green, lantern red, Persian blue,
poppy yellow.)

When a room is occupied by a Lord, it is also vased with flowers
and contains a pair of birds, doves usually, though sometimes crows.
A lute, *shamisen,* or other stringed instrument is present and small
bowls of spice—ginger, cinnamon, sage, vanilla bean, clove—are set
about. When a room is not occupied, it appears hallow and spare.
The one bright spot of color is the stack of glazed dishes on the meal
table.

In the Ocean Green room I was shown, the floor was of quarter-
sawn tulipwood, light colored, straight grained, with a matte sheen,
as if holystoned. The long outer wall of sliding cypress panels was
complemented by a taller cypress wall facing the courtyard, constructed to admit light and air in the same way. The interior walls
were of unfaced stone. In the Ocean Green room, each was a single

piece of micaceous granite. As well as I could guess, these massive but consoling walls were founded first and the rest of the house then built around them. How they were erected or squared I could not imagine. As was true elsewhere in this prefecture, a question was received as an impolite gesture, a condition under which I chafed, but only slightly. I was content to see and listen.

I was informed that in the Ocean Green room the evening meal was always the flesh of a winged animal.

From the Ocean Green room I was walked through a round orchard of loquat trees to see a Lantern Red room. The floor here was of clear larch, the walls of charcoal-gray basalt. The evening meal was the meat of a grazing animal. The empty basin of the hearth, the absence of candle stands, contributed to a feeling of repose or suspension in these rooms. On our way from there, in a southern portion of the grounds, we passed the entrance to a Poppy Yellow room, pointed out through a single lattice row of kumquat. Its dark floor was of mahogany and the pale walls were of a fossiliferous sandstone. The evening meal there, it was explained, was of vegetables, intentionally bland. The final rooms, the Persian Blue rooms, had floors of *li* oak. The outer wall of the one we walked up to was standing open and I saw within walls of brindled marble, the color of a flock of pigeons. The evening meal here was of carp or other freshwater fish.

In the courtyard of each house the Lords grow some flowers and vegetables, as they are inclined.

I was not permitted to look into any room that was in use—a Lantern Red room in one house, two Poppy Yellow rooms in other houses—so again must rely for these descriptions upon my companions. When a Lord steps into a new room at Change of Season, he finds lying neatly upon the tables several dozen bound and unbound Texts (in the Dobrit and other languages), along with dictionaries, paper, and pencils. The books, manuscripts, and folios of drawings all bear on a single culture—here my younger host vol-

unteered that the Lords were then reading, respectively, of Quechua, Tomachan, French, and Xosha peoples. It is the determination
and desire of each Lord to have at the end of three months enough
of an understanding of the culture in which he is reading to be able
to make up a single story, one that gives evidence of his study and
reflects his respect, but that demonstrates no enthrallment. On each
of the four evenings before Change of Season, the Lords gather at the
center of the gardens to listen to one story each night, recited before
a fire kept by two of the attendants. When the Circle of Women
speaks of the Prayer, it is to these stories told at the end of each season that they are referring.

My hosts pointed out that the Texts are not chosen solely on the
basis of impeccable scholarship but consist, instead, of a variety of
printed materials—novels, treatises on natural history, biographies
of politicians, works of reference, ethnographic documents, hydro-
graphic records, works of architectural theory. It is, too, a collection
chosen to match the strengths in language and metaphor of an individual Lord.

I chanced here one question: Were the stories the Lords told ever
written down? No, the stories were only spoken once, said my elder
host. She said, further, that in their reactions to the stories, the Lords
tried to reinforce in each other a desire to do well. And it was this
desire—to perform their tasks well, to read carefully, to give in to
the manuscripts, to think deeply—as much as the Litany of Respect
that the Lords produced, she believed, that kept War at bay.

As we walked toward the Gate of Entry, my younger host suggested I might wish to be alone for a few moments. I was grateful for
her kindness, and walked some steps back along our gravel path to
sit on a ginkowood bench. In my six years of travel, I knew I had
never before been in a place so peaceful, so eloquent. The evidence
of turmoil to be found in each country, including the one I was then
traveling in, was here absent. By virtue of their ferocious concentration and expertise, the architects and builders of this garden had

made all that line, shade, and color might do to compose the soul work, as if a terrified animal could be calmed completely and solely by what the eye beheld.

I ran my fingers along the precise joinery of the ginkowood bench, a plan of assembly that let the various pieces of wood expand and contract in the rain and sun but that did not compromise the bench's strength, its sturdiness. The alignment, the proportions, and the forgiveness of the joinery were exquisite.

I caught up to my companions at the attendant's house. As we turned together for the outer gate I said—if it would be permitted—I had one other question. How was it determined when a man was no longer fit to be a Lord of War? My elder host said that from time to time a woman in the Circle would visit a Lord and they would make love. The woman would sense a man's interior land in this way. She would discern in the act of love whether the man was gentle or not, if he was passionate and curious, whether he was generous. These men, said my host, longed sometimes, like everyone, to be with children, to occupy a less strenuous station. When a woman detected a shudder of hesitation in the emotions of love, she knew it was time to open a path for a Lord to return. The choice was the man's to make, but out of gratitude and simple respect the women did all they could to make this possible.

When a Lord is ready to return to the city, I learned, the four attendants secure the grounds and depart. The other Lords prepare a meal they all then share, using vegetables and edible flowers from their personal gardens. Afterward the three Lords begin walking their longtime companion through the grounds, playing their stringed instruments and each singing the phrases he recalls from all the stories the man has told in his years there. They walk and sing through the night. Just at dawn, before the city is astir, the Lord sets forth, passing through the outer gate and returning to the house that once was his only home. It has been kept undisturbed and now has been readied for him. After this, no one may inquire of him what he has done or what he thinks or feels. He plays a lesser or greater role in the affairs of the city, as he sees fit.

Some men, said my elder host, became again merely threads in the fabric of the community, and this, too, she thought, starved, angered, and humiliated the dogs of war.

Charlene Gilmore

Breaking Ground
A Vision of Alberta's Prairies

First publication

It's ninety-seven degrees out, and the late-July air is so dry that a deep breath might leave you choking. But we're bumping across a Pendant d'Oreille pasture 150 miles southeast of Calgary in the comfortably air-conditioned cab of Lee Finstad's green pickup truck. I can hear the truck's low belly being scratched by the tall grass growing between the parallel grooves of this old, winding prairie trail that curves and turns back, crossing itself at times. Even if I knew where we were going, it would be difficult for me to gauge our progress. The contrast of the meandering trail to the straight grid of the main roads is characteristic of rural prairie regions, but it strikes me now as unfamiliar, making me feel impatient and out of place. I squirm in my seat. Every time I've ridden through one of these pastures, I've been the same painfully self-conscious observer that I am today— part and not part of things.

Lee is my antithesis. The son of a rancher, he seems to have been born in boots, Wranglers, and a plaid shirt with pearl snaps, and he walks with that sauntering gait of a horseman that exudes a rare kind of peace with the ground under his feet. Lee was born and raised here, the fourth generation of a Norwegian family that was among the first settled in the area nearly a hundred years ago. Now a pilot with Canadian Airlines, Lee returns from Medicine Hat to the family ranch every chance he gets—lately, because of a pilots' strike. When I ask how long it will be before he returns to the ranch for good, he grins, adjusts his cap, and begins to muse. Flying from coast to coast, he's seen a lot of land, and he knows this place is special. "There's not much unbroken prairie left anymore," he explains, "though you wouldn't believe it from looking around here."

From our vantage point, prairie grassland is most of what you can see. As you drive north from Pendant d'Oreille toward Medicine Hat, Calgary, and Edmonton, grain fields begin to dominate. At this time of year, the naturally dusty, sage-colored landscape is interrupted by a patchwork of bleached-yellow fields thick with nearly ripe wheat and the dry brown ridges of summer fallow. In a history book from my hometown, Etzikom, a prairie hamlet forty miles north of the U.S. border, some longtime residents claim that on a clear day you can make out the Rocky Mountains on the western horizon. It never occurred to me to try, so I can't confirm or refute the statement; but I suspect an informed imagination. I do know that, as a child in Etzikom, I believed I shared every inch of my flat horizon with a girl in another small town who went to another small school, and who knew, when she looked at the bottom of her sky, that I stood on the other side. Which, of course, was true. And it wasn't.

My husband, Shane, and I are visiting my family in Etzikom for only ten days. Our official obligation is to visit—we haven't been in the area for three years—but it's Shane's first extended time here and I feel another responsibility to him: to *show* him the prairies. So today we've driven down to the Finstad ranch to see and photograph the native burrowing owl, a creature as "prairie" as anything. Lee's mother told me they often see the owls on the ranch. In fact, she said, a scientist from the Wildlife Board had recently flagged a few areas of their pasture as "protected." Lee has driven us to one of the spots, but we haven't yet spotted a single owl.

We spread out, stepping around sage and dragging our feet through clumps of short prairie grass, watching for any sign of movement. I'm looking for feathers, footprints, anything, but I sense Lee's patience wearing thin. As overwhelmingly gracious as he has been, Lee is less than enthused about the owl quest. "We see them all the time," he shrugs, experience easily dismissing Wildlife Canada's theories and population statistics. "It's too hot for them to be out. Bad timing."

The burrowing owl, found throughout Canada's prairie provinces, makes its home by occupying abandoned gopher holes and digging them out for a better fit. The bird is cross-looking, even for an owl: it has a spotted forehead marked by white eyebrows that draw down sharply to a point between its eyes; the contours of the owl's cheeks (more precisely, the large rings around its eyes) also meet there, creating the impression of a deep frown. A white collar of a stripe outlines its chin, and its chest is "barred"—an effect rather like miniature stratus clouds, except in brown against a background of white. It has unusually long legs for an owl and stands with an erect, stately quality. All this I've learned from photographs, drawings, and a handy bird guide. I have never seen a burrowing owl.

My quest to find this bird began just yesterday when we were visiting the Etzikom museum, a building that was my school from kindergarten through the sixth grade. Standing in the entrance after signing the guest book, I scanned a display of tourist brochures for ideas of places to take Shane, for anything that might open up this place to me in a new way. On a poster of endangered species was a photo of the burrowing owl, a bird that I hadn't even known existed and was now threatened due to diminished grasslands and the use of gopher poison. My belief in the prairie as a place of stability was jarred by this evidence of impermanence. I realized that the land and the life it sustains had changed, and that the sense I was trying to uncover was tied to a place that, just maybe, was beginning to disappear.

Just my luck that our short trip coincides with an extremely hot spell, and the owls enjoy this weather as little as Shane and Lee do. Returning to the truck, though, we discover that Lee has another plan. Farther back on the Finstad land are Indian teepee rings he wants to show us. They're all over this country, apparently, but I don't remember knowing this. I do remember a friend of my brother collecting arrowheads on his family's ranch in the Pakowki Lake area south of Etzikom, but I could never decide whether his collection was valuable, as collectibles are presumed to be, or common, since he found so many.

Returning home after eight years living in Vancouver and Honolulu and finally facing my ambivalence about the prairies, I'm beginning to learn that these terms—valuable and common—don't have to be uncomfortable together.

In a little while, Lee, Shane, and I are standing near the teepee rings and the remains of an old homestead on top of one of the highest rises in the area. Once you adjust to the *space* of it, the view is breathtaking: the Milk River flats lie to the south, several farms and ranches dot the patchwork of field and pasture to the north and east, and for miles around, small rises and dips like the one we're standing on ripple and crease this land I carelessly refer to as "flat." Lee has taken the binoculars from the truck and is scanning to the west.

"Yup, I thought I saw antelope over there."

I follow his gaze, searching the land for signs of wildlife, and see nothing. Lee hands me the binoculars. "On the other side of the road."

Blue . . . blue . . . and then the Sweetgrass Hills in Montana come into focus on the horizon. I lower my gaze until I find fence posts, and then the road. Back up . . . there they are, fifteen or twenty of them, all turned broadside so their white rumps are just barely visible lines defining their sandy bodies against the like-colored land. Lee is chuckling.

"See the buck? He's scoping us out from this side of the road."

I lower my gaze again until I feel I must be looking at the ground in front of my feet. Then I see him: large and close, standing protectively in front of his herd, watching us, motionless.

I hand the binoculars to Shane and refocus without them. The antelope are still there; the buck, standing two slopes away, hasn't moved. For a moment, I'm overwhelmed with relief and possibility. We've found something—we can point to it—we'll remember. The antelope have acknowledged us—the whole herd is watching. And I can *see* it.

Maybe, now, I can begin to piece a vision of this place together with the sense of it that follows me everywhere.

In the summer of 1909, the Canadian government made the ranching country between the Medicine Hat railway line and the Montana boundary—in the middle of which now lies Etzikom—available for homesteading. Pressure from immigrants desperate for land prompted the decision: ranchers with long-term leases were evicted, and as fast as the land was surveyed, it was advertised in land offices. Between July and September of 1909, and beginning with the southernmost land along the Montana border, three huge tracts were claimed in quarter-section portions by those fortunate to have been in the front of huge, rowdy lines of people at the Lethbridge land office. A September 1909 Lethbridge *Herald* article covering the land rush explained to prospective settlers that "the land is not of the most desirable, especially the southern townships, which are stony and rolling. The north townships are much better and contain a lot of first-class land." It went on to explain that a chute had been built outside of the land office to manage the crowds; it was "badly wrecked" in the rush.

The image of this office and its chute fascinates me, as does a copy of the final survey map of southern Alberta reprinted on the inside cover of Etzikom's history book. Place-names and landmarks are almost unreadable behind the surveyor's grid imposed over the map. The only areas that escaped the surveyor's pencil were Blood and

Piegan Indian reserves, far to the west in the foothills of the Rocky Mountains, and Pakowki Lake, nearer the Cypress Hills that spread across the Alberta/Saskatchewan border to the east. Perhaps to a farmer or rancher who refers to his fields by their section and quarter designations, this grid isn't strange at all. But when I stood on the Finstad land looking out over that huge blanket of grassland, there appeared no homestead boundaries, no obvious divisions of ownership carved into the land. Fences and roads probably follow some of the original survey lines, but overall the scene appears whole, intact, human life and its orders submerged beneath the surface. I cannot imagine very many people bothering, now, to break down the door of a land office to get a chunk of it.

From the earliest surveys in the late nineteenth century, this land was known to have bleak agricultural prospects. Described as sandy, stony, and washed-out in numerous reports, the soil sustained only sparse vegetation: the clumpy short grass, taller spear grass, sage, and thistleweed on the open plains; saskatoon bushes in the coulees; cottonwood trees in the Milk River flats. The most extreme southeastern corner of Alberta is in fact called the badlands, even dryer and more sparsely vegetated (and populated) than the Pendant d'Oreille and Etzikom areas. My Uncle Gordon, who farms and ranches in Pendant d'Oreille, told us that it would take fifty acres to graze a free-range head for a year if he didn't also supplement the animal's diet with commercial feed and put it out to community pasture for the entire summer. After the land rush in 1909, the Pendant d'Oreille area supported 140 homesteading families. Now, there are fewer than 10 families living modestly off the same land. Without regard for the nature of the land, the surveyor's grid of 1909 simply pinched the homesteaders too tightly, and before long many of those little square dreams were pushed right off the map. People who associate rural prairie life with a weary fatalism are not completely wrong; from a perspective of early settlement, failure is far more than half the story.

The whole story of the people who still live there is harder to decipher. On this trip I had wanted to ask some of my old friends how they feel about this place, what they think about as they cover fields on their tractors or cross a pasture checking cattle, how many circles they trace in a day. But as soon as I was back, I knew that to ask would be to cross the boundary into a very private subject; most of the time, these just aren't things people talk about. I happened to overhear an unusually candid moment, however, at a social gathering the weekend before we left. A group of my friends' fathers were casually chatting about crops and cattle, answering Shane's much more practical inquiries about the machinery and implements. Gary, a middle-aged farmer, prompted by the topic of conversation and perhaps what he perceived was an outsider's naiveté, suddenly began to talk on an entirely different level. A farmer was always behind, he said, always a day behind the weather, a year behind the newest machinery. "I'm just tired," he finished. "Sick of the whole thing." He received no sympathy in response, no encouragement or advice—only uncomfortable, slightly impatient stares at the ground. I sensed that Gary might have lost, or perhaps never had, the thing that could counter his frustration and defeat: an understanding of what prairie farming offers in return for the toll it takes.

In many ways, my Uncle Gordon represents the kind of person who understands the need for discipline and perseverance that the land imposes on its residents, and has the vision gained from enduring its harsh conditions. For some time, Shane and I had been hoping to go horseback riding during our short time in Etzikom, and as soon as word of our desire reached Uncle Gordon and Aunt Myrna, an invitation was extended. We arrived in the late afternoon on a Monday, eager but poorly prepared for my uncle's idea of a ride. Shane, my sister SheriLynn, and I were soon outfitted in long pants, socks, cowboy boots, and jackets. Tentatively we made friends with our assigned mounts while Uncle Gordon and his teenage daughter, Renae, saddled the horses and hooked up the twenty-foot horse trailer. We were not taking a little trot through the back pasture, as

I'd expected: we were going to check on the cattle and count the bulls. Because of the dark clouds that were gathering on the western horizon, Uncle Gordon had decided to drive us as far as the pasture gate with the horses in the trailer behind.

Shane and I rode in the cab of the Dodge Ram with my uncle. As he casually maneuvered our caravan over the freshly graded gravel road, then around deep ruts in a trail that followed the fence of a wheat field, Shane asked him questions about his operation: how many head of cattle he had, how many acres of farmland and pasture. We were incredulous at the figures, multiplying 350 cattle by, hypothetically, 50 acres per head per year. Uncle Gordon, recognizing the formidable appearance of the operation when converted into numbers, supplied us with what seemed to him the more important explanation for why and how everything worked. "I do it all for the kids. I don't mean I make them feel they have to stay for my sake. I'm surprised they're as interested in it as they are. But I've made all this so that if they want it, it'll be here for them." Renae, sixteen, was following us in the four-by-four with SheriLynn. We had just driven through the small coulee where I knew Renae dreamed of one day building her own house and raising a family.

We parked and unloaded the horses just as a few heavy drops of rain began to fall. We mounted and were on our way, riding west into the brewing storm and the beginnings of a spectacular sunset. I rode a small but wide-bellied white mare, and Shane a chestnut-colored stallion. Uncle Gordon and Renae flattered all three of us on our horsemanship. SheriLynn giggled and jostled most of the way, her feet hanging limply in the stirrups as if they were mere footstools. Shane bounced unevenly but effortlessly to the rhythm of his horse's lively trot, leaving the horse to its own whims. Sneaking glances at Uncle Gordon and Renae, I tried desperately to recall the little I did know about riding.

In this concentration, my mind returned to a summer fifteen years ago when I spent a lot of time riding with my friend Julia, who was staying with a family that lived a few miles from Etzikom. Every chance I got, I went out to visit. We would curl our hair, don our best jeans, and occasionally sneak Western shirts from her older sister's closet, then get a pail of oats to lure the horses in from the pasture. Though we weren't supposed to, we always rode bareback. Sometimes we would race along a strip of fallow between two rows of trees in a small grove, hugging the horses' necks tightly, their muscles smooth beneath our cheeks. When we could only catch one of the horses, we would double as far as we could, letting the horse run faster and faster until one or both of us slid off the side. We thought highly of those horses for always slowing down just before we fell—it seemed an oddly sympathetic gesture in response to our wild escapades.

But even with saddles and a slow pace, we had a beautiful ride that day. My sister settled into her saddle, I forgave my mare her girth, and Shane experienced sheer pleasure the whole time, his muscles paying the next day for his disregard for technique. The rain steadily increased, and by the time we turned around we were all soaked through. Teeth chattering and legs quivering, I was overwhelmed by the stark beauty of the scene through which we rode: over knolls, through creases, and along the sides of hills to a point on the edge of the Etzikom coulee that overlooked Pakowki Lake in the bottom. We rode alongside wary cows and distracted calves, the whole time beneath a sky brought close by its deep shades of blue, purple, and gray, a border of orange and pink just beginning to form around the edges of the clouds.

When it storms like this on the prairies, you feel most certainly the flatness of the land; you can watch a cloud bank approaching from so far away that it actually seems to be creeping along the ground. I'd always loved storms from indoors; the raging chaos beating on the roof and windows while I stayed fearless and secure inside. I don't think I'd ever been quite so *in* a storm as during this ride. It felt new, and strange. I shivered and shook intermittently, partly from cold, and partly from the battle inside of me between the urge to seek shelter and a desire to feel the wildness of the storm.

Although I was raised in the rural community of Etzikom and most of my friends and family were associated with rural occupations, I held for many years the same stereotype of prairie life as many outsiders. For most of my youth I had witnessed farms suffering from lack of rain and ill-timed natural phenomena such as a surprise snow and freezing temperatures in May, or a late-August snow in the middle of harvest. And I'd become accustomed to the cycle of planting and harvesting thwarted by bad luck. I'd grown used to farmers' grumbling, disappointment, and—occasionally—their defeat. During the eighties, many farmers were forced by circumstances to sell or lease their land and move their familes to the city.

But this summer those images of loss and disappointment faded as I tried to imagine a land restored to productivity and hope. Pakowki Lake rose in my mind as the perfect symbol of this transformation. It was really an eight- or nine-mile swamp, never more than five feet deep, but we children proudly hailed the lake the warmest in Canada. I learned to water ski there, and one of the best ice-skating parties I remember was on Pakowki. It was at night, and we built a huge bonfire on the ice, roasted hot dogs and marshmallows, and skated for miles in the dark. I'm lucky to have any memories of the lake at all, because more than fifteen years ago it dried up.

But this year, Pakowki came back. Before Shane and I arrived, my father told me that the lake was filled with water again and Ducks Unlimited reported more waterfowl breeding on it than ever recorded. On our way to the Finstad ranch, Shane and I stopped on the small bridge that crosses the end of the lake and watched hundreds of these ducks swimming among the rushes, sitting on their nests atop beaver lodges, waddling about on the alkali-stained shore. When we moved too quickly, a mother duck in a nearby clearing flapped wildly in circles on the water's surface, the brood of ducklings that had flanked her weaving their way into the rushes. In another clearing of rushes, a muskrat appeared briefly on the surface of the water a few times, watching us more easily than we were able to watch him. I was thrilled to see this expanse of water interrupting the dry prairie, inviting back all of this life that I only remembered seeing in "dugouts," the deep, rectangular pits gouged out of the land as watering holes for cattle.

A month after we left, my father reported to me again on Pakowki Lake. Twenty-five thousand of the ducks that had lived and bred there during the summer—nearly one-half of the population— were dead from botulism poisoning. The disaster was brought on by a perfect combination of conditions: endospores (a form of the botulism bacterium) in the alkaline soil of the lake bottom, the spring runoff that had refilled the lake, August's extreme temperatures, and the nutrients supplied by the ducks. The botulism endospores are a dried and hardened form of the bacterium that can withstand incredible extremes of temperature and lie dormant for years, even centuries. My father told me that in the language of the Blackfoot Indians, "Pakowki" means "bad water."

Place-names in southern Alberta are often sources for local history and information about the land. The name "Pendant d'Oreille" (now pronounced pon-der-ay) is a good example. The coulee that extends south and west from Pakowki Lake received this name from the Blackfoot (Sik-si-kah') Indians following a battle with the intruding Pendant d'Oreille tribe from the south. The coulee and lake seem to have been a center of Blackfoot life and culture. On the Pakowki shores, more than 150 teepee rings remain in one camp, some as large as fourteen feet in diameter and all intact enough that the door openings of the tents can be plainly distinguished as a gap in the perimeter. Other artifacts remaining near Pakowki Lake include parallel lines of stones and boulders, eighty to three hundred feet in length, each one ending at a cairn. Apparently these stones mark the burial places of great chiefs. As my brother's friend knew, the area is also rich with smaller items, such as spear- and arrowheads and the remains of small domestic tools.

In contrast to the knowledge and history these native Indian names contain, there is relatively little known about the previous inhabitants themselves. Information is often speculative, anecdotes are short and inconclusive, and, most significant of all, there are no native people left in the area to remind us of their presence long ago or to relate stories from their past. What is known is the story of the tragic last years of their presence in the Cypress Hills, a series of three flat-topped rises that extend 130 kilometers in an east-west direction across the Alberta/Saskatchewan border.

Rather than offering an insight or description, the name of these hills preserves the error of the French-Canadian explorers who mistook the hills' lodgepole pines for their cypress tree, common in the east. Indian names for the hills include "Thunder Breeding Hills" and, from the Blackfoot, "Earth over Earth." Completely surrounded by plains, they rise to an elevation of 4,800 feet. Some say that after the last ice age, forest covered all of the land between the Rockies and these hills. As the climate warmed, the forest was overtaken by grasses except in the higher elevations—now the Cypress Hills. The wetter, cooler climate in their heights allowed eighteen species of orchids to survive that aren't found anywhere else in the province except in the Rockies. Other people dispute the likelihood of grasses encroaching on forest, favoring instead the theory that, like the Rocky Mountains, the hills escaped submersion by the ice sheet and the resulting denudation that left the surrounding plains covered only by grass.

To me, the significance of this feature of the landscape is the escape it offers from the bare, dusty prairie, but also the role it played in the final dispersal of the Indians who had lived on the plains. The Cypress Hills were home to Blackfoot, Cree, Assiniboine, and Gros Ventre Indians. All tribes apparently lived peacefully together for many years in the hills. In 1877, just two years after the Canadian government established a Northwest Mounted Police post in the hills to regulate the whiskey trade, Chief Sitting Bull and approximately 4,000 Sioux fled to the Cypress Hills for protection following the Battle of Little Bighorn. Chief Crowfoot of the Blackfoot Indians and Chief Big Bear of the Cree welcomed him, but pressure from the Canadian government and fear of conflict forced them to withdraw their gestures of protection, and in 1881 the Sioux were forced to return to the United States. The Cypress Hills also sheltered a small number of Nez Percé who, in 1877, alone completed the journey to Canada begun by Chief Joseph and members of the tribe who had refused to be moved from traditional lands in Oregon to an Idaho reservation; Joseph and most of his people surrendered to the U.S. Army near Montana's Bear Paw Mountains, just forty miles from the Canadian border. Within the next few years, the Canadian government signed treaties with the tribes in the hills and with those living on the surrounding plains, which effectively removed them from the region and isolated them on reserves in the Rocky Mountain foothills.

At great cost was this unassuming region transformed into what it is now: a land from which so much is expected and much has been received. No single person, place, or moment in history can teach me the means of this exchange and transformation, or allow me to participate in the unspoken activities of the prairie.

During one of our reminiscent moments months after we left Etzikom, Shane grew quiet as I spoke with a tinge of homesickness about the spirit of the place and the people living there. Trying to assemble his own sense about the people he'd only briefly come to know, he found what he wanted to say as I remembered aloud our conversation with Uncle Gordon the day we went riding.

What I hadn't realized about Gordon, Lee, and the other men, Shane said, is that they like to work. They want to have more to do in a day than they can do. They want to drill holes in the earth and put up a section of fence where there wasn't any before. Certainly they want to pass the land on to their children, but it's a changed land—improved, enlarged—that they want to pass on. They want to make a mark on the earth that will last.

Inside I raged—at my slowness to reach this articulation, at the time and effort I'd had to spend to even approach this understanding. But perhaps most of all at my willingness to dismiss the obvious as shallow, as stereotype. I know these men; I've lived among them.

At a small dinner party shortly after we returned from Canada, Shane and I met a couple who were traveling around the world with their two-year-old son. We were all curious about how the boy had adapted to travel, to the confusion of time zones, to being away from home for so long. His mother described how, at every place along the way, they showed him on a globe exactly where they were, where home was, and where they were going next. "But I don't know how much he really understands," she concluded.

The others—scientists, a doctor, and a nurse—began to discuss childhood perceptions of culture, distance, and time. As I thought about the globe, the mother's finger tracing the path of the airplane, and the little boy watching, being told that now he was on the pink spot and tomorrow he would be on the green . . . the door to a memory opened in my mind. "Does he know that he stands on the *outside* of the globe?" I asked.

For a few awkward moments, I tried to explain. As a child, I visualized myself living on the inside of a ball. My earth enwrapped me, spread out and up and around the sky, and God was somewhere in the middle.

The dinner conversation stopped, considered me. I tried to make the others see my child self, suspended headfirst inside the earth, joined to me now by the soles of our feet.

But I was left behind, swamped in my memories of this old confusion. I remembered how I used to turn to the west every time my mother asked me to close the east windows. And how still, every time I look at a map of even my own province or country, I experience a dizzying flip-flop before I can make sense of it. Long ago I had decided I must suffer from a strange form of dyslexia, when actually I was simply looking at the earth's surface from the opposite direction as most everyone else.

Last winter, my parents sent photos to me of our family home and of Etzikom, taken from various vantage points after fresh snowfalls or while such phenomena as sun dogs and harvest sunsets marked the sky. One photo in particular caught my attention, though it was far from the most interesting in the package. It was taken from the road less than a quarter mile north of Etzikom, just far enough to include the whole town. On the left, my parents' home was visible on the outskirts of town with the museum's windmills in the background. On the right, you could see the grain elevators criss-crossed by the chicken-wire backstop of our old baseball diamond. It was the photo's proportions that drew and puzzled me. The town itself— eighteen years of my life and the intended subject of the photo—lay in a narrow, horizontal strip less than a half-inch tall on the three-by-five-inch photo. Most of the picture was of the sky.

Later, on the telephone with my parents, I described my reaction to the photo, how strange and *large* the sky appeared to me. After a moment's pause, my mother said, "I guess, when you're here, you just look at the things around you."

I couldn't remember ever being startled by the sheer size of the prairie sky in quite the same way that I was when looking at that photo. Of course, everyone who lives in the prairies watches the sky regularly—for signs of rain or reprieve from a hot spell, for frost, snowstorms, chinooks. Some, like my father and me, would watch it for the particular spread and color of an autumn sunset, the throw of light from a late-afternoon sun dog, the reaching, clawing dance of the northern lights on a clear night. But our observation aspired to a relatively small moment of connection compared to what this photo seemed to make possible. I wonder that we didn't walk hunched and bent under the weight of such blue.

How certain and finite my heavens once were, and what a shallow casement the earth containing it. After so long of stepping gingerly in my world and looking about so selectively, I finally understand what a lonely and confining space I'd been trying to occupy; what a precarious position it is to balance between all these powerful forces, between such overwhelming features of land and sky. As I tap at the shell of my childhood universe, I find that I'm in a world huge with possibilities.

In Etzikom's history book is a black-and-white photo of an early settler standing chest-high in a field of thick wheat. It reminds me now of the field I stood in several years ago so that my sister could take a photograph. I had wanted to know what I would look like standing in the wheat and framed by the flat prairie horizon.

In this old photo the blurred heads of the wheat soften the lower edge and a few stalks in the foreground seem to come right out of the picture, reminding me of how the bristles brushed my arm and caught in my shirt as they bowed to a small whirlwind passing by. The settler has grayed hair pulled back into a bun, and her face is beautifully weathered. The sleeves of her worn and faded dress are pushed to her elbows. Her feet sink a little into the dry soil; a line of footprints weaves through the stalks to the place where she has stopped. When she walks away, she shakes each foot to empty the dirt that has spilled into her shoe.

But as she stands in the photo, she smiles. She's been looking at the things around her, and you can see in her face that she's let go of something for the view.

The wind lifts a wing of hair from behind her ear.

Rick Kempa

The Wind

from *Puerto del Sol*

We live on a hill that rises from the middle of a sprawling little city in Wyoming, in a land of much sky. Ours is one of a row of town houses, by no means a romantic dwelling, but it's modern, efficient, comfortable, and built with at least some attention to the weather. The view is what recommends it most: the swirl of town lights beneath us; the interstate—dividing line of the world—in the middle ground; the angular horizon of buttes and crags, and on the best days, in one particular notch in the bluffs, north-northeast, the far-off glint of the Wind River Mountains.

Being a confirmed view man, one for whom the top of a tree or mountain or double-decker bus has always been alluring, I am willing to put up with a lot of abuse for the sake of my horizon—the higher rent, for instance, that is affixed to a housing complex called "Hilltop Manor." But hand in hand with the view comes the other legacy of living closer to the sky, the most obvious fact of life on the hilltop, the wind.

All of nature has ceded this territory to it. Nothing grows taller than knee-high up here, even in the best of times. The seedling of any sort that manages to sprout here is destined to be a dwarf. The antelope in their restless grazing periodically scour this place, the birds alight on eaves and wires in a calm hour, but except for a few rodents that hide beneath rocks and a few humans behind walls, no creatures live here.

Even we humans have granted wind its dominance, limiting our spring-planting projects to ground huggers like grass or shrubs. This is not to say that our sights were always so contained. I'd like to see the architect's vision for this place, concocted in some controlled-air dream factory in Denver. The six cherry trees, one in front of each town house, are evidence of our initial false assumption as to who or what would rule here. As spindly and squat as the day they were transplanted, they are growing downward, if at all.

No matter where one goes, folks are always bragging about their weather, and we're no different. Ours is not your ordinary wind, we say. We've seen it blow holes in billboards or flip over trucks on the highway like they were empty cardboard boxes. It's been known to take a freight train and put it in a ditch. Last summer in one of those mean dust raisers that pass for thunderstorms around here, the wind pummelled a two-story house being built a little ways down the hill, until it collapsed into a pile of twisted wood.

When we meet in the grocery store by chance, even before we ask about the kids, we talk about wind: "Ain't it something out there?" "What do you think is behind it?" Memory can be as compelling as the thing itself. Whatever else the weather might be doing—bitter cold or dusty drought—we remind ourselves, "It could be worse." Or if it's been nice too long, the cashier is sure to say, as if it's the Official Company Line, "Enjoy it while you can. You know it won't be long until . . ."

Or we joke about it, make it the butt of our bareboned humor. "It's snowing sideways again," someone will say, frowning out the window. We tell the thin-skinned newcomer that if it ever stopped blowing, "everything would fall over." We talk about the flakes that leave the clouds just this side of Utah and touch ground four hundred miles east, in Nebraska.

But at times wind is the fact of weather that one must take dead seriously. "It's a wonder the wind / don't tear off your skin," Utah Phillips sings, and that's no lie. Arctic air set into motion can literally burn or bite. Layers of skin can lose their life in a quarter hour's time. Protrusions like noses or tips of chins can be in mortal danger, anesthetized first, and then, in a stroke as clean as any surgeon's blade, excised.

Skin grows back or scars over, but once the wind's been under it, it stays there. Once you've been out driving on that open road fifty miles from anywhere and had to fight the wind with all your might to see who turns the wheel, or once you've been caught short-sleeved several hours up-trail on one of those days that started out so perfect, so blue, that you forgot the wind was out there (it *was* out there, prowling around the blue, quiet only because there was nothing for it to rub its back on), once *you've* been out there, you come to know that the wind is an animal.

When my wife, Fern, and I moved to the hilltop, we included the front and back yards in our homemaking plans, thinking, like the Denver draftsmen, that the outside world was ours to shape. Shrugging off the absence of trees, we bought patio furniture so that we might better enjoy the view. But the chaise longue shuffled around the deck without asking leave, the chairs flip-flopped daily through the dog's minefield, and the table with its umbrella threatened to take to the sky, passengers and all. We learned to fold and store the chairs each night, and we bolted the table down, but the wind whirling through the umbrella made an eerie high-pitched sound, causing the dog to bark and the neighbors to mutter. When I complained to a friend about these matters, she looked at me with eyebrows raised and exclaimed, "But the wind hasn't even started blowing yet!" Taking her comment as a warning, we changed homemaking tactics, sold off the lawn furniture (Barely Used! Lowest Price!) and, like the cherry trees, surrendered the outside space. We instead invited the best of it indoors by hanging prisms, sun catchers, and plants, and by frequently scrubbing our windows.

When the wind finally came that made the first ones seem like wisps, our task became one of trying to keep it out. It took us by surprise at first, in schizophrenic October, the month of sunbaked afternoons and frost-tinged nights. One morning I found the kitchen window open and papers strewn across the floor into the living room. My first thought at seeing the disarray was of burglars, for I distinctly remembered reaching over the sink the night before to turn the crank that drew the window closed. But the screen, still in place, belied that notion. A few minutes of on-site chin rubbing gave me a likelier answer: apparently I had left the window slightly ajar, and the wind, as insinuating as a screwdriver in a gloved hand, had approached at a certain precise angle and pried it open.

On another night, in November, when the wind shifted out of the north, icy pillars of air filled the house and sent me running downstairs to find the front door flung wide. Again, the fear of man beset me, more urgent this time. With my dog at my side and my clenched flashlight doubling as a nightstick, I searched every cranny of the house before I was satisfied that, again, the culprit was the wind. This time its assault had been premeditated: first it had threaded through the mechanism of the lock to see that it was not turned, then probed the latch to find it hadn't clicked, and finally had backed off, summoned its strength, and thrown its shoulder against the heavy wood.

This skirmish signalled the start of our winter's war. Armed with heavyweight plastic and duct tape, I sealed all the windows on the inside (which meant, of course, saying good-bye to the clear, clean light). When the wind mounted its offensives, the plastic bulged and strained like full-blown sails, and the tape that held the edges down began to come unglued. It was frightening to see how the air between the glass and the plastic was not static, not "the extra layer of insulation" I had been told it would be, but rather a restless, alien body striving to get in, vanguard of the invading force.

Every day I patrolled the borders, tape and scissors in hand, sealing off the icy little arrows that had pried up the tape or pricked the plastic. I nailed strips of wool along the edges of the door, so that it took a major exertion simply to open it. By Christmas, closets became refrigerator-freezers, and we joked about hanging our coats on the outside to avoid entering them. Then the joke became reality, as we surrendered those dark spaces and instead lay our coats along the bottom edges to trap the air inside.

One January night I sat on the sofa with a blanket draped around me and simply paid attention to the movement of air, the violence of it outside, beating the walls like drums, rattling the metal vent caps on the roof like cymbals. Inside, too, in spite of all I'd done, the cold air freely moved. I got down on my hands and knees to feel for its source, and the futility of my season-long defense became clear. In the cracks between the baseboard and the wall, long, thin planes of icy air seeped in. A jet of it surged in through each electrical outlet. The wind even infiltrated the molecules of the wall itself: the plaster was frigid to the touch.

At that moment, my season-long efforts seemed more the work of a madman than of a devoted homeowner. I felt a sudden, weird kinship with Bobby, the introverted boy-next-door of my youth, he of the famous obsession. All summer long, he prowled his back porch with a fly swatter, squashing every beady-eyed bug that landed on his wall. So diligent and so accurate was he that I kept expecting his work to be done, the world to be flyless. But no; every morning brought a new hatching, more toil for the slaughter boy. Similarly, no matter which way I turned in my poor wind-shriven home, the influx of cold awaited my petty efforts. "Shoddy construction," Fern complained, but I took the higher perspective, as I continued (how could I not?) to insulate. Ours were the labors of Sisyphus. We were part of a long tradition, Bobby and I, which bestowed dignity if not meaning on our work. There was something ennobling about carrying on while faced with the truth of the old Chinese proverb: "There is no wall through which wind cannot pass."

The storm arrives one April night, a dark tide moving against all that is anchored, making the whole world scream, seeping into our po-

rous dreams and playing havoc with them. In between my deep
dives, as I approach the surface where trees are hissing and rainwater
is smacking the window in waves, I think, "Hmmm. The street
cleaner is out—how strange" (especially because I have never seen
a street cleaner in this town). Fern, meanwhile, is imagining that she
is lying in a small boat in a big surf, close to shore but getting no
closer, being pushed toward it and pulled away from it at the same
time. She sees the butt ends of the oars sticking out of the oarlocks
above her, she wants to row, but she can't sit up; it's like her back is
glued to the boat's bottom. And all around her and under her, separated only by some thin planking, is the crushing, thumping,
seething force.

Claire, our three-year-old, trots into the room, yelling, "Mama,
Papa, there's animals outside!" We assure her there's not, that it's
"just the wind," that she should go back to bed. But as I draw her
close for a hug, I realize she's trembling, and I see the glint of alarm
in her eyes. What is the wind to a little girl but an unseen animal
flinging its body against the house? I haul her aboard, settle her in
between us.

She promptly sleeps, but not Fern nor I. Of our three dreams,
Fern's is the one that compels our wakefulness. Even in the house, in
bed, being in the windstorm is much like being in the surf. The
panic, the threat of imminent drowning, is absent, but there's the
same sensation of helplessness, smallness, engulfment in something
with no beginning or end, with only variations in intensity. Relax for
a second, and the next invisible thrust will convulse you, unbalance
you. The whole damn house might get torn from its moorings, like
Dorothy's.

"To him that hath no home, no wind is friendly," Montaigne
wrote, and the wind moves Fern to commiserate. She imagines other
people out in it—the hitchhiker cowering under a bridge, the mo-
torist stranded on the interstate. She projects ourselves out there:
"What if we were living in a tent?" she suddenly blurts. And what a
thought that is, to have nothing but a thin sheet of nylon between us
and it, the fabric flapping, bulging, the air streaming in through the

seams, the terrifying tautness of certain lines of pressure. With a shiver, she moves toward my side of the bed. Her feet are so frigid they could keep an ice pack cold. She rummages for the heavy blanket at our feet, pulls it over us, gets my half as well because that's too much weight for me. Claire, half-smothered between us, lets out a yelp.

Once I spent a night and a day on a Carolina beach during a nor'easter, a windstorm fierce enough to test the limits of any tent, except I didn't have a tent. I was sandblasted down to my eyeballs and scoured on the inside too. A nor'easter is a gale wind that blows in from the North Atlantic in the fall, a dry run for the wetter, fiercer storms that'll come from those parts in winter. It's a wild, ceaseless thing that whips the waves to frenzy and idles the fishermen, easily deserves the name of "storm."

Time and again in the course of that eerie, moony night, I moved from behind one clump of dune grass to another, in a futile search for a niche of calmness. It didn't exist, of course, outside of the rented walls. No matter where I threw down my sleeping bag and crawled into it, the incessant hiss of sand in motion—louder always when you get down to its level—filled my ears. "Today's sand flat is tomorrow's dune," an old-timer at the chowder hall in Okracoke had said to me with a wink, when he heard I was heading down to the water. Out in the storm, where all I had to do to make a pillow was tilt my head and let the sand flow in under it, there was no reason to think he was speaking metaphorically. How many of these particles would it take to bury me, backpack and all, I wondered— five hundred million? A billion? Whatever the number, it seemed within an easy night's work of that wind. I ended up wandering, like the ghost of a drowned buccaneer, up and down the beach and through the empty streets of the old seaport, waiting for the first pot of coffee to call me in.

"The wind in one's face makes one wise," wrote the English poet George Herbert. This wisdom has nothing to do with words: yell into the wind and hear what happens. Nor for that matter does it have to do with thoughts. Wind can get your thoughts aswirling just like everything else, but it's one thing to be moved, and quite another to be organized.

But the wind will do what no other creature is allowed to—it will touch your eyes. The prophet touched the eyes of the blind man and he saw; he was forever changed. A hitchhiker I plucked from an Idaho highway one November day was so wind-battered that he couldn't answer the commonest traveller's questions—clutching for my atlas when I asked where he was going, staring and staring at it until it became clear that he didn't know *where* he was going, other than east, the way of the wind. His eyes, which had been facing into the big blow, were neither red nor swollen, but wide open—the pupils huge, unfocusing. They were *touched,* no longer organs for seeing but for feeling. He was obviously out of his element in the controlled air of the car, and when, soon after, I pulled over where our roads diverged, he plunged headfirst out the door like a grateful skydiver.

The wooden gate outside our bedroom is being flung over and over against the side of the house. Our neighbor's second-floor storm window breaks loose and plunges into our driveway, where it explodes. Impossible to lie still! Wrestling free of the sheets, I prowl the dark house, window to window, peering out—at what? The body of the wind is not the wind; the animal is invisible. I place my palm on a pane, hold it there, then watch the imprint generated by its heat disperse.

The presence of the past, with me in ways more real, more permanent than memory, the way one's lovers are: a night on a beach, the wildest night of the most potent, most unfettered season of my life. I'd travelled twenty-five hundred miles by foot and by thumb from the Arizona desert to be there at the dividing line of earth and water, simply to be there. That the line was a frothing, pounding pit of violence made it all the better; the last thing I wanted or expected was tranquillity.

I mounted the last dune to its crest, where the wind that knew no land came across to touch me, took off my clothes there, and faced into it. Under that big moon, the blue-black water shifted and pulsed and broke into flashing, flecking silver. The sand held an unearthly luminescence, moonlight conjuring moonscape. I was the first man, the only man, and even the existence of my own body seemed uncertain, for the wind did not blow against it so much as through it, flushing out my cells, imparting a vibration to all my molecules. Arms outstretched, head raised, I gave my voice—no melody, no message, just voice—to the wind.

For as long as we have lived here, our neighbors have had a string of clay bells hanging from the eave of their porch. Each bell (there are five of them) is of a particular weight and timbre, so that they ring, in endless succession, a line of music that has imbedded itself into my mind as the first bars of a nursery song: "Mary had a lit . . . , Mary had a lit . . ." Only the fiercest wind waves, flinging them all together in confusion, disrupts the pattern, and even then not for long. I listen hard between each crest for the feisty little string of swimmers to grasp at, gasp for, achieve their melody.

In a solitary, receptive hour, this interplay becomes the pure strains of collaboration, wind and man working for once toward the same end. Musicians know that if the thing between them is going to have a life of its own, if it is going to *take off,* they must act not only on *it,* but on each other. So, too, in the ferment of the night. The hand that made the bells translates brute force into pattern. Consciousness, in whatever being it resides, always aims for this, to impose itself on the world. The wind, neither harnessed nor humanized, has an equal potency, improvising, insisting with its wild forays on its own preeminence, but above all—or rather below all—imbuing the inert matter with life, translating clay to chime.

But the wind is an animal, a body in motion. I awake suddenly and completely, without it (surprised as usual that sleep had claimed me). In its place are the far midnight sounds: the shudder of boxcars coupling in the train yard, trucks groaning on the highway as they downshift for the climb out of our valley. Most of all I hear, in the underlying, unsettling quiet, the passage of the present. The world grows larger and larger. Heat disperses, stars pile on stars, that intolerable infinity approaches. Suddenly I yearn for wind, as one does for a bedmate: part shield, part company. The wind is most felt in its absence.

Susan Ewing

Riding Whitewater, Seeing Shadows
Divining Hells Canyon

First publication

Hells Canyon lies carved into the heart of the Columbia Basin like a divine inscription. Among themselves, Nez Percé people call it the Place of Shadows—a name far more understanding of the land's capacity to hold darkness and light.

This remote shadow-catching, shadow-making place forms the border between northeast Oregon and west central Idaho. Hells Canyon isn't on the way to anywhere. If you're there, it's because that's where you were going. It's where I was going.

On the Idaho side, I followed the Snake River north; or, I followed a permutation of a river that had been fattened into a reservoir by Hells Canyon Dam, a dozen miles ahead. Approaching the dam was like approaching the portal between twentieth-century here-and-now and the lost horizon. On my way across the concrete threshold I stopped my truck to look up the reservoir and down the river. The reservoir bore all the trappings of hydropower: cables, chain link, cab-over campers, fishermen in lawn chairs, and rock-chucking children. Downstream of the concrete spillway, the Snake River hissed back to life. I kicked the flanks of my Ford and drove toward the wild side.

Hells Canyon drew people to itself six thousand years before Christ drew disciples. Before Western expansionists brought the hell of greed and conquest, this was a home place. The Nez Percé and those who came before hunted, gathered, found shelter from winter, and marked rocks with notice of their passing. Pictographs, petroglyphs, and burial mounds fill the canyon with watchful spirits.

Shortly after crossing the dam I reached the end of the line. There are no roads through the seventy-nine-mile canyon slithering away from the dam, although two Forest Service roads and three rough tracks provide limited river-recreation access. Most nonmotorized float trips begin here, just below Hells Canyon Dam, where the river is let out of its bag for a while. Hells Canyon holds some of the most renowned whitewater rapids in the United States. Depending on release levels from the dam, this portion of the Snake may channel the largest volume of water of any wilderness river in the contiguous United States. The natural water volume is more than double that of the Colorado River. Whitewater gives me butterflies, and as I met my party at the boat ramp, a monarch migration was fluttering through my belly.

For the next three days my tribal unit would consist of four oarsmen and about a dozen paying customers from such oppositely remote outlands as New York, New Jersey, Boston, and San Diego. We would be traveling in three seventeen-and-a-half-foot wooden dories, plus one rubber raft for gear; no motors, no cabins, no windshields, no radios. With their upswept ends, dories drift gracefully as floating feathers. It was late afternoon and after much organizing of gear and safety instruction for us passengers, the boats were loaded. Two ravens watched us set out into the convolution of land, water, and light.

Through the canyon the river averages about fifty yards wide.

The depth varies; holes of nearly two hundred feet have been measured, although in some places the water is shallow enough to see the smooth stones tiling the bottom. Rocky and sandy beaches appear along the semiarid riverbank as do occasional abandoned homestead buildings and groves of cottonwoods. For much of its length, the canyon is more like a football stadium than a sheer chasm. Geography-sized benches fold down from the surrounding mountains like wide bleacher seats; creek draws define the sections.

Swooping swallows drew us down the river, crisscrossing before us in pursuit of low-flying insects. Every drifting minute brought a new view. Varying elevation and slope orientation create a patchwork of alternately timbered and open-country ecosystems that abut like neighborhoods of differing character. Ferns in one block, prickly pear cactus in the next. Larch, fir, and pine string down the mountainsides to meet hackberry, cottonwood, sumac, and sagebrush.

Peregrine falcons have accepted this land's hospitality, as have cougars, mountain goats, lynx, golden and bald eagles, bats, black bears, rattlesnakes, and the nation's largest, free-ranging, nonfed elk herd. Giant white sturgeon live in the Snake's canyon-cradled belly, one of the few remaining places to find the riverine aborigine.

Maybe because there is so much room here, or maybe because the land has something it wants to say, the country takes its voice in extremes: Hells Canyon is the deepest river canyon on earth, rising a treetop over 8,000 feet from the river to the tallest adjacent peak in Idaho's Seven Devil Mountains; the Grand Canyon is half a mile shorter. The Snake River drinks from forty tributaries spread through six states to become one of the largest rivers in the nation. A land of extremes, yes. But an embracing land, full of grace.

Too soon we landed at the first night's camp, a comfortable, riverfront swath of beach. Setting up my blue tent in violet evening shadow, no hint of hellishness was to be found, only the steady, soothing burble of flowing water. The Snake is born in the Wyoming

Rockies of Yellowstone National Park and passes on into the Columbia River more than one thousand miles later. It's the kind of river you can lean on—sturdy and quick to regain its composure between numerous, frothing rapids. Oh, the rapids. My butterflies roosted fitfully through the night, until . . .

"BREAKFAST!"

The call echoed from Idaho to Oregon and back. David Sears—trip leader, breakfast cook, and former football player for the United States Army—tipped thick coffee from a gallon-size pot into my plastic mug.

I dished up eggs and cereal, plopped contentedly on the ground with the family from Boston and reinsurance guys from New York, and ate with gusto. Motivations have changed with the centuries, but human beings are still drawn to Hells Canyon. They come for solitude and wilderness. Some make the long trip here for whitewater adventure—nature's reminder that people aren't always in control. Whitewater is why Laura from San Diego came. A pink clip held her hair in a makeshift nest on top of her head.

"I wanted a little violence, you know? Nothing too serene. Something to remind me we're not always the dominant force. You know what I'm saying?"

I said I thought I did. Today she would get what she wanted in the form of Wild Sheep and Granite rapids. These two foaming furies range between Class IV and a fat Class V, depending upon water levels. Class VI tops the scale and has been described as "almost by definition a near-death experience." This was not a fat-V day, thank you very much, but there was no shortage of hydraulic fluid.

Oarsmen not putting on breakfast attended to their boats: bailing, sponging, arranging, packing, puttering—and finally sitting, looking out over the water, gathering the river into themselves. After breakfast, camp was transformed from a homey colony of tents into a pile of dry bags, metal boxes, and canvas sacks, ready to go. I relish the nomadic rhythm of river life. Set up camp, settle in, strike camp, move. Set up camp . . . move . . . move . . .

Just above Wild Sheep rapids we pulled off the river to scout the drop. The sight of whitewater was seductive and we were quickly back to the boats.

"Hatches secure? Life vests tight?" Our oarsman, Ric Bailey, called the final check. I took the questions as rhetorical. Bailey never took his eyes from the stack of water, submerged rock, and trough before us. Heading toward the fall, he pushed the boat into an exuberant pirouette.

The Snake lifted the dory then twisted away, plunging us into a green and white hole. Water roiled into the boat, washing across bare legs and sneakered feet. We bucked and rolled, hooting and hollering, looking over the bow toward the sky, then—*WHUMP*, stomach-sucking fall—toward China. Walls of river collapsed on our heads, striking thunderous chords of roar, hiss, and groan. Thick water slapped my body and stole my breath. Bailey hauled hard on the oars, fighting for passage.

A few more carnival-ride slams and dips and we coasted out of Wild Sheep. The roar subsided like a window had been shut against the noise. Suddenly, all was serene. Through a screen of wet hair I counted all bodies aboard before I began to bail. Scoop, pour. Scoop, pour. Scoop, pour. Finally—scoop, scrape, pour, as the bailer hit bottom. Scoop, scrape, pour. More river rhythms.

Riders were unanimously drenched and exhilarated; oarsman was evaluative.

"I didn't end up where I expected to, going in," Bailey frowned. "It's new every time."

About two miles downriver we approached Granite Creeks rapids, biggest water of the trip. Laura should be having a good day.

I smelled them first: a dense scent of fresh water worried by a hint of pestled rock. Then the coming rumble. Again, we pulled over to scout. Climbing to an overlook, the oarsmen stood apart from each other studying the tumult. At last, they called out their navigation opinions over the noise of the rapids. My butterflies were somewhat appeased that all opinions agreed, although I tightened my life vest against their fluttering.

Sears was first through. He executed the run handsomely, to the full glory of the dory.

Our turn.

"Hatches secure? Life vests tight?" The questions no longer seemed rhetorical. We stormed a castle seemingly built of shattered glass, running through the halls and great rooms in a feast of light, water, noise, and motion. Like other of life's corporeal pleasures, it was over entirely too fast.

Scoop, pour. Scoop, pour . . . Scoop, scrape, pour. Bailey pulled a deep breath into his fort of a chest, revived by the perfect run. The rest of us chattered inanely, wearing the cocky smiles of survived experience. We pulled into a downstream eddy to watch as the third dory took Granite in a run as lithe as its young, dark-lashed oarsman. Sunlight cobbled the river; brightness curved in behind my eyes and dripped down my throat.

That night we made camp by McGaffee's cabin, a deserted homestead and registered historical site. Nonnative interest in Hells Canyon country essentially began with the discovery of gold in the 1860s. Settlers followed miners, coming in with the Homestead Act of 1862 and more liberal Desert Land Act of 1877; not surprisingly, 1877 is also the year the Nez Percé were finally forced out.

Before the gold rush, the government had set aside for indigenous peoples a reservation of several thousand square miles that included Hells Canyon and the adjoining Wallowa Mountains. If the canyon is the heart of this country, the Wallowas are its soul. As homesteaders and entrepreneurs flooded west, government negotiators proposed treaty revisions that would take most of the reservation land back. A minority of Nez Percé chiefs agreed to the revisions, but Old Joseph and Toohoolhoolzote, chiefs of the Wallowa and Hells Canyon bands, rejected the treaty changes.

Old Joseph died in 1871 and young Joseph—"Thunder Rolling from Mountain Heights"—promised his dying father that he would never sell the people's land. In 1873, the United States government ruled that Joseph and the other nonsignatory chiefs were not bound by the treaty revision, but two years later, President Grant reversed the declaration, ordering Joseph and the others to a reservation in Idaho. The Indians ignored the order to leave and one year later another treaty conference was called. Toohoolhoolzote spoke for the Nez Percé:

"The Great Chief made the world as it is, and as he wanted it, and he made a part of it for us to live upon. I do not see where you get the authority to say that we shall not live where he placed us."

Government agents responded by locking the old man up. The Nez Percé finally, agonizingly, agreed to leave if Toohoolhoolzote were freed. Upon his release the people were given thirty days to vacate their land of all memory. And so it happened, that around the first of June, 1877, Chief Joseph gathered his four hundred people in the north end of Hells Canyon and crossed the runoff-swollen Snake into Idaho and exile. They were joined along the way by the chiefs Toohoolhoolzote, Looking Glass, and Whitebird. Early in the exodus violence erupted and the refugees became fugitives. The chiefs and their bands resolved to join Sitting Bull in Canada.

Five months and 1,400 harsh miles later, Chief Joseph was defeated in the Bear Paw Mountains of Montana, forty miles from the Canadian border. One of his wives had been killed earlier at the battle of Big Hole. In surrender, he said: "I am tired of fighting. Our chiefs are killed. Looking Glass is dead. Toohoolhoolzote is dead. . . . The little children are freezing to death. . . .

"Hear me my chiefs. I am tired; my heart is sick and sad. From where the sun now stands I will fight no more forever."

Joseph and the other survivors were taken to reservations in Oklahoma. In 1879, Joseph traveled to Washington, D.C., to request that his people be allowed to return home.

"Suppose," he told the U.S. Congress, "a white man should come to me and say, 'Joseph, I like your horses, and I want to buy them.' I say to him, 'No, my horses suit me, I will not sell them.' Then he goes to my neighbor, and says to him, 'Joseph has some good horses. I want to buy them, but he refuses to sell.' My neighbor answers, 'Pay me the money, and I will sell you Joseph's horses.' The white man returns to me, and says, 'Joseph, I have bought your horses, and you must let me have them.' If we sold our lands to the government, this is the way they were bought."

Eventually, many Nez Percé were relocated to reservations in the Northwest. Joseph, placed on the Colville Reservation in Washington state, was forbidden from returning to the land where his father was buried.

"I love that land more than all the rest of the world," Joseph had told Congress.

Embracing land, full of grace.

These days, the spiritual shadows being cast across the canyon are from opposing camps of whites: those who would preserve the status quo, and those who would preserve the place. Currently, the 652,488-acre Hells Canyon National Recreation Area is managed by the United States Forest Service for broadly defined multiple uses including logging, grazing, and jet boating. The Hells Canyon Preservation Council (HCPC) wants the canyon and river, the recreation area, and the adjacent backcountry areas on public land—the complete Hells Canyon ecosystem—to be designated as a 1.5-million-acre park and preserve. The park and preserve designation allows hunting, but restricts other activities not compatible with the preservation of wilderness. HCPC would like to see the proposed Hells Canyon/Chief Joseph National Park and Preserve placed under the authority of the National Park Service—an agency it feels is better suited to protect the canyon's nature.

Although they're federal kin, the Park Service and Forest Service have different agendas. The Park Service, under the Department of the Interior, has been instructed to protect and preserve. The Forest

Service's marching orders from the Department of Agriculture have been to extract and utilize. If they were brothers, the Park Service would be a catch-and-release fly fisher, the Forest Service a gill-netter.

Designating Hells Canyon a National Recreation Area in 1975 did prevent the canyon from being flooded by proposed dams, but it was thought the recreation area designation would also ensure that eco-system protection was given priority in management decisions. HCPC and others, however, accuse the Forest Service of subsuming environmental considerations and using the recreation area as a "commodity grab bag" of timber and rangeland, and allowing unlim-ited jet boat use on the river while restricting the number of floaters. Power boating has become a 22-million-dollar industry for the local economy, and many area families also support themselves with tim-ber and ranching dollars. But HCPC, also locally organized and headquartered, argues that continued levels of logging and grazing will exhaust resources and that unregulated jet boating will erode the beaches and the peace, leaving no jobs *or* trees, *or* wild country to hand down to future generations.

Oarsman Ric Bailey is executive director of HCPC. "They're wearing the country out," he told me during our first evening on the river. "I don't want to see the essence of this country driven out by roads, RV parks, jet boats, airplane overflights, stumps, and cow shit." Wearing a torn T-shirt, river sandals, and unpremeditated stubble of beard, he looks more like a troubled, latter-day Lancelot than an executive director. The former logger, firefighter, and long-haul truck driver has been jousting with the Forest Service for four-teen years.

"I love this place," Bailey said. "And the other people who live here, who don't agree with what I'm doing, love this place too. It's just that we have a different vision of what our relationship with it ought to be. We don't have to tear down a place in order to make a living."

I left the boats on the third river day and spent the next couple of days alone, hiking out to the canyon's rim. The river becomes more accessible below the point I was dropped off, and increased encounters with cow herds and jet boats confuse the wilderness experience. Later I heard that on their sixth, last, day on the wild and scenic Snake, my fallen-together family had been passed 110 times by power boats.

There is another reason to consider the well-being of Hells Canyon, more elusive than arguments of politics, economics, or environmental fervor: This land is alive—not in the sense that there are animals and plants and running waters, but in the sense that walking here takes extra attention because you're balancing across a living being.

I spent a few days in Joseph after my hike out of the canyon and, on one day, drove the gravel road to Dug Bar—the river crossing where Chief Joseph and his people took their first, sad steps toward exile. There are a few campsites, wind, and many spirits. The rough Dug Bar road climbs, drops, and switchbacks across the arid Imnaha Canyon down to the Snake. The Imnaha River, beautiful little sister to the Snake, wears her own canyon like the loveliest doeskin dress. It wasn't the extraordinary vistas that pressed my heart—it was the tactual, transcendent emotion of the land itself.

Down by the river I rested against a solitary fence post long since freed from attachments or purpose. A canyon wren hopped onto a rock at my feet and considered me with a tiny, serious face. We were alone until a trout rose to a bug at the river's edge. Across the Snake, columnar basalt held up the steep hillside like a vertical-timber retaining wall. The wren went back to its business, picking at lichen in a nearby rock pile. A jet boat roared by and the wren disappeared, as did the trout and the river's own patterns of swirls, boils, and ribbons.

Some people hear voices at Dug Bar. I heard the *dzip* of lazuli buntings and the restless rustle of river and leaf. When no voices came, I pulled in sounds from the powwow I had stumbled onto the night before in Joseph. It was Chief Joseph Days and most of the white crowd had gone to the rodeo, but no one in the powwow crowd seemed to mind, or even notice, my minority pale face on the top bleacher in the small, high school gym. I had sat tight against the wall to absorb the vibration of the drums. No surface or molecule of air was left unfilled by song and drumbeat; dancers moved around the music like planets around the sun. Singers, dancers, drummers, and onlookers had come from reservations in Idaho, Oregon, and Washington. In final ceremonies the emcee honored elders and warriors of the Gulf War and Vietnam.

I didn't hear voices at Dug Bar, but my ears rang. I thought about the powwow drummers and dancers, some of whom may have been descended from Toohoolhoolzote, Looking Glass, White Bird—or Thunder Rolling from Mountain Heights, who had begun to die here at this crossing place, where I waited with the steadfast Snake. In time, patterns returned to the river. Embracing land, full of grace; a wren.

Rick Bass

Yaak

The Land that Congress Forgot

from *Montana Magazine*

Some anthropologists say that our species began in forest homeland before venturing out into grassland, while others say our beginnings were in the savannah, and that we were then driven into the forests for sanctuary.

I don't really care which version is accurate, for I like where I am now, and it makes me feel right. It used to bother me that I loved the deep forest more than the sylvan meadows. I would acknowledge that there was some familiar longing, some sparkling blood affinity, whenever I came upon some small opening in the woods, some place of light. But still, I loved the symphony and magic of the deep woods best, and for a while this seemed to suggest to me—if the savannah anthropologists were correct—that I was a misanthrope, turning back and away from the human race, that I was more ape than man, and that I had shaken off old loyalties.

But truth is truth, and after a while it didn't matter—I love where I am now, and that's what's important.

I live in the Yaak and it is dark and rains a lot and the trees are big. There are mysterious assemblages of animals, groupings and relationships found nowhere else in the world. It is my home and I do not think any longer I will rush out into the bright meadow, lemming-like.

It's up on the Canadian border, and on the Idaho border too; it lies within Montana's boundaries like the corner pocket of a pool table; but if you were to fall asleep and then wake to find yourself in Yaak, you would not recognize it as being anywhere you had previously been.

The big trees climb in tangling diverse fashion over the tops of the low mountains (not unlike the Appalachians); there are only a handful of peaks in the Yaak that push up above treeline. The highest peak, Mount Robinson, is only 7,500 feet tall; the river bottom is around 3,000 feet. Troy, the nearest town, possesses the lowest spot in the state at 1,800 feet.

The Critical Link

There's so much I don't know about this valley; there's so much that nobody knows. I'm learning the geology of it, and I plan to learn the plants and flowers. I want to learn about the soil, and about how the black bears interact with the grizzlies up here, how the wolves and coyotes get along together, and the wolves and the lions. I've seen mountain lions chasing coyotes off their deer kills, in the Yaak; I've seen two bald eagles battling a golden eagle in midflight, with Mount Henry's snowy crest in the background. It's a predator's showcase; I've seen wolverines and lynx, martens and fishers, weasels and owls. Everything eats something else, it seems, up here on the Canadian line, and I'm reminded of the old saying, "The closer you get to Canada, the more things'll eat your horse."

True, there is only a small double-digit population of grizzlies—ten? twenty? thirty?—and a single-digit population of passing-through wolves; and a dozen or so bull trout, down in Pipe Creek, beneath the achingly huge clearcuts bladed out on the 60-degree slopes of national forests, clearings that are now only memories of ancient cedars, and the soil and fungus of those old forests opened to blazing sunlight and aridity, followed by the slaughterous rains and runoff . . .

But those few wild individuals who remain in the Yaak are super-survivors, with genes as good as gold. They have survived the thousand miles of new roads built here since the 1970s, and the shuttling back and forth of their roadless areas; having to abandon one sanctuary and move to a new, stranger one. They are almost always moving around, trying to make rhyme and reason out of those locked gates. Many of the larger animals—the bears and wolves—have come down into the Yaak from Canada's reservoir of wildness, and possess precisely the migratory abilities, the pathfinding urges, that will be required for our wild corridors to be linked back together in the West, for a genetic flow of health, of vigor and strength, to stretch as uninterrupted as possible once more from Canada to Mexico. I'm convinced that the Yaak is, and must continue to be, one of the cornerstones of this linkage—the most unique, atypical valley in the narrowest "bottleneck" of the Northern Rockies. I believe strongly in the old saying that a chain is only as strong as its weakest link, and I guess this is as good and important a place as any to mention that the Yaak doesn't have a single acre—not one square foot!—of protected wilderness.

I'm not going to waste space or time, won't dignify this wrong by going any further than to say that the reason is purely political—big business—and that it scorns biology. To me, it is a slap in the face of God and nature to pretend or argue that the Yaak is not wild, is not wilderness.

Hidden Gems

There are areas in the Yaak I sometimes take friends to, intersections of seemingly invisible factors that conspire to create magic; places

where I have seen elk, grizzlies, bull moose, lions, grouse, and coyotes all bedding and living in the same area, no more than 20 acres
apart from one another. Everything lives together, here—everything is all crammed in on top of everything else. It's a small valley.

A lone woodland caribou drifts through the valley occasionally,
doubtless following the ghost scent of the herds of caribou who once
lived here, but began to be pushed out earlier in this century. (The
last verified sighting in Yaak was in 1987.) One year when I shot a
spike elk, far back in one of the roadless areas, I returned with my
backpack to the startling sight of 30-plus ravens, 2 golden eagles, and
2 coyotes feeding on my elk, and the hide had been dragged off a
hundred yards, with fresh bear scat leading me to it . . .

It all comes together here; the rain crashes into the mountains
and the forest types crash into one another—the Pacific Northwest
mixing with the Northern Rockies—and what comes from all this
cataclysm is the deepest wildness, the wildness of truly wild animals.

In addition to the traveling individuals who have survived in the
Yaak, there are survivors who have learned how to hole up in those
remaining core security areas. The largest trophy bull elk I've ever
seen has bedded in the same spot for four years in a row. (Needless
to say I've never been able to get up on him in hunting season.) These
last secure roadless areas in the Yaak are the perfect size for elk security—large enough to hold and protect them, not so overwhelmingly large that they can't be hunted—but if these areas are whittled
down any further the elk will leave, but will have no place else to go.

Between 25 percent and 40 percent of the valley's grizzly population may be denning in one particular roadless area, and still the
Forest Service is planning to build roads into this core, with a below-
cost sales program whose purpose, I'm convinced, is to initiate long-
term access into this last place.

Ah, but now politics is crashing into biology.

It's not just the animals who hole up and hide in this jungle. We
do, too, the human residents. It can be a pretty rough existence for
us, as well. There are those of us who trap, who tan hides, who try

to log small green slip sales; those of us who build log and frame homes, who fix small engines, who hunt and garden, who teach, who guide hunters and anglers, who write, plant trees, tend bar, preach, raise sled dogs and bird dogs. Our livelihoods are as diverse as the animals', though one commonality we have is that we all work for ourselves—there aren't any big-corporation employees and that in itself is its own form of wildness, neither bad nor good, but simply wild and strong, if not rich.

We're all pretty much reclusive, up here—we shun crowds, which is why we're here, instead of in Libby or Troy or Missoula or Butte, or *anywhere* but here. The Yaak is full of what we all refer to as "characters"—brimming overfull with them—but it seems to violate the spirit of the place for me to put any one of them before the other 99 and to profile any of them, to haul them out, kicking, into the light. I should speak only for myself, only of my own loves.

Life in the Rough

I want to stress that this is not a travel piece. It is information, is all. I've been asked to write lots of travel pieces about the Yaak. I always decline. It's not a place to come to. It's a place to save. And it's ours, Montana's.

There are two bars—the Dirty Shame, and, across the road, by the river, the Yaak River Tavern. There's the mercantile, which sells gas and canned goods, and sometimes has a couple of cartons of eggs, a half-gallon or two of milk, and some cheese. There's a volunteer ambulance barn, a two room schoolhouse in the upper Yaak, plus a two-room school down in the lower Yaak, near the old mining camp of Sylvanite.

There's a fishing guide—Linehan Outfitting—and a big game guide, McAfee Outfitting. There's one cemetery, a small lumber mill—it burned, right before the fires of '94 in which 2 percent of the forest burned, in varying degrees of intensity—but the mill is being rebuilt. I've bought rough-cut lumber from the mill and love the feel and smell, love knowing that the wood I hold in my hand has come from the valley in which I live.

A couple of guys here have skidders, dozers, backhoes; a few others are carpenters. Several residents tan hides and sew the deerhide into moccasins, pants, shirts, jackets; Tom Oar and Nancy Weaver sewed several outfits for some Hollywood movies. There are a handful of trappers up here, working the lonely snowy ridges. Sometimes, after a good snow, you will see hand-lettered signs propped up beside the winding roads: WARNING. SLED DOGS AHEAD.

It's as much a place of indigenous peoples as may be left in the Lower 48—a place of hunters and gatherers of mushrooms, venison, antlers, berries. It's a good land for craftspeople, a good place to take one's time with a single piece of wood, or with anything, rather than getting in a rush and making mistakes. I have a friend, Jesse, who in the coming year plans to begin carving totem poles; he wishes to make perhaps five or six of them per year.

The school bake sale, a 4th of July pig roast, the Super Bowl party, an occasional wedding, and election day down at the ambulance barn—we see each other, if not regularly. Our paths cross, our paths are twined. We're connected, even if invisibly, just as Yaak is connected to the rest of the state and the rest of the Rockies, even if invisibly.

Wilderness Issues

Many of us are hermits, or shy, or reclusive because we simply live here for the solitude. Engagement in political struggles is, for many, not a healthy choice. It's not why we're here. Often I feel as if, in working to protect the last roadless areas, I've allowed my private, healthy self—the one capable of great happiness and peace—to be lured into some place of turmoil, of never-rest.

But it is my home. There would be turmoil, also, if I didn't try.

We—those of us working with the issue of wilderness, and roadless lands—understand the arguments, and the fears. Never mind that if every standing piece of merchantable timber in the 7,000-acre Grizzly Peak country were cut it would provide the mill in Libby only about two or three weeks of timber. Fears are always bad, or worse, than realities, and led by Steve Thompson of the Montana Wilderness Association we drew up a proposed McIntire/Mount Henry Conservation Reserve, in honor of two of the valley's 1930s homesteaders, the actor and actress John and Jeannette Nolan McIntire. The stated purpose of this area, which has been hammered hard by huge corporate clearcuts, would be to dedicate its use exclusively to sustainable, small-scale logging, rather than continue to let the international companies work it. They've had their chance and have been harsh; now the proposal is for locals to work it—horse logging, roadside salvage, helicopter logging and selective timbering. Additionally, the remaining roadless core would be protected intact for its roadless values, and streamside repairs as well as road reclamation would begin, in efforts to repair water quality.

This proposal was included in the bill sponsored by Pat Williams last year—he said that the Yaak has "been hammered" and that he intended to "protect a small sliver of land between clearcuts." The bill passed the U.S. House of Representatives with overwhelming bipartisan support (over 300 votes), despite an aggressive run against the McIntire/Mount Henry area by a representative from Oregon, Bob Smith, and one from Alaska, Don Young (who now chairs the House Committee on Natural Resources and Public Lands).

The bill then stalled and died in the Senate, receiving the support of neither Montana Senator Conrad Burns nor Senator Max Baucus.

Thompson described the area as "one of the few wild places in the Lower 48 in which all of the original pieces are intact; native old-growth forests, grizzly bears, bull trout, mountain lions, cascading waterfalls, and even a newly discovered fungus closely associated with the yew tree that manufactures the cancer-fighting drug taxol. In the last few years, wolves have ventured back into the wild Yaak Valley from Canada."

According to the *Missoulian,* Cary Hegreberg, vice president of the

Montana Wood Products Association, called the dedication of the proposed small-logger area "unconscionable," and said it was a slap in the face of unemployed millworkers.

And so it goes on, that battle with which we are all so familiar.

Deep Timber

I have so many stories to tell of the Yaak, with hopes of more to come. A mountain lion running a coyote off the lion's fresh deer kill. An elk herd in the backcountry. A great gray owl sitting on a snag in the deep woods, seemingly the size of a man, watching me approach. Rivers and creeks and waterfalls, grizzly prints in the snow on a ridge one October—fresh tracks that measured $6\frac{1}{2}'' \times 12\frac{1}{2}''$. A trophy whitetail staring across a ravine at me, deep in the backcountry, one snowy dusk . . .

The Yaak is wilderness, and the Yaak, though atypical to our state—atypical to the world—carries the spirit of Montana, the spirit of a place without borders, even if many of the lands here do have roads binding them, carving and cutting into these last places.

The big timber companies, some of whom have already abandoned the state, have successfully sold much of the public on the idea that environmentalists such as myself believe that logging is bad, even evil. I don't have sixty or seventy thousand dollars lying around to donate to some senator, but I do have a pen and paper. I do have words that come against the power of their huge campaigns, I can say that I use wood, and love much about the culture of logging. I love the rip of a saw, the muscularity of it—the smell of wood, the sound and sight of wood. I love going into Rosauer's parking lot in Libby, 60 miles away, and seeing the guys in suspenders and hard hats, with the chainsaw oil and gas cans looped together in the back of their pickups, and a saw tool roped to the gas can. These to me are as much a part of the culture and a part of the wild as the lions and bears and wolves.

That is the truth, just as it is the truth that 500-year-old larch trees are not needed for toilet paper. *That* tired argument. It is also true that jobs in timber would last longer if more work were done on the trees that are cut here, instead of shipping logs, raw, to Asia. I want a new business in Lincoln County. I want a value-added industry, something that will allow us to take our time with the wood we cut, rather than just shipping it off raw, faster and faster. I yearn for bookshelves and kitchen cabinets made of Yaak lodgepole.

You can't talk about the Yaak without talking about timber.

You can't talk about the Yaak without talking about wilderness and wild things.

Where is it all going to settle? What is going to be taken from us, and what is going to be left?

Who has the Yaak on their minds, and who has it in their hearts? Sometimes these are not the same thing.

To me it is a sacred place, and I am worried for it and troubled by its history, and worried for its future. It still belongs to us—that wildness, a kind of which we do not see much anymore—but it is being lost to us quickly, is being bought and sold by those who neither own nor know it.

It makes me want to howl. Whether we love the grassland country, the wet jungle, or the in-between, a precious thing is being left to us.

We keep trying our damnedest to come up with solutions, and we keep getting thwarted—all sides, all beliefs, all of us, except the road-builders and the numbers-people in Washington.

Terry Tempest Williams

Statement before the Senate Subcommittee on Forest & Public Lands Management
Regarding the Utah Public Lands Management Act of 1995

First publication

Mr. Chairman, members of this subcommittee, my name is Terry Tempest Williams. I am a native of Utah. My family roots run deep holding me in place—five, six generations of Mormon stock run through my veins. Our family has made its living on the land for the last six decades laying pipe in the Utah substrate. We are a family of pipeline contractors and although I have never dug the ditches, I love and care for the men who do: my brothers, cousins, uncle, father, John Henry Tempest, my grandfather, John Henry Tempest, Jr., who is in his ninetieth year, even my great-grandfather, John Henry Tempest, Sr. We understand the power of continuity and our debt to these lands that have given us livelihood. As a Utah family, we would

like to enter into the *Congressional Record* personal letters, four generations worth, of why we care about wilderness, why we do not favor Senate Bill 884, and why we want more wilderness designation
in Utah, not less. Some of the letters are forthcoming, some I have
brought with me. With a large, extended family I trust you can appreciate the organizational logistics. These letters represent men and
women, Republicans and Democrats alike, registered voters and
voices too young to vote, but not too young to register their opinions. They are individual and original, some sealed, some open. It is
a gesture of sincere concern for what we hold dear.

I appreciate this time to be able to share with you some of my own
thoughts about the Utah Public Lands Management Act of 1995.

It is not a wilderness bill that the majority of Utahans recognize,
want, or desire.

It is not a wilderness bill that honors or respects our history as a
people.

It is not a wilderness bill that honors or respects the natural laws
required for a healthy environment.

And it is not a wilderness bill that takes an empathetic stance toward our future.

It is a wilderness bill that lacks vision and undermines the bipartisan principles inherent in the Wilderness Act of 1964.

Quite simply, in the name of political expediency and with eyes
capable of seeing only through the lens of economics, our public
lands in Utah are being sacrificed. Our congressional delegation has
told you that this issue must be resolved, now, that this debate over
the wildlands in Utah has torn our state in half. But I prefer to take
the artist Frederick Sommer's approach when he says, "Quarreling
is the cork of a good wish."

What is it we wish for?

In Utah, there was a man with a vision. He dreamed of a civilization bright with lights and strong of belief. He knew the indus-
trious nature of work and picked the beehive as his symbol. He loved
the land he saw before him, a landscape so vast, pristine, and virginal

that he recognized it as the kingdom of God, a place for Saints with a desire for home. The desert country of the Great Basin and Colorado Plateau was an answer to prayers of spiritual sovereignty.

He sent families north into the mountains and south into the valleys where red rock walls rose upward like praying hands. He said, "We will create Zion among the wilderness." And with great stamina and imagination akin only to communities committed to faith, the building of culture among the pioneers began. Humble ranches, small businesses, and cottage industries of silk and wool sprung up, and a United Order was dreamed.

Brigham Young, the colonizing prophet of the Mormons, brought with him not only a religion and a life but a land ethic.

"Here are the stupendous works of the God of Nature, though all do not appreciate His wisdom as manifested in his works . . . I could sit here for a month and reflect on the mercies of God."

Time. Reflection. Mercy. I do not find these qualities revered by our forefathers in the Utah Public Lands Act of 1995. There is little gratitude extended on behalf of these sacred lands.

Only a few generations ago, Utah was settled on spiritual grounds. It is ironic that now Utah must be protected on spiritual grounds for the generations to come.

What do we wish for?

To be whole. To be complete. Wilderness reminds us what it means to be human, what we are connected to rather than what we are separate from. "Our troubles," the Pulitzer-prize–winning scientist Edward O. Wilson writes, "arise from the fact that we do not know what we are and cannot agree on what we want to be . . . Humanity is part of nature, a species that evolved among other species. The more closely we identify ourselves with the rest of life, the more quickly we will be able to discover the sources of human sensibility and acquire knowledge on which an enduring ethic, a sense of preferred direction, can be built."

Wilderness is both the bedrock lands of southern Utah and a metaphor of "unlimited possibility." The question must be asked,

"How can we cut ourselves off from the very source of our creation?"

This is not about economics. This is not about the preservation of ranching culture in America. And it is especially not about settling a political feud once and for all. This is about putting ourselves in accordance with nature, of consecrating these lands by remembering our relationships to them. A strong wilderness bill as recommended by Congressman Maurice Hinchey, HR 1500, is an act of such consecration. At a recent family gathering, my uncle Richard Tempest, a former Republican state senator, said simply, "Wilderness is a feeling."

Mr. Chairman, if you know wilderness in the way you know love, you would be unwilling to let it go. We are talking about the body of the beloved, not real estate. We must ask ourselves as Americans, "Can we really survive the worship of our own destructiveness?" We do not exist in isolation. Our sense of community and compassionate intelligence must be extended to all life forms, plants, animals, rocks, rivers, and human beings. This is the story of our past and it will be the story of our future.

Senate Bill 884 falls desperately short of these ideals.

Who can say how much nature can be destroyed without consequence? Who can say how much land can be used for extractive purposes until it is rendered barren forever? And who can say what the human spirit will be crying out for one hundred years from now? Two hundred years from now? A few weeks ago, Yosemite National Park had to close its gates and not allow any more visitors entry. The park was overcrowded. Last week, Yellowstone reported traffic grid locks in the Lamar Valley, carloads of families with the wish of seeing a wolf. Did our country's lawmakers who held the vision of national parks in the nineteenth century dream of this kind of hunger? In the same vein, can you as our lawmakers today, toward the end of the twentieth century, imagine what the sanctity of wilderness in Utah might hold for us as a people at the turn of the twenty-first century?

We must act with this kind of vision and concern not just for our-

selves, but for our children and our children's children. This is our
natural heritage. And we are desperate for visionary leadership.

It's strange how deserts turn us into believers. I believe in walking
in a landscape of mirages, because you learn humility. I believe in living in a land of little water because life is drawn together. And I believe in the gathering of bones as a testament to spirits that have
moved on.

If the desert is holy, it is because it is a forgotten place that allows
us to remember the sacred. Perhaps that is why every pilgrimage to
the desert is a pilgrimage to the self. There is no place to hide and so
we are found.

Wilderness courts our souls. When I sat in church throughout
my growing years, I listened to teachings about Christ walking in the
wilderness for forty days and forty nights, reclaiming his strength,
where he was able to say to Satan, "Get thee hence." And when I
imagined Joseph Smith kneeling in a grove of trees as he received his
vision to create a new religion, I believed their sojourns into nature
were sacred. Are ours any less?

There is a Mormon scripture, from the Doctrine and Covenants,
section 88:44–47, that I carry with me:

> The earth rolls upon her wings, and the sun giveth his light
> by day, and the moon giveth her light by night, and the stars also
> give their light, as they roll upon their wings in their glory, in the
> midst and power of God.
>
> Unto what shall I liken these kingdoms that ye may understand?
>
> Behold all these are kingdoms and any man who hath seen any or
> the least of these hath seen God moving in his majesty and power.

Without a philosophy of wilderness and the recognition of its inherent spiritual values, we will, as E. O. Wilson reminds us, "descend farther from heaven's air if we forget how much the natural
world means to us."

For those of us who so love these lands in Utah, who recognize America's Redrock Wilderness as a sanctuary for the preservation of our souls, Senate Bill 884, the Utah Public Lands Management Act of 1995, is the beginning of this forgetting, a forgetting we may never reclaim.

John Calderazzo

Sailing Through the Night

from *Orion*

*Thoughts which day turns into smoke and mist stand about us in the
night as light and flames; even as the column which fluctuates above the
crater of Vesuvius, in the day time appears a pillar of cloud, but by night
a pillar of fire.*

Henry David Thoreau, "Night and Moonlight"

For more than twenty years I've been thinking about a few seconds
of film. In a newsreel taken in Asia during the Vietnam War, a
saffron-robed monk sitting in the lotus position allows himself to be
doused with gasoline. Suddenly his bright saffron robes explode into
an even brighter orange, and flames begin to climb his neck. Yet
somehow he continues to sit without moving or crying out, continues to meditate even as the terrible fire shoots up the side of his face.
Finally, he crumples to the side, a human torch illuminating the un-
real horror and waste of war.

That film clip was a cultural and generational marker of the late
1960s, and anyone who saw it is likely to see it again, probably without wanting to, in the unruly theater of memory. The older I get, the
more I am haunted by those flames.

Or I should say I am haunted by the monk himself, an anonymous
and middle-aged man, maybe younger than I am now. Often these

days I lie awake at night and listen to the wind roaring out of the mountains and over my comfortable Colorado home, wind that occasionally roars like fire, and I wonder what brought that man to make that decision.

I mean the man himself, as much as I can separate him from his monkish traditions of social responsibility and sacrifice. A mother's son full of bravery and fear and desire—had he lost hope in a world full of war? Or was he mostly affirming life, believing that his final act would engender other acts to stop violence? Or was he gripped by something completely beyond my understanding, an emotion or a way of thinking like an invisible color on the spectrum of human experience, a bright band of light shimmering in front of me that somehow I still haven't learned how to see?

Or maybe it's not the monk I am haunted by. Maybe it's me, my confusion about how to handle the seemingly endless bad news of the world. I have come to probably the halfway point in my life, a life blessed mainly with privilege and good fortune, yet more and more often I worry about how I'll get through the rest of it without giving in to cynicism or self-indulgence or despair. And until I learn to find some balance between action and acceptance, I suspect that I'll keep throttling myself with questions about suffering and heartbreak and the darker exhalations of the human soul.

I'm five years old, and I'm squatting on the sidewalk, watching black ants pour out of a crack in the cement. They're running everywhere—frantic, insane, incensed. At the urging of my friend Herb, I've just reached down with a stick and scrambled their hill.

"You know," says Herb, in his sly, older-boy voice, "ants don't sleep—not ever. And if you're not careful, they'll follow you home, just to get even."

That night I pull the covers over my head and scrunch my face into the pillow. The ants are coming—I can practically hear them marching down the sidewalk. Eventually they'll find our house, squeeze under the front door, file up the stairs, and climb the bed legs. They'll swarm into my nose and mouth, they'll gnaw my eyes. I lie awake in the heavy darkness, wondering if I should sneak downstairs and cram a towel under the door, or wake up my parents and little brother and confess to the catastrophe I've wrought, this wrathful army of insects bearing down on the house.

I wonder how often insomnia starts that way—not necessarily in a childhood in Dachau or Somalia or Bedford-Stuyvesant, but in some half-forgotten moment, an absurd pang of guilt that the routine cruelties of the world transform over the years into a firestorm of worry, into hours of working out the permutations of disaster, into an unwise but inevitable blurring of private and public dread.

Or maybe all of this is fueled by getting older. Or by a visit to a doctor—say, for a case of poison ivy. In my case the bubbly rashes were an amusing and slightly embarrassing affliction for an adult who should have known better, an outdoor guy who should have looked before wading into the backyard hedges to pull weeds. Amusing until the moment I felt the doctor's cold finger press into my back and heard him say, "What's this? This I don't like *at all*."

His finger pressed into a black spot the size of a quarter, a mole that somehow my wife SueEllen and I hadn't noticed. Melanoma, a surgeon soon confirmed over the telephone as I sat silent and alone in our kitchen one afternoon. Malignant.

Even after I had it cut out, along with a hand-size chunk of skin, the surgeon said that there was a chance, always a chance, that a rogue cell might have worked itself deeper in, so that sometimes even now, nine years after the surgery and with statistics piling up on my side, I lie awake wondering where that pinprick of darkness might have gone, that death star sailing through the infinity of my body.

We bomb Baghdad. On television, dream images of green, glowing rockets slide across the night. Then we invade. Even after I pull away from the set and try to walk off my anger, I hear the muffled shouts of hungry and abandoned Iraqi conscripts who've been buried alive in long trenches, tractored into the earth by the hundreds. The teen-agers who helped do this to them look into the camera and say, as they've been told to say, "We got a job to do, and when we finish we'll be outta here."

I watch friends speak at peace rallies in town, and I think: I should join them up there, I'm articulate and not shy, I should write letters, I should make phone calls, I should march, I should fast. In 1989, with willpower alone, a skinny young man in China stopped a row of enormous tanks—didn't we all see this on television?

Then I think, What fools we are to keep yammering at each other, the naïve or the already-converted, or the philosophically dispos-sessed, or the hard-up-for-thrills-of-the-Sixties. In China, those tanks rumbled through Tiananmen Square anyway. The damage in Iraq and Kuwait has already been done. And besides, Saddam's a killer and a sociopath, even if our main interest in suddenly getting rid of him is fueled by oil, not justice.

A woman I know and like takes the microphone and starts waving her arms, as though she really thinks she can redirect the gales of history. Where does her optimism come from? More than twenty years ago, an Asian monk decided to die an awful death, and a year later, a boy I knew in high school, a star hurdler, lost his legs in the Vietnam highlands. The war went on forever.

The woman at the microphone talks and talks. I rock on my heels, my fists jammed in my pockets. Then I wander off to find a beer.

For three nights now, winds have boomed like surf against the bed-room wall. They rattle the double storm windows next to my head. Fifty miles an hour, sixty, seventy—they plunge from the high coun-try through narrow canyons into our moonlit valley, the meeting point of mountains and plains. No matter how many pillows I bur-row under, I can hear our big cottonwoods creaking and cracking, waving their limbs like dervishes.

I'm desperate for sleep, desperate not to wake SueEllen. Last night, after hours of being elbowed and kicked, she pulled me close and whispered, "Those elk we saw last week when we walked in the meadow—remember? How still they sat with the sun on their backs, and wildflowers everywhere, Queen Anne's lace, Indian paintbrush, mountain bluebells . . ."

SueEllen's night mantras: meditations on loveliness, haiku just for me. Often they help. But not last night. Or tonight—the gusts roar in from some far corner of the universe, and our big blue spruce shudders and lashes the window behind my head. It's a tree the previous owners planted after the neighbor's picnic table, lifted by the wind, came flying through the glass.

I close my eyes and try to think of good things—my marriage and job, deep friendships, our small cheerful nieces—but suddenly I'm staring at the ceiling, then out through the backyard window and up into the blades of our windmill. On calm nights the windmill stands against the stars like a giant silver daisy shining in moonlight. But tonight the blades are flying. They blur and turn into a propeller, a murderous flower whirring, whirring.

A squall starts whining in my skull, prying loose nightmares, ragged clots of thought: Amazon forests bulldozed to extinction, a midnight call—aren't they always at midnight?—saying a friend has died in a car wreck, a monk sitting in robes of fire.

This is the time of night when anything can come sailing through the window, when one thought multiplies to infinity. This is the time of night when tumors grow.

"Oh, John . . . ," sighs SueEllen, twisting away from me to salvage what she can of her sleep. So I throw an arm over her and watch elk drift through green mountains, feel my cross-country skis glide over diamond fields of snow.

I think of Zach, the son of good friends. One afternoon when he was about two, he and I, out walking, found a golden aspen leaf on the wet sidewalk. "Look," I said, peeling it off the concrete, holding it up by the stem so he could watch sunlight stream through it. Then I let it go. The leaf butterflied down, danced and flipped in the sunlight. When it landed, Zach jumped with delight, his eyes huge, his blonde curls flying. You'd think it had fallen from the only tree on earth.

"Again!" he said.

I picked it up and let it drop.

"Again!"

By his fourth request I was bored. But by the sixth or seventh something had begun to happen. As I watched Zach lasering in, I found myself slipping into his way of seeing things. And finally, like a small boy, I saw something astounding: a golden leaf falling out of the sky.

Sometimes, when sleepless nights come in binges, I find myself preparing for the night during the day. I work hard at my teaching job, which I love, and then make sure to exhaust myself by riding my bike miles up the canyons or around and around our valley. I skip the television news, cancel the newspaper, cut back on coffee. For a year, I drink nothing alcoholic.

Or: Sitting cross-legged in front of the television, I sip Jim Beam while a psychologist says that long-time pessimists develop more chronic diseases than optimists do. It doesn't help that I write magazine articles and essays about the forests of Thailand shaved clean of elephants and tigers, or read about a computer that will simulate the constellations fifty years from now, when filth in our own atmosphere will keep us from actually seeing the stars.

Even as I write, even as I jet off somewhere to tramp through a jungle that seems always to have shrunk down to a green dot, even as I scribble in my reporter's notebook in the glare of the malignant sun, whose greasy light I keep trying to scrape off my arms, I realize that I've grown slightly ill. At night the fever only rises.

And so I've come to California to learn how to wash dishes. With maybe a hundred others, environmental activists mostly, I'm listening to Thich Nhat Hanh, a Vietnamese monk and teacher who is sitting cross-legged on a low stage. He's flanked by flower vases and wisps of burning incense. His brown robes hang motionless from his thin frame.

"We need to be mindful of the present moment," he says slowly. "We need to be aware of what is happening to us right now. For example, if I am washing the dishes, I should pay full attention to the dishes. If I rush through them just to be done, or if I keep thinking about the tea I will drink when I'm finished, then I'm not capable of being fully alive during the time I'm washing the dishes."

I close my eyes and see big-eyed Zach staring at the wet sidewalk. A golden leaf blots out the blue sky.

I open my eyes and see Thich Nhat Hanh smiling at me. It's an exceptionally intelligent smile that radiates inward *and* outward, a practiced Buddha smile that nevertheless looks as guileless as a glass of water. It comforts me in this room full of people I don't entirely trust, this room near Los Angeles with too many men my age wearing ponytails and more women in serapes than I've seen in years. The place is festering with goodwill, and I keep expecting somebody to break out a guitar.

But I suspect that one of the people I don't entirely trust is *me,* me with all my knee-jerk biases. There are damn good people here, I tell myself, pragmatic and tough-minded visionaries, a lot of them, who just need some rest from years of seventy-hour work weeks. Still, I can't shake the notion that I'm sitting inside a colossal cliché. "The Sound of One Lung Coughing"—that's what I'd call the story I could write about this week. On the other hand, meditation is one of the most difficult things I've ever tried, a slippery slope I can't seem to hang on to, and I don't know if I'm strong enough to make it through the week.

Here I am, though, sitting cross-legged on a cushion like everyone else, my knees aching.

I try smiling back at Thich Nhat Hanh, but I feel stiff. He looks as unwrinkled as a teenager, yet he's at least in his mid-sixties. Chairman of the Vietnamese Buddhist Peace Delegation during the Vietnam War, exiled from his homeland for his war resistance, he was nominated by Martin Luther King, Jr. for the Nobel Peace Prize and has worked with war refugees for twenty-five years. Somehow he's found a balance between action and acceptance, a way to neither retreat from the world's suffering nor let it burn him up from the inside.

"If I am chewing a string bean," he tells us, "I should be mindful of the string bean. I should give it my full attention so it will reveal its true nature to me. If I am chewing the string bean and thinking of baseball, then I'm chewing . . . baseball!"

I laugh with everyone else. Thich Nhat Hanh's laughing, too. A thousand tiny muscles in my face begin to let go. Later, when I close my eyes and try to meditate, I can feel the room fill up with breathing, a great orange glow.

The Serbs bomb the Croats. Hunger bombs Africa. Another window-rattling, sheet-twisting night, the windmill flying. The full moon burns my face with a lunar tan, blue and dangerous.

I hear a long rumble, or maybe I make it up. It comes from the Bellvue Dome, a spectacular rock formation shaped like a giant ramp that walls in part of our valley. Its red cliffs face our house; the ramp slopes off to the east and the Great Plains. The Dome is the first foothill of the Rockies, the first great rise in two thousand miles, and not that long ago it was used by the Arapaho to kill bison.

I hear them now, animals rumbling up from the plains. Heads down, they charge into a wind they barely notice because leather-clad hunters are yelling and flapping animal skins to funnel them uphill. Their eyes swivel with fear.

Now they're galloping over the edge, shaking the earth. They snort and scream, paw and stamp the air. A river of fur pours over the cliffs. The wind blows out of the mountains over miles of bison, a continent of animals surging toward the cliffs under enormous dust clouds. Behind it all, dimly visible, come lines of covered wagons, then railroads, steam engines puffing west.

The wind rises, and somehow I realize that I can control it, whip it into a hurricane. So I do: I make it blow up until it stops the bison in midfall, then pushes them back over the Dome and back out onto the grasslands, which are tossing and rolling, rolling. The wind slashes the wagon covers, lifts the wagons and flings them back over the horizon. It rips up the iron tracks and the trains. Yes, I tell myself as I lie in bed smiling at the ceiling, the tracks are flying up from the ground, and now I'm sending the wind over the earth's curve and through an arc of time, I'm sending it to Asia, where it blows out a wooden match that is poised to make a man in robes turn into fire. . . .

This is my ghost dance, a desperate act of imagining that annihilates the past and edits the future. Like the plains Indians of the 1890s who were cornered into dreaming back a lost continent full of animals, I cling to this vision.

But I'm beginning to wonder if I'm just chewing baseball. Dancing back and forth through history and stopping anywhere but here—right here in the present moment—didn't work for the Sioux, so why should it work for me? The moon is beating down and SueEllen is breathing beside me. The time is *always* right now. Why can't I let the wind just be wind and not the stirrings of the apocalypse?

"Give me silence, water, hope," writes the great poet Pablo Neruda. "Give me struggle, iron, volcanoes." After puzzling over those lines for years, I think I'm starting to see what he means. I'm writing a book about volcanoes, maybe an odd topic for an English professor. But volcanoes, I'm beginning to think, are incendiary with hope.

I fly to Italy and climb Vesuvius, which smothered Pompeii. I sit on the broken and burnt-red rim of its crater and watch steam hiss from small cracks. In Sicily, I drive a car around the base of Etna and buy tomatoes from an old woman sitting in a field, its soil rich from centuries of nourishing ash. She looks like my father's mother, who died years ago. Over her shoulder, the volcano rolls with smoke, hard black lava rivers stretching for miles. Thousand-year-old towns and vineyards sit on lava slopes that once simmered and welled like tar a hundred miles below the earth's surface. The woman smiles at me and the tomatoes explode in my mouth.

On the island volcano of Stromboli, I walk along black pebbled beaches that shine like sealskin. Fishermen drag their boats from the water, and every ten or fifteen minutes I hear what sounds like a dragon exhaling. Faces turn to the sky. It's the mountain erupting, the earth breathing fire and putting out new earth—the newest anywhere. At night, in a boat bobbing offshore, I watch orange lava splatter from its summit.

I begin to *feel,* not just understand, how winds can move under the ground. I don't mean Colorado mountain squalls or even the fiery gusts that Aristotle and Pliny the Elder thought blew through the center of the world, causing earthquakes. I mean centuries and centuries of rock wind, sirocco of iron and granite, glowing lava zephyrs, stone currents. And mountain ranges and continents that have been bulging up and wearing down for more than four billion years.

I'm finding solace in the liquid nature of rock, in the impermanent nature of everything.

Give me volcanoes, iron, hope.

Back home one afternoon, I hike in a river basin full of changing aspens. A cloud sliding over a far ridge reminds me of the glacier that once carved out the valley. I stand very still, just breathing. I inhale, and down slides the glacier, a long white tongue that soon fills up my view. I exhale. The ice pulls back, leaving a valley full of newly minted elk and flowers. Miles below me, deep in the earth, I can practically hear the grinding of continental plates coming together and tearing apart. Yes, it's good to know that North America has been a drifter, a pilgrim, too.

My eyes are opening to time in fast-forward and reverse, atoms that swirl through dreams and disappointments, a man's flesh turned to fire to blowing ashes to tough new grass, a house-sized boulder rearranging itself through millennia as surely as a cloud. Is this a kind of world-breath, a kind of optimism? I begin to see it even when I stand in my shower at home, the shiny plastic curtain a world map whose green and orange continents buckle with an offhand sweep of my arm, whose once-unclimbable mountains crumple or flatten out in my soapy hands.

A volcanologist I know tells me that even the planet's crust bulges out under the moon's pull. The universe breathes; everything sails along in its wind: rattling windows, rogue cells, bison, rainforest, bombs, eruptions of hatred and peace and goodwill.

I need to remember to remember this.

One summer morning after a passable night's sleep, I get up, shower, and sit on the edge of our patio, my bare feet on the grass. I'm clipping my toenails. After a while, I notice something moving near my feet. It's one of my toenails—upright, luminous as a sliver of moon—and it seems to be wandering off, as though it's decided to walk to Kansas. It bumps slowly along through the shadowy grass. I lean forward, bend down. It takes me a while to find the ant struggling underneath it, half its size. The tiny legs work furiously.

A second later I see my own death.

I don't mean a cold finger in the back or even the dying itself. I mean the steady fires of decay and regrowth, the redistribution of myself—light, heat, bones, hair, heart—into the great wide windy world. "If only I could be like the tree at the river's edge, every year turning green again," says the Cold Mountain poet of China. I used to wish for that, too, of course, and most of the time I still do. But then I remind myself that even a redwood breaks through the earth as a redwood for only a moment or so before falling back into the immensity of time.

I sit on the patio and watch my toenail walk away. I smile. I almost wave.

Carolyn Kremers

Trapping Wolves

from *Place of the Pretend People:*
Gifts from a Yup'ik Eskimo Village

For twenty years, I dreamed I could not remember the combinations to my lockers—my book locker, gym locker, music locker—in junior high, high school, college, graduate school. I would reach for the dangling lock and dial three numbers. When the lock didn't open, I would try again. I would try all the combinations I knew and then start making them up, hoping to hit the right one. Each time the lock stuck closed, my heart beat faster. My hands began to shake. After several minutes of this random circling, I would panic. The mind that I trusted, that I had come to rely upon, had gone blank.

I knew that this dream of forgetting was trying to tell me something. But until I lived in Tununak, I did not understand what.

Inside my dream, two girls from Tununak call out in unison, "Three! Try three!" Janie is almost tall enough to reach my gym locker, on the top row in the women's locker room at the university in Fairbanks, but Melanie isn't tall at all. She's short, a little sister.

"Next is twelve," says Janie.

"Yes, try twelve," says Melanie. "And then . . . ?"

I think perhaps they are right, so I try moving the dial to three and twelve,

*but of course they aren't right. Anyway, how would they know? And what are
they doing in Fairbanks? Suddenly, I am surprised.*

"How do you know my locker combination?" I ask.

"Oh, we've watched you open it so many times," says Melanie.

"Remember?" Janie says. "At the post office."

*Indeed, they have. Whenever I return to Tununak from a trip, they like to
tell me I have "lots of letters" waiting in my mailbox. Standing on tiptoes, Janie
can see the edges of envelopes—mostly junk mail—through the little window
in the top row.*

*"And pictures," she says. "Your pictures did come! May we see them? May
we visit?"*

Children in Tununak always knew when I returned from a school
district meeting in another village, or from a band trip or Christmas
vacation. They would see me from their houses, out the windows,
coming up the frozen river from the airstrip, in a sled behind the
postmaster's snowmachine, or the store owner's, or a friend's. Or if
it was a nice day, one of those spectacular ice-blue days, when you
flew in from Bethel, and Tununak seemed the most sparkling place
on earth—no city crowds, no strangers, no stores full of gew-gaws;
no lines to wait in, no dirty snow; all sky and newly open water,
blinding white sculptures and crystals, room to move and breathe;
people who said hello and smiled, people who laughed—if it was
one of those days, I would want to walk the mile home from the airstrip. Someone on a three-wheeler or snowmachine would offer to
take my duffel bag. He would drive through the village and up the
hill and drop the bag at the foot of the giant drift outside my door.
Then little kids—Melanie, Jenny, Jack, or Martin—would spy me
walking through town, grab my hands and skip beside me, taking
two steps for my one.

I wasn't used to being noticed like that, loved like that: being
waved at so much, having people at the post office and the store and
the church and the school say "Welcome back!" and "How was your

trip?" I had grown up in Denver, a city of half a million people, and I came from a disciplined, white middle-class family where only my mother talked much. Before moving to Tununak, I had spent eight years trying to be a classical flutist, practicing, practicing, often alone. I had never lived in a community as intimate as Tununak, and I had never met anyone like John Hoover-on-his-knees.

There were three John Hoovers in Tununak: John, Jr., John, Sr., and John Hoover-on-his-knees.

John had had polio. He walked with legs bent double, toes pointed to the sky, each knee centered over a large padded ring sewn to the top of each of his long sealskin mukluks. No one had trapped him in a wheelchair and no one stared. There were no wheelchairs in Tununak and even if there were, John would not have been able to get around in one. Snowdrifts in winter and mud in spring made going to the post office hard sometimes, even for me.

John did not need a wheelchair. He preferred his knees, his three-wheeler, his boat, occasionally a sled or a plane. He would walk on his knees up the construction ladder at the school to get scrap plywood and two-by-fours. He spent hours gathering driftwood at the beach, especially after storms, then hauled it home, lashed with bungee cords to the back and front of his three-wheeler.

Sawing wood outside his steambath, John always noticed me walking. He would put down the saw and maneuver past his grandson and the woodpile, balancing sturdily on his knees as he thrust his weight from side to side. Then he would throw back his head and laugh.

"Halloo, halloo! You came back. Is good weather today, eh?" he would say, taking off his glove and reaching up to shake my hand. Or, "Taking a fresh air, eh? Good, good!"

John was happy with who he was, at peace with the things around him. How could I tell him he unlocked something, made me thankful every day for my long, blue windpant legs, for polio vaccine sugar cubes in the first grade?

———————

"We knew you were back," Janie says inside my dream, " 'cause your mailbox was full and all of a sudden it got empty." She comes down from her tiptoes.

"When you were gone, we couldn't have no singing," pouts her little sister, flopping onto the locker room bench. "We had to read. Will we have music tomorrow?"

"Try it again," Janie says. "Try three."

But wait.

My mailbox in Tununak doesn't open with a combination, it opens with a key. So how do these girls think they know the numbers?

They don't know them. They can't think of the third one and it isn't 3–12, anyway. Now it is coming back to me. Of course I know it. The combination to my gym locker is 4–14. Four . . . fourteen . . . thirty-six. I know that combination. Why, then, do I keep forgetting it?

It's December, in Fairbanks, and I am no longer dreaming, I'm awake. The bed is moving. The two-story house shakes, creaks, for several seconds. Again. I am moving in the blue flannel sheets. Earthquake. It must be, for I have felt earthquakes before, years ago, in California.

Green numbers on the clock say 2:00 A.M. At first I am frightened. Will there be more tremors? And bigger ones?

Where is Dan? Still out on his trapline? He hasn't telephoned for two and a half weeks, since before Christmas. Is he safe? How strong was this quake? Are people lying dead in Anchorage?

I wait for more, but there is nothing. I am relieved. In the dark I turn on the clock radio to see if there is news.

Yes, I felt that earthquake, too. A three, surely, perhaps a four. Three people called in and said they also felt it.

This is comforting, to know that others are awake and talking at 2:00 A.M.

Everything is fine. The building is still standing, everything is still standing. More music.

I turn the radio off, try to sleep again, to dream. But I am tired of sleeping alone. When I am fully awake—out of bed, going about the day—I don't let myself think this way. My mind takes over, and feelings get locked out. What is the combination I forget?

Breakfast in the tar-papered eight-by-eight cabin at Jubilation Creek in the Alaska Range. *Three-Minute Brand Quick Pan-Toasted Oats, Great Flavor Since 1910.* The door is cracked open. March. It's like a Colorado day: sunny, blue sky, clear. Already thirty degrees.

Today, Dan and I begin a three-day ski trip to Leonora Creek. We're going to follow a forty-five-mile snowmachine track, one of the loops on Dan's trapline, and we're going to get sunburned faces. We'll try out the *pulk* he put together on Sunday in my landlord's garage, with five thousand parts from Fred Meyer's discount store.

Dan says the Laplanders invented *pulk*-ing—a method of pulling gear and children on sleds behind skis—and that *pulk*-ing has become a popular sport in Scandinavia. In Fairbanks, though, a Norwegian *pulk* costs $580, so Dan bought a yellow plastic kiddie sled for $9.99 at Fred's. He attached a ten-foot plastic rod to each side, making two handles like a rickshaw, then cut small slits in the rim of the sled with his Buck knife. He threaded black nylon straps through the slits, and I sewed them in place with dental floss.

Wrapped in a tarp, tightly strapped down, our gear should be secure.

We set out for Leonora around noon, but the *pulk* keeps tipping over on the slippery trail. The load is probably sixty pounds, and it's packed too high. After an hour, the plastic fittings that hold on the long handles crack off.

I favor giving up on the *pulk* idea. It seems cumbersome and silly to me. I think we should just carry packs. But Dan asks me to ski back to the cabin to get trapping wire and cutters, while he dismantles the sled.

Forty minutes later, I return and find the contents of the sled piled neatly on the track, the broken fittings unscrewed, ready for repair, and Dan covered with snow.

"I decided to try some telemark turns," he says, laughing. "There's a nice hill up there."

Dan can fix anything, which he does, bare hands twisting wire-cutters in the cold, and soon the rickshaw handles are reattached.

We pack the load more carefully, heavy stuff nestled on the bottom: the red food bag, Stanley thermos of coffee, backpack full of warm clothes, our two sleeping bags zipped together in a big stuff sack. In the middle are the three-pound Bibler tent, cook kit, Whisperlite stove and fuel bottle, orange-handled bow-saw, two foam pads, emergency mukluks and boots. Bungeed on top: the pistol (rabbits, grouse, ptarmigan?) and ax, covered by Dan's blue fleece mitts, and the trap-setters.

The trap-setters look simple. Just two pieces of two-by-two, each a foot long, each shielded at one end with a steel plate. From last year, though, I remember how they are used. A red fox moans. I don't want to think about her. I pull on my pack, not yet feeling the twenty pounds of clothes, gorp, water bottle, and camera inside.

It's lucky I stole five minutes to eat a granola bar after finding the wire in the cabin. Dan forgets to eat lunch sometimes or even to drink water.

After only a few hours, he gets very good at *pulk*-ing. His blond hair and strong frame, fused with his tenacity, remind me of a Viking. Attached to the sled by the rickshaw poles, he gets so he can ski down hills and clamber up them without too many falls.

In the evening it starts snowing on the campfire. Snow falls all night, and all the next day and the next night. You can hear crystals sprinkling on the tent under the tree.

I have always liked this kind of listening. Similarly I am attached, still, to the treeless tundra of the Bering Sea coast. How do things get inside, so deeply, so fast? Out on the tundra, space can be heard and time, as they roll unbroken over hundreds of miles of green mosses and tiny ferns, neon flowers—delicate, rugged—or wind-blown ice and snow, clean-bracing air. In summer, bees drone under riots of mosquitos. Feathers, bird eggs, tea leaves, and spiders hide in the grass. Berries grow to be gorged—pink, red, blue, black—and thousands of ducks, geese, cranes blot the sky, honking, honking. Everything gets wet, fog rolls in and winter, and there is not a tree or person anywhere.

I think I will always be drawn to the tundra's open mystery, to places like Tununak and Port Clarence, to the Bering Sea. Perhaps this intimate association is why I still marvel, even after two years in this Interior, at such rich forest. Spruce, birch, aspen, alder, an occasional clump of cottonwoods.

Both nights we camp under a hundred-foot spruce on a thick bed of boughs, something I have never done. With his ax, Dan hacks branches from three sturdy trunks, and at first I feel guilty. You can't cut at trees like that in Colorado. The land isn't big enough. I try not to listen or watch. Soon, though, Dan asks me to haul the boughs into piles around the rim of the hole he's excavating in the snow, under the tree. The snow is waist deep and more, so I keep my skis on, tromping around with no poles, hauling boughs, then whole, gray, fire-killed spruce trunks for fuel.

How can entire dead trees be so easy to uproot? They lift out of the snow like matchsticks.

"It's likely this fire was set by the Copper River Athabascans a hundred years ago," Dan says, pointing out young trees, shoulder-high, sprouting among the old ones. "The Athabascans knew that burning down trees would improve browse habitat for the moose."

From up on top of the rim, I hand Dan branches, one by one. In the same careful way that he helped build the school addition in Tununak, he weaves a thick bed of Christmas-scented boughs, all interlaced in the same direction. "Shingled," he says.

We spread a blue plastic tarp over the boughs, then pitch the small green tent. No stakes or fly, just poles, slipped inside the Gore-Tex seams. Pup tent style. My REI thermometer, which only goes down to minus twenty, says plus eighteen degrees.

Spring is a blessed time in the Interior. In March, the sun comes up at seven, stays up until seven, and gains seven minutes a day. Temperatures soar above zero, dipping only at night, and there is little wind. When you ski all day, work all evening making camp and dinner, wear the right layers, and crawl into a down bag with all your clothes on, you don't get cold.

Dan is a fast, good cook. We drink instant chicken ramen soup for dinner both nights, three cups each, huddled by the fire, and I get to snooze an extra hour in the mornings while he melts water and makes oatmeal. He says that getting out of a warm bag is the hardest part of snow camping, but at least it's light outside, not dark until ten or eleven, like mornings in winter.

After we leave, marten will come and sniff at the fire pit. I wonder if moose will bed down here, but Dan says the boughs will be covered with snow, and they are, as soon as we roll up the tent.

This has been a hard winter for moose. Even with their broad hooves and long double-jointed legs, they get tired plowing through chest-deep snow. They burn too much energy digging for buried willows and other browse. Dan says the cows, especially, get tired and depleted. They'll bear weak calves and be easy prey for wolves and bears. We don't see any moose, though, only their ghosts: tracks and droppings, clipped willow tips, places where they've bedded down.

In fact, we don't see any animals. Just tracks, which are almost as much fun: short-tailed weasel, mink, fox, marten, ptarmigan. River otter, hop and slide, hop and slide. Snowshoe hare, boing-boing on all fours. Squirrel, arctic vole, tiny shrew. The bears are asleep, and Dan says the wolves have been gone from this area for weeks. They roam a wide range.

Beside the trail, a pile of brown and black feathers and a bloody gizzard reveal the fate of a spruce grouse. "Goshawk took it," Dan says. I ask how he knows. He says he can tell by the brushmarks of the wing tips and the wingspan, and by the way the hawk swooped in low for the kill, skimming a snowdrift a few yards away.

While Dan skis on, I stop to collect some of the grouse's feathers for the small jar in my living room. They will add good spirits to the white and gray feathers already there, dropped by the round-eyed snowy owl we watched last summer at Port Clarence. Feathers are like shells and bones: pieces of life you can bring home and keep inside, to remind you of all that isn't there and all that is.

I've learned that you can't just stuff feathers in your pocket, though. They have to be handled gently or they'll get pulled out of shape, like a pie crust or a person. I zip the feathers carefully in the Eskimo-style pocket of my nylon anorak, planning to transfer them that night to my eyeglasses case.

I love to ski hard all day. It reminds me of my father and the trips we took in Colorado. "Up in the high country," he called it. We did some magnificent skiing up passes and mountaintops, twelve and thirteen thousand feet high. We would climb steadily almost all day, up a four-wheel-drive road or a hiking trail, then ski several hours down. Then climb back into my father's red Toyota Landcruiser and head for Denver and my mother's homemade chili.

I guess I just got used to Dad's Victorian/German/no-nonsense drive. He would pack a lunch the night before, wake up at five, drive several hours to our destination (no coffee break), hit the trail, and not stop until he got to wherever he was going. Lunch was at the top and not before—unless, of course, one ran into "inclement weather," as he called it. I don't think I knew that there were other, more circuitous routes to one's destinations—and that those routes might be worth taking—until I lived with the Eskimos.

Dan is a lot like Dad. He doesn't get side-tracked easily and he never gives up. The *pulk* is a good example. But Dan is malleable, partly because I'm not his daughter. For instance, I can usually get him to wait until seven to wake me. He says his inner alarm goes off at five, just like my Dad's, and I believe him. He doesn't have the heart to shake me from my dreams, though. He says he just lies listening to my breathing until it lulls him back to sleep or until the light tells him it's seven. Whichever comes first.

Sometimes I do funny things, sleeping on the trapline. I get scared. Last year at the Tetlin River, when snow slid off the roof of the Visqueen shelter, I jumped out of the sleeping bag. I thought the woodstove had exploded and the whole shack was on fire. This year I sat "bolt upright," Dan says. I dreamed I was on my skis and falling through ice and no one was there to help me. I jerked away from the crumbling edge so hard, I woke sitting up.

When I do these things, Dan always says, quietly, "Steady," as if he hadn't been sound asleep himself. He puts his big arms around me, pulling me back inside the bag, and as soon as I realize I've been dreaming, I burst out laughing. These things never happen when I'm alone at home (do they?). But the trapline gets down inside your soul, like feathers, like shells.

Curled in our bags in the tent, we wear too many clothes to make love. It's like hugging a Green Bay Packer, Dan says. But inside the tar-papered cabin, with our half-zipped sleeping bags fluffed over thick foam pads on the floor by the stove, things are different. There we are slender, like dancers, like reeds by a water's edge, played by a breeze or a gale.

Last summer in Port Clarence, I dreamed I was flying on two bungee cords, over Hindu streets crowded with tenements, balconies, roosters, past the end of the city, over a jagged, red sandstone wall. I sailed out past lichen-covered granite cliffs I could touch, or miss by leaning slightly to one side. I held the sharp hooks of the bungees in both hands but I could not feel them, only the two cords slung beneath me like a swing. I had to pay attention or I would tip and fall out. But I could fly higher than I ever had before without the cords, and I did.

I flew over tree-covered valleys—ponderosa? spruce?—toward the long white line of a distant mountain range. After a long time, I landed on top of a densely wooded hill and walked down the dirt road to a cedar-covered house.

Inside, standing in my stocking-feet on warm tiles next to a yellow fire, I played a song on my flute. The song was intricate and ornamented, all from memory, and I played better than ever before.

The second day, we cross Leonora Creek and enter a forest of widely spaced white spruce, taller and bigger trunked than usual for the Interior. If I stepped off the track and waded over to one, I wouldn't be able to put my arms all the way around it.

"These trees have been growing for two hundred and fifty years," Dan says. "They may never have seen a skier glide by."

I smile. Such space and time.

We ski contentedly through the forest, then onto what Dan says is the first of a chain of lakes. I'm terribly thirsty. We have drunk all the snow Dan melted at breakfast, and there will be no open water until we reach the river.

Breaking trail ahead of Dan, I spot a sudden, small hole. I slip off my pack and take out the liter water bottle. Leaving my pack on the track, I ski toward the hole. Dan catches up, steps off the track, too, his skis apart, then stops.

"Be careful around a hole like that," he says.

"I thought we could fill up this bottle real quick," I say back, not listening, my eyes on the hole. I step closer, as if drawn by a magnet, and poke hard at the hole's edge with my pole.

"I said be caref—"

Before he can finish, the snow-covered ice that I'm standing on breaks with a muffled thump. I gasp and jump back on the track, the water bottle almost slipping from my hand.

"You're not paying attention!" Dan says, raising his voice. "Listen to me. Never walk up to a hole in the ice with your feet together. Keep your skis apart. This is a spring hole. See those bubbles coming up?"

I look at the water this time, instead of the hole. Yes, now I see three thumbnail-size bubbles rolling up, slowly, steadily, like translucent marbles, breaking at the cold surface.

"The moving molecules create heat," Dan continues, his voice not softening, "and the heat melts the surrounding ice. All the ice under this snow is probably weak. It could be almost melted away. Otters usually know where each of these holes is. Watch for their tracks and don't go so near without thinking. You've got to pay attention out here!"

Three years ago, I would have argued. I would have made excuses for my mistakes. Now, when Dan reaches for the bottle, I give it up wordlessly. I have not yet learned to laugh, always, at my misfortunes, as my Eskimo friends do, but I have learned not to argue.

Dan takes the plastic bottle and, advancing carefully with his skis in a vee, scoops out another hole with his pole. He fills the bottle, but the water is cloudy brown. I put the bottle in my pack anyway, not drinking. We can boil the water later if we have to.

He's right to have gotten upset with me. I frightened him. Clarity comes to a fast-beating heart.

Awkwardly, we move on without saying more. So much lies underneath, waiting to be seen, to be understood. We're so alike and yet, we're not.

To be able to ski hard all day and then sleep on spruce boughs at night, not go home, that's paradise. I keep thinking how the photographs will look. Nothing but cold, hard work. Dan dragging the *pulk*. Wet mittens steaming on sticks over transparent flames, that weak way fire looks in daylight against a soot-blackened snowbank. Me waxing skis in the wind at the top of a ridge, the pink slopes of Mt. Sanford and Mt. Drum, glacier-footed, towering behind. The long white expanse of Jubilation Lake turning pink in the setting sun, spruce-ringed, the snow broken only by a single snowmachine track. The stacked woodpile outside the pocket-size cabin. Water that must be hauled from the river four miles away. Cold orange moon a day after full, cold stars flung across the sky, cold green band of northern lights.

It is hard work. But it's not *all* hard work. It's being so tired, all you want is to lie down on the spruce boughs. But both nights the tent has to go up first and the soup has to be cooked and eaten, and savored going down. The body has to crawl into the bag, take weight off muscles, lie still, horizontal, released like a heavy fish into open water.

You wake in the morning and there are no pinched shoulders, only the heady air when you step outside the tent. And on the third day, the sun glints off white hilltops, and patches of blue sky shine through where the clouds have rolled back.

We ski all day, take turns breaking through five-inch powder, reach the Gulkana River, poles tapping on ice.

"How many thousand pole-strokes do you s'pose we've made in forty-five miles?" Dan asks, with a laugh.

Our faces fry in the sun's reflection. Eyeless in dark glasses, oily hair plastered to our heads, we stop on the river to shed clothes. I stand on my gaiters in stocking-feet and pull down my expedition-weight long underwear. Just as I step out of the bottoms, a red and white Super Cub on skis skims the treetops. The first sign of civilization in three days. The pilot tips a wing and the passenger waves.

"Looks like Carl or his brother, Harry, from Glennallen," Dan says, raising a quiet hand. "They're probably counting moose and wolves for Fish and Game."

Have they seen our trail, I wonder, waving too, then pulling my fleece pants back on. Will they notice our circle, the outlines of our spruce beds, the holes in the wacky snow? Do they have any idea how it feels to step off the track and sink in? Do they think we're crazy?

Out here I forget stacks of papers to grade, my checkbook to balance, books to read, writings to revise. I even forget how much I want to play softly the high notes on my flute. Out here, something else plays. Two hundred fifty wolves run these mountains, have been counted from the air.

_____

We ski on. We haven't found any wolves in the traps, nor have we seen any droppings or paw prints.

"Will you trap here again next season?" I ask, as we round a bend in the river. This is the first year that Dan has trapped in the Gulkana River area, and it has not been easy to establish trails in such deep snow. He has worked hard since before Christmas and the earthquake, gradually learning the lay of the land and the ways of these wolves.

A wolf is not easy to trap, even for someone as experienced as Dan. The wolf is intelligent and alert, with a keen sense of smell and sight. It notices everything: human footprints, the smell of dirty gloves or contaminated metal, unusual depressions or lumps in the snow.

Twenty years ago, Dan spent a winter trailing the Cheslina wolf pack in Alaska's eastern Interior, documenting in notes and photographs the wolves' behavior. He was inspired by David Mech's research on Isle Royale in Michigan, research the first of its kind. Dan felt that Mech had not addressed certain aspects of the relationship of wolves to moose, and he wondered whether Mech's findings could be applied beyond the microcosm of an island. For five months, he followed the pack along the Cheslina River and over the surrounding mountains. He traveled on snowshoes without a tent and camped every night in a snow trench lined with spruce boughs. Although the data he collected differed from Mech's, it pointed to the same conclusions. In order to survive, an adult wolf needs food equivalent to almost one moose per month.

It will take Dan years to become as familiar with this part of the Gulkana River as he is with his other trapline on the Tetlin River, near the Cheslina. He has not trapped enough wolves here yet to impact the moose population. In a few months, more than enough pups will be born to replace the eight wolves that Dan has caught this season. Trapping this area again next year, though, should make a dif-

ference for the moose. That's what the Department of Fish and
Game hopes, anyway.

"I don't know," Dan answers. "I'd like to trap here again next
year, but it depends on whether the new land-and-shoot law gets
overruled. If it doesn't, it'll be too easy for people to come in here
with Super Cubs and work these packs with guns. There are lots of
lakes around here, just right for landing, and I don't want to have to
deal with that. It takes away all the freedom and space, for the wolves
and me. Do you know what I mean?"

I'm thinking of the cabin we'll be sleeping in again tonight. There
is no lock on the door. Tacked inside is a handwritten note from the
man who built the place. It reads:

> This trapline is registered with the Alaska Fur Trappers' Association.
> This cabin is located on public property. It has been registered as a
> trapping cabin with the State of Alaska and the Department of Fish
> and Game since 1978. You are welcome to use it.
>
> Signed,
> Rick T.

Late in the afternoon, we leave the river, climb a long ridge, and drop
down on the other side. Except for my father, I can't think of anyone
else who would have enjoyed this trip. Books say that cross-country
skiing is one of the most vigorous forms of exercise, that it's almost
as much work as running a marathon. According to books, we're
burning about 680 calories an hour per hundred pounds of body
weight.

We take turns breaking trail, and fantasize about our favorite
trapline dinner, macaroni and cheese with hot dogs. Neither of us
usually eats meat, except wild, but out here hot dogs are irresistible.
Kept frozen in a tree, then sliced and tossed with boiling macaroni,
the buttons swell to twice their size. Tonight they'll explode in our
mouths, peppery bursts of protein and grease.

Trudging past Jubilation Lake, almost home, Dan breaks into a

chant like an army captain. "Dogs! Dogs! Nitrate dogs! Huh! Huh!
Dogs! Dogs! Nitrate dogs!" He's waking all the squirrels. "Sing it!"
he calls, and laughing, I do.

On the way out by snowmachine the last day of my visit, we will
check more of Dan's traps. Forty miles from the nearest road, we'll
fly across acres of fresh powder and chains of lakes, me bending
knees to keep balance on the back of the sled. Hatless in the sun, I
will drink for hours the powder that sprays my face, as if I were
water-skiing.

We'll come to the place on the east side of Ragged Mountain,
where Dan heard a pack of wolves at Christmas "not a hundred
yards away," howling in the night. Somewhere on top of the mountain, two other wolves had started the chorus. The pack near Dan
sang so powerfully, they shook his soul, and mine when he told me
over the long-distance phone. Their echo shakes us now. It's a sensation that lifts, like shaking the hand of John Hoover-on-his-knees.
A resonance, not a toppling.

Today there are no wolves in any of Dan's number nine traps, only
scraps of black fur and bloody bones in one—all that's left of a cross
fox, eaten by another fox.

"Sometimes they eat their own," Dan says, shrugging. He smiles.
"Not the best trapline etiquette."

Secretly, I am glad that, for a second season, I have visited Dan's
trapline and I have not seen a trapped wolf. I've never seen a wolf in
the wild, not even in Denali National Park. Only captured ones:
whole skins in my living room before Dan takes them to the fur
dealer, or pieces made into Eskimo ruffs and mukluks.

The wolf is a spirit. It has run into my soul. I want to hear it howl,
see it lope. I want to catch the flash of its amber eyes, the growl behind its teeth. But it will reveal itself in its own time. Perhaps I do
not want to face a wolf in a trap. Am I afraid to see its dead body,
whole? Would I rather see only its tracks and droppings, find its
moose kills, imagine its shaman sound?

"What happens to the bodies?" I ask Dan. "You know, the meat. Do people ever eat it?"

"Not unless they're starving. People use wolf carcasses for wolverine bait or feed them to their dogs."

"Is that what you do?"

"Yes." He looks at me. "There was a time when *Homo sapiens* fit, when we had a niche in the circle of life," he says, gently.

Dan is a biologist turned trapper, outdoor adventurer, seasonal construction supervisor. He grew up in the countryside of Michigan, hunting, fishing, trapping. For a few years, he worked as a waterfowl biologist, but he did not like being indoors, bound to lists of data and a paper calendar.

"I'm trying to rediscover that niche," he says.

I want that niche back, too. I want balance. But I'm thinking of the day or night that we'll check the traps and find a wolf in one, how you'll have to shoot it before releasing its leg from the trap. I hadn't realized that's another thing the pistol in the pulk is for. You'll pry open the jaws of the trap carefully, with the two trap-setters, freeing something heavy and warm, like the red fox last year, only bigger. I'll want to touch it. And the spirit of that warm dead wolf will seep inside me, like feathers, like spruce boughs. Flying through deep powder, it will unlock doors, and some of them will be dangerous.

"A wolf weighs almost as much as you do," Dan says when I ask, "anywhere from ninety to a hundred twenty pounds. I can pick one up, but you probably couldn't very easily, except maybe over your shoulder. Any large dead body is hard to handle before *rigor mortis* sets in. Have you ever tried to lift a person who's unconscious? That's how a dead wolf feels."

He senses my reaction, can see it in my eyes. With his ski pole, he draws a circle in the snow and little arrow marks along it every inch or so. "Everything between each of these marks is the same stuff, the same matter," Dan says. "When something dies, its matter can't be distinguished until it takes on a new life form."

He taps my head gently, rests his hand in my hair. "Where does any of this go?" he asks. "Where do we go?"

I know that the wolves Dan catches aren't going anywhere. I know that their matter is staying right here, in the circle, and so is mine. Intellectually, I know all this. But what about the pain?

Dan looks at me again. I think he has been expecting this.

"Eskimos believe that an animal has a spirit," he says slowly, "but they also believe in using all of that animal, in natural ways. They see themselves and the animal as part of an interlocking design. We try to take the design apart."

I'm thinking of a sunny spring day my second year in Tununak. I was sitting at my desk after school, taping together photocopies of sheet music for my band students and wanting to get outside. I had only a few pages left. A young man came into the room, someone I had seen in the village but had never spoken with. He looked like he was in his early twenties. I was pretty sure he was a Washington.

"Excuse me," he said. "I heard you have a new piano. May I try?"

"Of course," I answered, standing to shake hands. "You're welcome to play."

He said his name was Andy. I told him my name, but he said he already knew it.

"Everybody knows who you are," Andy said, smiling. "You're the music teacher." He slid onto the piano bench, and I sat again at my desk.

The piano was an electric Roland with a full-size keyboard. It stood on four shiny black legs, like an acoustic spinet. The year before, I had asked the principal if we might purchase one.

"The school district may not approve the money," Phil said, "but it never hurts to try."

I ordered the model I wanted out of a catalogue from Chicago, and the $2,100 piano arrived by barge, in two cardboard boxes, the next summer.

The Roland was well-suited to the bush. It could be dismantled and hauled anywhere in Tununak on a sled or a three-wheeler, and it didn't mind bumps or cold. It never needed tuning, and students could plug in earphones and practice without being heard.

"There was good hunting today," Andy said from the piano bench, as though we were already friends. "I got lots of ptarmigans. Maybe forty-six. I think it was, because I took two new boxes of shells. And when I came back there was only one shell left. And I missed three times. So that makes forty-six good shots, right? Forty-six. That's pretty good. Mmm, those ptarmigans taste delicious. It was beautiful out there. Today was very beautiful."

"How many birds did you see?" I asked.

"Oh, I don't know. Maybe three hundred. Or four hundred. It was like a snowstorm flying, so much white in the sky."

Andy put on the earphones and began to experiment. I thought about forty-six ptarmigan. He said he had hauled them on his three-wheeler in a big plastic garbage bag. Images of white pioneers shooting the passenger pigeon to extinction flashed through my mind. I was happy for Andy, but also a bit horrified. Forty-six ptarmigan seemed too many for one person. Then I realized, of course, Andy didn't kill them all for himself. They would be shared with members of his family, many of whom had families of their own, and with friends and other relatives. There was more to the circle than I could see. Women were already sitting on the floor, plucking birds.

Late April. Dan and I are sitting at the table in my apartment, finishing breakfast. The table is oak, solid. I can feel it under my elbows and hands. We've been talking about the circle again and about Black Rapids Glacier and the Denali Dash, a 150-mile ski race over two passes in the Alaska Range. Dan leaves for the race today with a fully loaded *pulk*.

He shows me a picture he took in Port Clarence last summer of our friends Rebecca, Simeon, and Annie. Grandfather, grandmother, grandchild. Inupiat. They're standing close together, wind combing the wolf ruff on Simeon's white parka, Rebecca smiling, fall-colored tundra stretching behind. Little Annie wears somebody's giant pink mittens, synthetic, not fur. She reminds me of the girls in my dream—Melanie and Janie—and of all the other children who used to grab my hands and skip and laugh and sing with me in Tununak. These designs are interlocking. They cannot be taken apart.

We get up from the table and Dan gives me a hug. Tightly hugging him back, I can hear something playing, something playing very well. The circle, like the song, is not the mind, the body, or the soul. It is all of them together, and more. Instinct, intuition, dreams. A celebration.

It's as if we're back out on the trapline the last day of my visit, having lunch, which Dan remembers this time without prompting. Neither of us wants this day to end. We're perched on the black vinyl seat of the snowmachine, drinking coffee from the thermos, munching honey-dipped peanuts and raisins, bits of dried pineapple, an occasional chocolate star, the sun refracting, refracting. Dan tells a story of the time he was driving his truck down a dirt road, when a great horned owl soared out of the bushes with a rabbit in its talons.

Dan caught sight of the rabbit's face, its startled black eye glued toward the ground. "Four legs curled tight under its belly like landing gear," he says.

The owl soared ahead of the truck "for at least half a mile," before veering back into red willows, the rabbit still taut, airborne, legs like landing gear, ready to bound away any moment it might touch down.

Suspended over the white lake, we laugh like we used to in Tununak, running down the beach, before we got to know each other this well. I'm surprised at my laughter, that I don't just feel sorry for the rabbit, even though, at the same time, I do. I'm feeling the circle and the song—the mirror, not the rabbit; the reflection, not the form. I know it must have been hard work for that owl to fly with that rabbit, and the rabbit was scared. I do not want pain, do not choose it. But there is more to the circle than I can see.

In the old days, the Eskimos had no doors, and later, they did not lock them. I want to believe this: that mind, body, and soul are one, inseparable, and that the combination will not be forgotten . . . even when it cannot be remembered.

Jerry Dennis

The Music of This Sphere

from *Wildlife Conservation*

My wife and I moved to the country in search of quiet, I think. It's difficult to remember. We settled into a century-old farmhouse surrounded by meadows and orchards and a large yard filled with maples. And we brought the children with us. The children, of course, brought along their usual noise. Little has changed since our days in the city except that we have much more snow to shovel in the winter and a lot more lawn to mow in the summer, and the neighbors do their own yard work with tractors instead of Toros. Much of the time, Gail and I still must shout to make ourselves heard.

Our first night in the new house, with the children upstairs asleep at last, Gail and I lay in the darkness in the unfamiliar bedroom and admitted that achieving silence is probably a vain aspiration. The wind was up, blowing off Lake Michigan, vibrating the aluminum storm windows in their frames and making the house hum as if it were suspended from tuning forks. During the blaring distractions of daytime, while we unpacked and the kids were turned up to full volume, we hadn't noticed that the furnace in the basement ignites with an alarming bang, followed seconds later by the same noise in triplicate, like someone hammering the ductwork with a mallet: BANG! . . . bang bang BANG! I got up and investigated, but all was well with the old oil burner; it moaned and throbbed in proper fashion. On my way back to bed, I stopped in the kitchen for a drink of water and discovered that after a few hours of disuse the faucet turns on with a sputter, a hiss, and an explosion of spray, followed by a low intestinal groaning of pipes deep within the house.

That night I had a realization: Silence might be the voice of eternity, but in the mortal world every important thing asserts itself audibly. Silence is not only ungolden, it is unnatural. Like a vacuum, it is abhorred by nature. The very continents beneath our feet groan and grumble like barges of timber bound together with hemp. Scientists who submerged microphones in the oceans during the 1940s were surprised to learn that the seas abound with a cacophony of chatter. More recently, researchers aimed their instruments toward space and discovered that the sun and stars hum with gonglike resonance and that the Big Bang still echoes across the universe. Noise is everywhere and relentless. The music of the spheres turns out to be a grand clamor.

The clamor is great even in the animal kingdom. In April, during the first warmish nights, the tiny tree frogs known as spring peepers begin chirping their mating choruses near the pond across the road. They seem to begin all at once, as if someone flipped a switch. And for such small creatures, they put out a lot of volume.

Such volume is not unusual during mating season, when the males of many animal species are highly vocal advertisers of their vitality. If territory is intruded upon, the roar of an elephant seal, the bugle of an elk, and the bellow of a bull alligator serve as "ownership displays" to warn away rival males and avoid physical conflict.

Vocal displays also attract mates. Male songbirds sing their signature melodies to identify themselves to females of the same species. Male grouse stand erect and beat their wings rapidly, compressing air into a surprisingly loud "drumming" that begins slowly and ends rapidly—about 50 beats in 10 seconds. A humpback whale sings songs lasting from 6 to 30 minutes each, repeated for hours at a time, which can be heard by other humpbacks through many miles of water. A male cicada attracts mates with its shrill, buzzing call made by vibrating drum membranes over cavities on each side of its thorax.

Mating calls go on even when an animal would be decidedly better off staying quiet. Ruffed grouse reduce the risk of advertising for a mate by drumming at sites surrounded by thick cover to protect them from owls and hawks. Frogs of Central and South America are preyed upon by bats that hunt them by listening to their calls and determining which frogs are edible and which are poisonous. The frogs are caught in a dilemma. If they stop calling they fail to mate, but if they call recklessly they die. The only solution is to be very alert and become instantly silent if overhead motion or sound is detected.

It is not only during mating season, of course, that animals make noise. Within a caucus of crows you might hear calls of warning, which send all crows in the vicinity winging to safety, calls of distress if a bird has been captured or injured, or assembly calls, which attract crows from all directions to mob a cat or hawk. Blackbirds give at least two alarm calls: a drawn-out *eeeeee* when a predator is spotted overhead, and repetitive *chuck, chuck, chuck* when it is on the ground. Social animals use various vocalizations to signal alarm, warning, distress, or food, and to maintain and challenge the hierarchy of dominance within a group. Wolves may howl to assemble the members of a pack, to communicate with other packs, or even, in the words of one researcher, "for the heck of it." In many parts of the world, nearly constant background music is made in summer by the scraper-and-file stridulations of crickets, grasshoppers, and katydids. These singing insects—or fiddling insects, their music is never vocal—are highly expressive. Songs have been identified as common (expressing, perhaps, nothing but well-being), seeking (performed by males trying to locate females), rivalry (between competing males), disturbance (caused by persistent rivals), courting (by males who have found females), and reduced (just before and during mating).

Many animals make warning sounds to avoid potentially harmful conflict. A dog growls, a cat hisses (which is effective, it has been theorized, because it imitates the hiss of a snake; a cat even swings its tail back and forth in a snakelike way), a scorpion squeaks as it arches its tail, and a rattlesnake activates its rattle with a sudden buzz. Many tropical geckos make loud clicking or squawking sounds and lunge at enemies to frighten them away.

With all the noise going on in the world, surely it is a mistake to think that children should be seen and not heard. Our kids won't run shouting through the house forever. They will grow and move their noisy selves elsewhere, and someday (too soon!) my wife and I will wait eagerly for grandchildren to visit so we can give them battery-powered fire trucks and drum sets and games that employ clappers, gongs, bells, and whistles. We will plan our lives around Sundays and holidays when the still hours are pushed away again by voices raised in laughter and conversation.

What if the record of our lives is kept in a kind of musical score, every spoken word a note, every speech a bravura, every stomp of foot and clap of hand a ringing counterpoint? Maybe, in our final moments, the entire score is played back at proper speed and we recognize where we should have added volume, where we should have given the brass section freedom, where we should have pounded chords with abandon.

There is little quiet in a house with children. I listen now as my sons pass down the hallway outside my office door, each boy bracketed within his personal zone of noise. Nick squeals in mock appeals for rescue as Aaron shouts, "I'm going to make lunch meat out of you!" They run to their bedroom, slam the door, and begin whacking tennis balls against the walls with hockey sticks. It is the sound of well-being. Every parent learns to dread the unexpected silences. They mean injury or misbehavior, a toddler drawing that long breath before a bawl of pain, a three-year-old dragging the dog to the toilet for a bath. I say children should hoot and holler, wail and whistle, bang, stomp, and clatter. The noise of my boys in action has become music to my ears. I find it as soothing as birdsong.

Ann Zwinger

Bright Angel Trail: Coda

from *Downcanyon*

For Christmas my eldest daughter, Susan, and I give each other a hike down the Bright Angel Trail, a couple of nights at Phantom Ranch. We will walk back up the South Kaibab Trail on winter solstice, the end of autumn, the beginning of winter, the rounding of the year when Sun prepares to leave his Winter House. We start down, knowing a major snow is coming in on a huge outbreak of polar air. Scathing winds. A wind-chill factor of ten below. I question my good sense in going. There may not be enough clothes in the world to keep me warm.

The Bright Angel Trail follows the Bright Angel Fault, a fault that simply on the basis of accessibility is the best-known in the Grand Canyon. Walking inside it helps one understand the other great fault systems to which there is no easy access. Once below the rim the wind mercifully abates. Sun lights the Coconino Sandstone and snow outlines ledges on the damp Hermit Shale like chalk lines on a blackboard. Not quite ten miles from rim to river, the elevation drops from 6,860 feet at the South Rim to 2,400 feet at river's edge. With each footstep, we go back 20,000 to 30,000 years in time.

Because the path is so narrow, hikers must flatten against the cliff wall while the "scrawniest Rosinantes and wizened-rat mules," as Muir described them, pass by. The eighteen miles of trail that the mules travel are doused yearly with 8,000 gallons of mule urine and 117 tons of road apples. I shouldn't grouse: Charles Silver Russell, trying to do a photographic run of the river in 1915, had a steel boat built, which he and his helpers loaded on a dolly to cart it down the Bright Angel Trail. Every time the mules came by, the men had to jockey dolly and boat off to the side and cover them with canvas so as not to scare the mules. It took a week to get it down and then Russell wrecked it at Crystal. Twice.

Even in December the cottonwoods at Indian Gardens hold their leaves, although most fade to dirty yellow. They were planted by Emery Kolb, who maintained a darkroom here to avoid having to pay for pumping water to the South Rim (water issues from Roaring Springs, just below the North Rim, and runs by gravity to Indian Gardens). After taking pictures of tourists on their mules, Kolb would race down the trail to Indian Gardens, develop and make prints, and sprint back up to the top by the time the riders returned, all prints seventy-five cents each, thank you very much.

Clouds begin to filter across the sky. Sunlight washes the far buttes but shadows wallow in the canyon. We've picked up six more degrees. Even in December while snow garnishes the Kaibab, brittlebushes and one sweetbush bloom, both cheerful brassy yellow. The change from prehistoric path to commercial trail transpired in 1891, when miner Ralph Cameron and others improved it to allow access to copper mining claims. Cameron (it was originally called Cameron Trail) operated it as a toll trail. When the courts declared his claims invalid, the trail became, in one instant, the property of Coconino County, Arizona, and *its* toll road.

In 1902 the U.S. Geological Survey established a trail from the North Rim down to the river, connecting with the Bright Angel Trail, and called it the North Kaibab Trail. One crossed the river in a boat "lent by a friendly prospector" at the only crossing between Lees Ferry, eighty-nine miles upstream, and the Bass Trail, thirty-five miles west. By 1903 the trails had become such a regular route that the county upgraded the river crossing to a steel rowboat.

After the National Park Service took over administration of the

Grand Canyon in 1919, it decided to replace the boat with a steel suspension bridge. Harriet Chalmers Adams, on assignment for the *National Geographic,* came down on mule back to write about its construction. Getting building materials down was a logistical nightmare. Eight mules carried the twelve-hundred-pound cables that were anchored into the walls eighty feet up. As today, wooden planking floors the bridge, and wire mesh cages the sides for protection. Adams took a canvas boat across to "Roosevelt camp" (now Phantom Ranch, which got its name from early surveyors who noticed a ghostly haze that often hung in the canyon in late afternoon), and exited by mule up the North Kaibab Trail.

Failing in its first attempts to acquire the Bright Angel Trail from Coconino County, the Park Service, from 1924 to 1928, built its own toll-free trail and crossing: the South Kaibab Trail, which connects with the North Kaibab Trail via the bridge. Upon completion of the South Kaibab, Coconino County, scarcely in a spate of public dedication, sold the Bright Angel Trail, which it had gotten for nothing, to the Park Service for $100,000, a *very* tidy profit.

We lunch at the top of a series of switchbacks called the Devil's Staircase, relishing the last sunlight before we enter the shadowy murk along Pipe Creek. Across the way the line of the Great Unconformity bears witness to what the earth did with its yesterdays, Tapeats against Vishnu, sandstone against schist, a familiar, friendly juxtaposition that has come to mark my eons in the Inner Gorge.

Pipe Creek chortles down the Pipe Creek Fault, a branch of the Bright Angel Fault system. The trail crosses a vein of salmon-pink Zoroaster Granite with big chunks of milky quartz, one of the proliferation of Zoroaster dikes and sills in the Bright Angel section. Lichens spatter paint a swath of deep red granite. Being damp intensifies the lichens' color, rendering them vivid gray green against the darker rock, ruffled edges markedly brighter with new growth. Scraps of brilliant chartreuse map lichen vibrating with color on this cloudy day, scabbing the surface with a near Day-Glo brilliance, growing above a webbing of cracks vivid with moss.

As Pipe Creek nears the river, Vishnu Schist begins to look like marble cake batter, swirled in ribbons and stripes: the Pipe Creek migmatites, a transitional stage between metamorphic and igneous rock. White lines swirl into dark gray rock with overtones of purple, undertones of navy blue, no orderly layers like a sandstone or a shale, but rock molded and welded, puddled and re-reworked, sunbaked and frost-split. Bands of white quartz flecked with red outline rounded knobs, and wider bands of crimson beribbon it. Sometimes the lighter lines are as steady as a stretched string, other times as quirky as a corkscrew, recording in turn a white quartz lizard, a red granite ankh, a silvery snake, a gray sneeze, a purple sniffle.

Wind shoots off the river and whips every bush and grass stem with a vicious, malevolent intensity, seeming to come from everywhere and all at once. Clouds bullet across the sky. I start across the old footbridge over the river at Bright Angel Creek. Despite the cold I stop at midcrossing. The river makes a big curve downstream, posing that old evocative river question: what's around the bend? Horn Creek Rapid, that's what. For some peculiar satisfaction, I'm glad I know.

Susan and I hurry along Bright Angel Creek, eyes tearing from the wind, too chilled to talk. Bright Angel was originally called Silver Creek for the silver "float," although the source of the silver was never found. Trout are spawning, a month or so earlier than those in Nankoweap Creek, just forty miles upstream. Two ouzels fly along the creek, darting and jabbering. Despite the presence of ouzels in almost every tributary stream in the canyon, it is still a treat to see them parading underwater as easily and perkily as other birds do on the bank. Snow flares through the cottonwood leaves, flakes the size of chads. Chicken wire wraps many of the big cottonwood trees along Bright Angel Creek to protect them from beavers—by the time Phantom Ranch was established in 1922, beavers had pretty well cleared them out.

We straggle into Phantom Ranch in day-darkening, spitting rain, altogether foreboding weather. After dinner, the wind tunes up to gale force, a wild Walpurgis Night. The cottonwoods clatter. Wind shrieks in uneven pulses and jagged crescendos. The ragged intervals between blasts create an erratic, irrational, breath-holding tempo that breaks the easy rhythm of nightfall. The latest weather forecast comes in with the last hiker: a foot of snow on the rim, blizzard conditions, all roads closed in and out of the park. That night winter knocks on the doors of consciousness, flaunting all its chill and bleakness, darkness and bitter corners, full of vindictive winds and treachery.

Two mornings later, still afflicted with truculent skies, belligerent wind, and clanging cold, we start up the South Kaibab Trail, leaving the river as the Anasazi did, on foot. Just before the Kaibab Bridge, some Anasazi tucked a small living space between wall and river. When Powell stopped here looking for wood from which to carve replacements for his eternally broken oars, he noted this site and wondered "why these ancient people sought such inaccessible places for their homes." The answer is, of course, that these were no "inaccessible places" to the Anasazi, who traveled this canyon freely and easily. Constructed on a talus slope about thirty feet directly above the river, the site has the highest elevation available of any place on the delta of Bright Angel Creek, the first space along the river downstream from Unkar Delta amenable to settlement.

Twice between A.D. 1050 and 1150 small groups of Anasazi farmers located here, encouraged by the same temporary increase in annual rainfall that allowed marginal agricultural land to be taken up elsewhere along the river. Although the steepness presented some leveling problem for the builders, siting here substantially reduced the chance of being flooded out by living too close to the creek. They situated carefully to take advantage of solar radiation and to free up the largest amount of potential farming area. Even the floods of 1983 did not reach its masonry walls. But the benches they farmed a quarter-mile down the creek no longer exist, having been modified when Phantom Ranch was built as well as by the December 1966 flood that also created Crystal Rapid. At its peak, the population here never exceeded fifteen or sixteen people, still a group large enough to build their own kiva.

When I take my gloves off to take notes, my fingers sting with the cold. In this confined chasm, the lack of sunlight and warmth congeal my marrow. Focused on my own discomfort, I recall the miseries registered in one of the two skeletons found here, that of a middle-aged Anasazi woman of my stature. The burial, rare in the Grand Canyon, was unearthed quite by accident when a construction crew was working at Bright Angel Creek in 1982. Typical of this egalitarian Anasazi society, only two artifacts accompanied the bodies: a Tusayan Corrugated jar, a cooking vessel of no special or decorative significance, and a bracelet on the arm of the juvenile.

The woman's skeleton bore marks of unusual trauma and degeneration. The atlas, named after Atlas, the Greek Titan who carried the heavens on the back of his neck, and the base of her skull were fused at the junction of the first cervical vertebra and the backbone. This fusion, a birth defect known today as Klippel-Feil Syndrome, is often hereditary and accompanied by other physical anomalies. In addition, the second and third cervical vertebrae were frozen into a single unit (now called a block vertebra), which put greater than normal stress on the neck, surely exacerbated if she used a tumpline. These fusions can reduce the size of the neural canal, allowing bone to impinge directly upon the spinal cord, which normally causes numbness and pain in the arms, weakness in the legs, sometimes muscle control problems, headaches, and blurring or doubling of vision.

Her left leg showed two fractures, one a stress fracture, probably from a fall while the left leg was extended, such as might have happened by losing her balance and pitching forward while stepping off a height. The full impact of the shock traveled through the knee while it was in an extremely vulnerable position, and when it healed with only yucca poultices to damp the pain, although movement was probably restored, osteoarthritic degeneration set in.

All her life she must have lived in pain, unsure of her balance, always walking in a blurred landscape. She bore pain without medication, misery without surcease, no hope of feeling better tomorrow, a bitter lot in this place of cold leavings. And yet, my instinct tells me that somehow she was a useful working member of her family group and did the work that she could do. I give her honor.

A short way up the trail I turn and look back down across the river to that small site squeezed in between river and cliff. Its emptiness on this chilling day epitomizes for me the Anasazi's final exodus from the Grand Canyon, for by A.D. 1200 there were no beginnings, only endings. Land expansion ended. The Virgin Anasazi branch disappeared. The uplands were virtually abandoned. Because there *was* someplace else to go, the whole population picked up and filtered eastward to the Rio Grande drainage, where their ancestors still live today.

The Southwest is unique in having a body of data—geological, climatological, palynological, tree-ring, and radiometric—that establishes in extraordinary detail the fabric of prehistoric climate unavailable elsewhere. A preponderance of the Anasazi movements on the Colorado Plateau neatly match known environmental changes, and all evidence verifies the hypothesis that environmental stress combined with overpopulation *does* trigger the kind of socioeconomic change and population dislocation that beset the Anasazi in the middle of the twelfth century. No evidence of warfare or aggression, no massive epidemics, no other catastrophic causes can be documented. The massive movement eastward ties clearly and directly to environmental deterioration exacerbated by too many people.

When the climate turns bad, no one then or now can make an arroyo carry more water, no one can lengthen a growing season, or raise a water table, no one can gentle violent summer storms. Arroyo cutting destroyed fields and pulled chunks of arable land into the river, lowered the water table, and left remaining lands high and dry. In most canyon tributaries debris caught high in shrubs and trees tells of fearful and fast torrents that reamed out a creek bed, clawed out the banks, and rattled the cobbles, destructive rampages against which, even today, there is no protection.

The Anasazi already employed strategies to deal with a falling water table, such as more rigorous use of agricultural ground, and soil and water control features to curtail erosion and conserve summer's rains. Anasazi farmers engineered a more drought-resistant maize, incorporated more fields of more aspects into their system. Their technology produced reliable yields in places that cannot support agriculture today. The failure of prehistoric southwestern farmers was not for lack of ingenuity or expertise but simply tells that the problems they faced were unsolvable.

Good times in the Southwest have a way of not lasting long; change blew in on a cruel, dry wind. Arroyo cutting begins when groundwater depletion is rapid, where valley floors are narrow and stream gradients high, a good description of most of the Colorado's tributaries here. No rain gauge recorded fewer tenths of inches over time, no data bank furnished comparative data, no climatologists forecast oncoming disaster or disagreed about global warming or global cooling. Tree rings narrowed in response to a less benevolent climate, a lowering water table paralleled diminishing rainfall, and an arroyo's steepening sides told of unmanageable erosion, narrowing the dry-farm belt to zero.

The mechanics of leaving, the breaking down of a settlement system, are complex. If enough people leave, the remaining population may be small enough now to be compatible with what the area can support, and those who remain gain more mobility, more territory, more lands upon which to hunt or gather. But there may be a point of no return beyond which a settlement cannot be maintained, when families choose not to be separated, when social relationships that depend upon contiguity cannot be held together long distance, when not enough people remain to carry out the necessary ceremonial roles, and when the exodus of people frays local exchange networks.

The casual nature of their leaving, taking some goods with them, leaving others, suggests an intent to return when conditions bettered as they had time and again in the past. But this departure was different. Even during short wetter intervals no one ventured back, perhaps because most arable lands were too damaged or were simply gone, washed down the river, along with a way of life.

Today is the winter solstice. Somewhere, far away, Sun begins a slow turn to the north, but here my boots squeak on the powdery snow. Body heat drains into an encompassing shuffling coldness, miles of growing cold, ascending into a colder, rougher-edged world, a shivered dark, always framed by those continuing icy vistas of such brutal starkness and terrible beauty.

The interminable zigzags of miles of trail unwind upward to a rim eternally out of sight, elusive, dangerously distant, perhaps unattainable. Blowing snow bites like pulverized diamonds across my face. The views build, illustrations in a wondrous fairy story of ice castles with cut-crystal spires, scrims of spun snow for ballets of ice crystals. Clouds canter into the canyon and out again with cymbal-clashing grandeur. Cold hones the world to a hypersharpness, as if it inhales the atmosphere and leaves this transparency, a gelid nothingness, the clarity of a vacuum.

We flatten against the cliff as the ascending mule garbage train passes us. For once I am thankful to see them. Their trail-breaking saves us from having to struggle through crusted snow drifted hip-deep. How such large four-footed animals make such a narrow track is beyond me. To stay in their path I mince and teeter, awkwardly placing one foot directly in front of the other.

At Cedar Ridge, a mile and a half from the top, a demonic wind explodes, unleashing razor blades of ice, ready to flash freeze a face on the instant. I jockey on a windbreaker over my down jacket. At the top when I take it off a quarter-inch of frost coats it inside like a frozen fleece lining. The temperature is 6°F.

I drop my pack and step to the edge of the canyon for one last look down into its shrouded silence. The sky dims early and the landscape shimmers with tender pinks and blues and whites. Frosty mists powder every turret. A stately pavane of snowshowers threads among farther buttes. Cold stings my nose and my eyes. In this terrible silence I see below me no silly lizards doing push-ups, no springtime bloom of redbuds, no little tree frog smiling smugly like a miniature Buddha, no bald eagle with a fierce yellow eye nailing a fat trout, no humpback chub ferreting out an existence between fast water and slow water, none of the animation of the canyon, only a final stillness, only a beckoning, deepening cold, an absence, beyond which there is no more beyond, and I step back, uneasy: in this terrible clarity of pure white light there is some kind of clarion warning.

Yet hypnotized by the singular beauty of the view, once more I step to the edge, wanting to make contact with the river just one more time. With the river out of sight and only this uncharacteristic preternatural silence, it takes an act of faith to believe that it even exists. Yet I know it is there, curling into back-eddies that chase upstream, nibbling at sandbars and rearranging beaches, always sculpting the perfect river cobble and fluting the limestones, dancing with raindrops, multiplying the sun in its ripples, taking its tolls and levies against the cliffs, pounding and pulsing with life that vitalizes anyone who rows and rides it, yesterday left upstream with a sixteen-hour lag, tomorrow waiting at the bottom of a rapid, today an intensity of being that runs with the river.

Into my cold-impaired memory flashes the picture of another ascent. One November, after two weeks on the river, I hiked out alone up the Bright Angel Trail. To keep warm I wore an outlandish assortment of layers, walked in scuffed boots, and labored under an ugly, bulging daypack. As I gained the asphalt walk at the top of the trail, the number of people dismayed me. After an idyllic two weeks spent at only two campsites, with time to wander far and alone every day, I felt as bewildered as Rip van Winkle must have: the world had gone on and left me behind. Maybe I didn't know how things like light switches and faucets and computers worked anymore. My head, my heart, my psyche lagged a dozen miles down in the canyon. I remembered John Burroughs quoting a lady tourist's comment that the canyon had been built a little too near to the lodge.

Out of one of the clusters of people stepped a nice-looking, neatly dressed, middle-aged woman, a question obvious in her face. I paused, uncomfortably conscious of how derelict I must appear. "Excuse me," she began, "is there anything down there?"

Sensing the sincerity in the question and wanting to be courteous, but overwhelmed by trying to put the richness I had always been blessed with "down there" into quick words, I could only mumble something about yes, there's a beautiful river down there, although the question so unseated me I'm not sure what I said.

The question haunted me, as questions like that often do, and the real answer came, as answers often do, not in the canyon but at an unlikely time and in an unexpected place, flying over the canyon at thirty thousand feet on my way to be a grandmother. My mind on other things, intending only to glance out, the exquisite smallness and delicacy of the river took me completely by surprise. In the hazy light of early morning, the canyon lay shrouded, the river flecked with glints of silver, reduced to a thin line of memory, blurred by a sudden realization that clouded my vision. The astonishing sense of connection with *that* river and *that* canyon caught me completely unaware, and in a breath I understood the intense, protective loyalty so many people feel for the Colorado River in the Grand Canyon. With that came the answer: there *is* something down there, and it cannot be explained in a listing of its parts. It has to do with truth and beauty and love of this earth, the artifacts of a lifetime, and the descant of a canyon wren at dawn.

Sometimes the "down there" is so huge and overpowering, the river so commanding, walled with rock formations beyond time, that one feels like a mite on a lizard's eyelid. And at other times it is so close and intimate: a tree lizard pattering little chains of prints in the sand around my ground cloth, a soldier beetle traipsing the margin of my notepad as I write by firelight, the trilling of red-spotted toads in iambic pentameter, cicadas singing a capella, the mathematical precision of leaf-cutter bees, a limestone cavern measureless to man swathed with yards of gauzy webs woven by tiny spiders. Often the "down there" encompasses contrasts between minute midge and pounding waterfall, between eternity in an ebony schist and the moment in the pulsing vein in a dragonfly's wing, a delicate shard lost in an immensity of landscape, all bound together by the time to observe, question, presume, enjoy, exaltate. The "down there" is bound up with care and solicitude, sunlight on scalloped ripples, loving life and accepting death, all tied to a magnificent, unforgiving, and irrevocable river, a river along which I wandered for a halcyon while, smelled the wet clay odor of the rapids, listened to the dawns, and tasted the sunsets.

Some of the things I know about the river are undefined, as amorphous as the inexplicable connection that seeps into my bones while leaning against a warming sandstone wall on an early spring afternoon, or the ominous rockfalls on a winter night giving notice of a canyon under construction, the ragged pound of a rapid that matches no known rhythm but has lodged in my head like an old familiar song, the sheer blooming, healthy joy of the river's refrain.

But one thing is defined and clear: the terrible life-dependent clarity of one atom of oxygen hooked to two of hydrogen that ties us as humans to the only world we know.

Rick McIntyre

The Wolves of Yellowstone: Year One

First publication

After years of research, hearings, and controversy, the U.S. Fish and Wildlife Service (USFWS) released the final version of its Environmental Impact Statement (EIS) report, "The Reintroduction of Gray Wolves to Yellowstone National Park and Central Idaho," in May of 1994. The EIS recommended the reintroduction of wolves into both regions, and the following month, Bruce Babbitt, the secretary of the interior, approved the proposal.

In early January 1995, American and Canadian biologists teamed up to capture twenty-nine gray wolves in Alberta, just east of Jasper National Park. After radio-collaring each animal, fifteen wolves were shipped to central Idaho and released in mid-January. The Idaho reintroduction was classified as a "hard release," meaning that the animals were turned loose immediately upon arrival at the release site. These wolves were primarily young animals at the age of dispersal, the age when they would leave their packs and seek out mates and new territories. USFWS biologists flew over the reintroduction area on a regular basis to monitor the animals.

As of the fall of 1995, nine months after the Idaho release, the wolves had not killed any livestock or caused other problems with the residents of the area. Like nearly all wild wolves, they are supporting themselves by hunting wild prey. This perfect track record during the first nine months of the project has proven that the dire predictions of opponents of wolf reintroduction, predictions that the wolves would immediately start killing large numbers of livestock, were wrong.

The Yellowstone reintroduction was handled in a different fashion from Idaho. It was a "soft release," an experimental attempt to break the normal homing instinct of established wolf packs. Because the prime goal of the Yellowstone project is to reestablish wolves in the park, it is important that the packs set up territories near the release sites, and the soft release seemed the best way to achieve that goal. Fourteen Canadian wolves, a total of three packs, were brought into Yellowstone, beginning on January 12, 1995. Each pack was placed in a separate acclimation pen for about ten weeks. During captivity, park rangers and biologists fed the wolves road-killed deer and elk twice a week.

All of the acclimation pens were located in or near Lamar Valley, a traditional range for elk, bison, and other prey species. The high density of prey animals available in this northeastern portion of the park once supported several wolf packs. The last-known native Yellowstone wolves were killed in this area in October of 1926.

But sixty-nine years later, in a new climate of tolerance, wolves once again began to roam Yellowstone National Park. Beginning on March 24, 1995, the Canadian wolves left their acclimation pens to explore the park. The first group out of the pens was the Crystal Bench Pack, consisting of six wolves, followed a few days later by the Rose Creek (three wolves) and Soda Butte (five wolves) packs. The events of 1995 in Yellowstone National Park were extraordinary on many levels. I will begin the story of the Yellowstone wolves with the epic, tragic, and finally triumphant story of the Rose Creek Pack.

The Rose Creek Pack

When the Rose Creek Pack was captured in Canada, the biologists could only locate the alpha female and one of her yearling daughters. Wolf hunting and trapping are legal in that area and humans recently had killed at least three members of the pack. Mother and daughter arrived in Yellowstone on January 12 and were situated in their own acclimation pen. On January 20, in an attempt to create a functional pack, the biologists placed a huge, 120-pound male wolf (known as "The Big Guy" to project staff) in the Rose Creek pen, hoping that he would pair off with the alpha female. No one knew it at the time, but that male did indeed bond with the female and bred her during the weeks they were in captivity.

In late March, the biologists opened the gate of the Rose Creek pen. At some point after they left, the big male ran through the opening and into the nearby woods. Soon, though, he realized he was alone; his mate had stayed in the pen, too afraid to leave. The biologists and rangers had used the gate to enter the pen, and the Rose Creek alpha female associated the gate with people. Her fear of humans, instilled by experience with hunters and trappers on her former range, caused her to stay well away from the open gate.

The big male returned to the pen and spent most of the next week trying to coax his mate out. His determined actions demonstrated the depth of his emotional bond with the alpha female. To him, the pen was a prison. Returning to the pen, after having escaped, likely seemed a very dangerous proposition to him. Since he had frequently seen humans outside the gate, the same humans who had captured him and placed him in the pen, his return would, in his mind, put him at a high risk of recapture. Despite this perceived danger, he loyally stayed put, trying to draw out his mate to share in the freedom he had achieved. During this time, the female's yearling daughter, perhaps due to her more limited experience with hostile humans, walked through the gate on her own and joined the alpha male.

The park biologists, unaware of the alpha male's departure from the pen, scheduled a trip to the site to see if the wolves had left, and if not, to drag in a fresh carcass. On approaching the pen they saw the alpha female inside. Assuming the other two wolves were also with her, the biologists pulled the carcass toward the open gate. Then they heard a loud, deep howl from behind them. Turning around, they spotted the huge alpha male, staring at them from a hillside. His howls seemed to say: "This is my area and my family. Get out of here!" Willing to abide by his wishes, the men immediately abandoned the carcass and rushed back to the road. To make sure they really were leaving, the defiant alpha male escorted them partway down the trail. For twenty minutes, the biologists, lingering by their truck, continued to hear his deep-throated howls.

Finally, after days of patient effort, the alpha male successfully lured his mate out of the pen. The yearling daughter traveled with the pair but soon split off and lived independently in the release zone, near her mother and stepfather. In late April, four weeks after release, the alpha pair explored the wilderness area just north of the pen. The project biologists did not know it at the time, but the female was pregnant and close to giving birth. As the pair approached the northern edge of the wilderness, they stopped and bedded down for a rest.

Later that day, April 24, 1995, the alpha male set out hunting for food to bring back to his mate. A short time later, a man shot and killed him. An eyewitness subsequently testified that Chad McKittrick, a forty-two-year-old unemployed carpenter from Red Lodge, Montana, killed the alpha male. McKittrick initially admitted killing the wolf but claimed that he thought it was a dog. Since the wolf's head and pelt were later found on McKittrick's property, his story is hard to believe. Who would kill a stray dog then save its head and skin? In early interviews with reporters, McKittrick indicated he would plead guilty, but later entered a plea of innocent. In late October a Billings, Montana, jury found him guilty of three counts of killing an endangered species.

Transmissions from the alpha female's radio-collar indicated that she stayed put in a small area in the foothills on the outskirts of Red Lodge during the days following her mate's death. Not knowing his fate, she waited in vain for his return. Two days after his death, she gave birth to a litter of eight pups, four males and four females, the first litter of pups born in the Yellowstone area in nearly seventy years. Having waited too long for her mate, she had no time to dig a proper den, her pups were born in a shallow depression on the cold, hard forest floor.

A few days later, on May 3, USFWS biologist Joe Fontaine, while searching for the alpha female, unexpectedly discovered the litter. "All of a sudden," Joe said, "I heard a whimpering kind of squeal. I lifted up a spruce bough, and here are eight wriggling wolf pups lying on the ground. I was surprised as heck to see them lying right there in front of me. When I saw the pups I just wanted to jump up and down and scream and tell the whole world." After a quick look at the tiny, week-old pups, Joe backed away. From a distance, he determined with his radio-tracking equipment that the mother wolf had returned to her pups.

The fatherless family, positioned along the wilderness border near the town of Red Lodge, was in a precarious situation. A mother wolf, especially one with eight pups, needs a mate and other pack members to hunt for her as she tends her young. If she herself left the litter in order to hunt, the pups could die of exposure, due to their inability to produce their own body heat.

To give the struggling family a chance of survival, the biologists filled in for the dead father by dropping off road-killed deer and elk near the litter. The alpha female quickly discovered the carcasses and made full use of the meat. When the pups were three weeks old, project leaders decided to capture the mother and litter and put them back in the Rose Creek acclimation pen. The pen would protect the pups from such possible threats as bears, mountain lions, and eagles.

The biologists captured the mother in a leg-hold trap early on the morning of May 18, but when Joe Fontaine went to gather up the pups, he discovered that she had moved them! Joe and the other team members frantically searched the surrounding area, knowing that if they didn't find the pups soon, all of them might die. Finally, after five hours of searching, Joe discovered the female's tracks and followed them to a boulder field. He then heard the pups whimpering among the rocks. All eight squirming pups were retrieved, and within a few hours, the mother and her litter were safely back in the Rose Creek pen.

The biologists released the Rose Creek family in mid-October, when the pups were twenty-four weeks old. In a wild pack, the litter is cared for and fed by the adults until the fall, the season when the pups begin to travel and hunt with older pack members. The release of the Rose Creek litter was timed so the eight pups could fend for themselves and travel long distances with their mother as they hunted.

Despite the premature, tragic death of the Rose Creek alpha male, he did not die in vain. He fathered the first litter of pups in the Yellowstone area in nearly seventy years. His mate, against all odds, and with the help of the biologists, managed to keep the pups alive during the first few critical months of life. The alpha female and all eight pups triumphed over adversity and tragedy. The alpha male's genetic legacy will live on in the park: As of late 1995, 36 percent of all the wolves in Yellowstone were his offspring!

The story of the death of the Rose Creek alpha male and the birth of his pups created a tremendous amount of sympathy for the wolves. This senseless killing inspired many local people to come out in support of the wolves and the reintroduction project. Recently, I was in Cooke City, Montana, a nearby small town not normally considered pro-wolf. Everyone I met talked about how they disapproved of the shooting of the father wolf and how they hoped that his killer would be severely punished.

Along with the eight pups born into the Rose Creek Pack, the Soda Butte Pack, who set up a territory along the northeastern border of Yellowstone, had one pup. Due to the stress of capture, no one expected any pups the first year of the project. All nine pups born in the spring of 1995 were still alive in the fall. The birth and survival of these pups is a great victory for the project and for the wolves.

The Crystal Bench Pack

The Crystal Bench Pack was the first complete pack to enter the park and the first pack to leave their acclimation pen. On March 24, these six wolves, consisting of a black alpha male, a gray alpha female, as well as three black and one gray male yearlings, stepped through an opening in the chain-link fence and began to explore the Yellowstone wilderness. The next day, perhaps in celebration of their release, they were seen playing in the snow a short distance from their pen. I was lucky enough to be one of the first to regularly observe these historic wolves.

I had worked in Yellowstone in the summer of 1994 and was planning on returning in 1995 from my winter job at Big Bend National Park in Texas. No government money was available for a wolf education specialist at Yellowstone so I took on the responsibility of raising my own funding for the position as I traveled around the country lecturing on wolves.

My prime goal for the 1995 summer, now that wolves were back in the park, was to see one wolf. I expected that if I did see one, it would be a brief glimpse at a great distance. But within eight weeks of returning to the park I had recorded 133 wolf sightings! During my first two months in Yellowstone, I saw the Crystal Bench wolves on 65 percent of the days I went out looking for them in Lamar Valley.

Once I realized the wolves were going to be visible on a frequent basis, I spent a lot of my off-duty time showing them to as many park visitors as possible. By early July, nearly four thousand people had glimpsed the Crystal Bench wolves. As had been my experience in Denali, the wolf sightings in Lamar Valley became very emotional events. Some people cried, others embraced family members, and a few hugged the nearest government official.

The wolves sometimes revealed themselves to visitors from areas of the country that have strong anti-wolf traditions. In mid-May I let a bus load of sixth-graders from Greybull, Wyoming, a small ranching town, watch the pack through my spotting scope. One of the girls, as she saw the wolves, yelled out to her classmate, "This is the most exciting thing I've ever seen in my life!" One of the boys in the group later sent the following note to me:

> I think it is neat to see *wolves* in Yellowstone. I think wolves are neat, the way they hunt. I live on a ranch and I don't mind the wolves being in Yellowstone. I feel that the wolves belong in Yellowstone so people can have a chance of hearing them howl or of seeing them. When I saw the wolves hunting an elk, I thought that was *magnificent!* I enjoy having wolves in Yellowstone.

When I was out in Lamar Valley, I sometimes felt a little like the press secretary for the Beatles at the height of their popularity in the 1960s. People constantly approached me and asked, "Where are they now?" "Where were they last night?" "What's their favorite food?" and "Where are they going to appear next?" Nearly everyone was overwhelmingly positive about the wolf project, and thrilled at the opportunity to observe wolves in the wild.

Play was the most common behavior we saw during our observations of the Crystal Bench Park. Such activity, often carried out as hundreds of park visitors watched, proved that the pack had successfully adjusted to their new territory and the presence of people.

Each day, for many weeks, we got up at 4:00 A.M. and drove out to Lamar Valley, just before sunrise, hoping to get a glimpse of the Crystal Bench wolves. We often went back out in the late evening and stayed until the very last light. During those excursions into the valley, I recorded scores of wolf sightings in my journal. An excerpt from my journal entry for May 24 conveys the playfulness of the yearling wolves:

Two of the black Crystal Bench yearlings are feeding on a freshly killed elk carcass. The other pack members left the scene some time ago. Having finished their meal, the young wolves begin to play. One yearling tears off a piece of hide and tosses it in the air. He watches it for a moment, then leaps completely off the ground and catches it in midair, the same way a dog catches a Frisbee.

The wolf then drops the hide, backs off, and pretends to stalk it. Lowering his body and moving slowly forward, he gets in position and pounces on it. He picks it up in his mouth and prances back and forth, then runs across the meadow. Periodically, he tosses it in the air and catches it as he runs along.

The other yearling comes over and chases the first one, who drops the bit of hide. His brother quickly snatches it in his jaws. Now the chase is reversed: The one without the prize chases the one with it.

The yearling holding the piece of hide outruns his sibling. At a point several hundred feet ahead, he stops and looks back. He then drops down, out of sight of his brother. When the other wolf runs up, the ambushing yearling leaps out of the grass and pounces on him. They spar with their jaws and wrestle across the meadow.

One brother sprints away, and the chase is on once again. When they next meet, one assumes the play-invitation pose common to both wolves and dogs: He lowers his front end but keeps his rear high, a position that makes him look like he is bowing to the other wolf.

After another wrestling bout, the two brothers take off running again. They streak across the meadow, side by side, sparring with their jaws as they run. They twirl and prance around each other with the grace of ballet dancers. Then one wolf slips and tumbles, bouncing across the meadow like a large, furry, black ball. He skids to a stop, untangles himself, and flings his body back into the game. I am amazed at his indestructiveness. He must have banged himself up but gives no indication of any injury or stiffness. The brothers continue their play session, lost in the exuberance of the moment, oblivious to the one hundred human observers across the valley.

When the Crystal Bench Pack left its acclimation pen in late March, the four yearlings were almost one year old. They would have hunted with the alpha pair during the previous fall and winter, prior to their capture in Canada. Serving as apprentices, young wolves watch older pack members as they hunt and learn by the example they set. They also learn by trial and error when hunting on their own. In Lamar Valley, we saw many examples of the Crystal Bench yearlings trying to learn the business of being a wolf.

The gray yearling wolf is traveling alone across Lamar Valley early one morning. Five adult elk spot him and chase him away. A few minutes later, he notices a bison bull bedded down in the meadow, facing away from him. With cautious, deliberate steps, the young wolf works his way toward the bull, always keeping well out of his line of sight.

The wolf's stalking works perfectly; he is now just a few feet behind the bull's rear end. For the first time, the yearling realizes just how big this bull is. Not sure what to do next, the wolf stops and stares at his quarry. Looking around for other pack members, he finds that he is all alone. Moving forward just half a step, he hesitates again and stops.

The huge bull senses that something is behind him. With a slow, gradual motion, he turns his massive head around and looks right at the wolf, just a few inches from him. Showing disdain for the yearling that is only one-twentieth of his size, the bull flicks his tail a few times, as if waving off a bothersome fly, then turns his head back and resumes chewing his cud. Admitting defeat, the wolf trots off in search of something more his size.

Elk are smaller in size but, like bison, can kill with one kick. Young wolves also have a difficult time figuring out how to attack an elk without getting injured. Until they do learn the proper method, yearling wolves often hesitate at the decisive moment. The following observation documents such a hesitation.

Three of the yearlings are out late in the evening. A small herd of elk appears, and the wolves immediately begin the chase. Like always, the elk easily outrun the pack. One large bull, however, chooses not to run and holds his ground as one of the black yearlings approaches. Stopping a few feet in front of the bull, the yearling now seems unsure of his next move. Looking back, he sees that the other wolves are still in pursuit of the fleeing herd.

Turning again to face the bull, the yearling moves a step closer, and then bounces from side to side on his front paws. He looks like he doesn't know how to handle the big bull. After staring at the wolf for a few moments, the bull turns and trots off. As he leaves, the frustrated yearling sits down and watches the elk depart.

This yearling could not decide what to do during the confrontation with the bull elk. As he would soon learn, something closer to his own size would be much easier to kill. An incident two days later, involving the entire pack, helped teach the yearlings how to successfully hunt and kill elk calves. It also taught one yearling how he could run interference for the rest of his pack.

The six Crystal Bench wolves encounter a herd of elk in the western end of Lamar Valley. One of the black yearlings is out in front, followed by the two alphas and the rest of the pack. As the wolves move closer, the elk stop grazing and watch the pack. The herd runs off when the first wolf is about one hundred feet away.

The black yearling and alpha female simultaneously spot a newborn calf struggling to keep up with the herd. As the wolves sprint toward the calf, the young elk gives up its futile attempt to catch up and lies down in the thick grass, trusting in its natural camouflage to mask its location.

The yearling and the alpha female arrive at the spot where the calf had disappeared. Like two golden retrievers trying to sniff out a ball in the grass, the wolves crisscross the meadow, frantically searching for the calf. The calf's mother senses something is wrong and leaves the fleeing herd, running back to her youngster. She charges straight at the two wolves, driving them away. The other wolves then arrive and join in on the search for the calf. They converge on the last-known location of the calf, but the mother elk continues to drive the six wolves away from that spot.

One of the black yearlings is now making a game out of the encounter. Whenever the elk cow charges and chases him away, he immediately returns and stands in front of her, daring her to charge him again. With her full attention riveted on him, she fails to see that three of the wolves have found the calf and have killed it.

As the pack begins to feed, the mother elk realizes what has happened and charges into the group. They scatter, just barely avoiding her deadly hooves. The black yearling races in front of the elk and seems to taunt her. With her attention again on him, she charges and drives him off. As soon as she stops, he comes right back at her. She goes after him again and again. Meanwhile, the rest of the pack is feeding on her calf. Thanks to the actions of the yearling, they are able to eat with a minimum of disturbance from the mother elk.

After the excitement of the kill ebbs away, the alpha pair engages in a greet-

ing ceremony. The female romps beside her mate, wagging her tail and licking the side of his face. One of the yearlings jumps in between the two alphas. They tolerate his interference and the three wolves run off, shoulder to shoulder, playfully biting and licking each other. The other three wolves follow closely on their heels.

As the weeks went by, I noticed that the yearling wolves continued to gain confidence in their speed and agility. At times, they even ran up to grizzlies and seemed to deliberately tease them, knowing the bears could not catch them. In mid-June, the yearlings successfully turned a play session into a cooperative effort to steal a carcass from a grizzly.

In late evening three of the yearlings, two blacks and the gray, are romping on a ridge. As they run to the east they frequently stop to wrestle and spar. Later, the yearlings, led by one of the black wolves, sprint at full speed toward a stand of aspen where an hour before a grizzly had killed an elk calf.

They disappear into the forest but I detect a flurry of activity behind the trees. The three wolves and a fourth animal, likely the grizzly, seem to be chasing each other.

A moment later, the black yearling, the one who had led the charge into the aspen, races out of the woods with the half-eaten remains of the calf in his jaws. The other yearlings burst out of the trees just behind him. All of the wolves are running as fast as they can toward a stand of conifers two hundred yards to the east.

The grizzly charges out of the aspen, in hot pursuit of the wolves. As the first black yearling dashes into the conifers with the carcass, his gray brother abruptly spins around to confront the bear. They meet face to face, just a few feet apart. The grizzly seems to be a young bear, only a few times bigger than the wolf. The yearling's refusal to back down confused the bear—it is not sure what to do.

After a few moments, the wolf casually turns around and trots after his two brothers who are now both in the conifers. The grizzly sniffs the ground, searching for the lost carcass.

Moving closer to the forest, the bear stops and stares toward the trees. A black wolf suddenly sprints out of the woods, straight at the bear. Startled, the *grizzly runs off, but only a short distance. It turns and faces the wolf and then slowly walks toward it. The yearling moves away from the forest, possibly trying to lure the bear away from the other wolves and the carcass. But the bear ignores the wolf and heads back toward the forest. The wolf, with its tail excitedly wagging back and forth, watches the grizzly move off. Then he charges again and chases the bear a short distance, before returning to the cover of the forest.*

At the edge of the trees, the grizzly pauses and intently stares into the forest. Slowly, the bear walks into the trees and disappears. All three yearlings and the bear are now in the forest.

About five minutes later, the grizzly reappears on the far side of the conifers. No wolves are in sight and the bear does not have the carcass. The grizzly continues on, apparently having given up on retrieving its kill.

Just after the grizzly departs, a black wolf emerges from the trees, carrying the calf carcass. Soon the other yearlings join him. They all bed down and the wolf with the carcass starts to feed. The other black wolf and the gray get up and play. A little later, all three wolves head toward the forest on the far side of the meadow. As they travel, two of them continue to play while the black wolf carries the carcass. They all disappear into the forest a few minutes later, just as it becomes too dark to see.

After numerous encounters with elk, bison, and grizzly bears, one of the black Crystal Bench yearlings now seems to be dominant among the four brothers. He is the one who snatched that half-eaten elk carcass from the bear and escaped unharmed with the booty. The other yearlings assisted him, but he was the instigator and the leader.

While watching the above incident last June, I speculated that this coming winter, when the wolf-mating season comes along, the widowed Rose Creek alpha female may notice that Crystal Bench yearling. She will need a new mate, one who could help lead her pack. A young male with the courage and ability to steal a carcass from a grizzly would be a good choice for the alpha male position.

But an event that took place in October proved my prediction wrong. Just before the biologists released the Rose Creek mother and pups, the gray Crystal Bench yearling, the one who stood face to face with an angry grizzly, showed up at the Rose Creek pen. Early signs indicate that the alpha female and pups have fully accepted him as a member of their pack. He is currently serving as the pack's alpha male and will likely breed the female during the next mating season.

As the new alpha male, the Crystal Bench yearling is also acting as the stepfather of the eight pups, the pups whose father died just two days before their birth. Unlike most other species of wildlife, adult wolves are very willing to help care for young that are not their own. The gray yearling will serve as a substitute for the Rose Creek pups' biological father, as he teaches them how to hunt and survive in Yellowstone.

After leaving their pen, the Rose Creek wolves settled into a territory that includes the western half of Lamar Valley. The Crystal Bench Park is currently using the eastern half of the valley. The extremely high prey density in Lamar Valley should easily support both packs.

Perhaps the black Crystal Bench yearling will pair off with the Rose Creek yearling female, the alpha female's daughter. If that does happen, they will move off and establish a territory for themselves nearby, in one of the many vacant wolf territories in the park. Wolves once lived along Hellroaring Creek, a valley just west of the current ranges of the Rose Creek and Crystal Bench packs. The yearling female knows that area well; the biologists often located her near the creek while tracking the movements of the packs. Since she has been successfully supporting herself in the area, she may bring her mate there, permanently settle, and raise a series of litters in the territory.

The Future of Wolves in Yellowstone

As I write these words, nearly seven months have passed since the release of the Yellowstone wolves, and during that time none of the reintroduced wolves has bothered any cattle or sheep. As in Idaho, the gloomy predictions of immediate and massive livestock losses never materialized. So far, the Yellowstone and Idaho wolves have proven to be model citizens.

The Environmental Impact Statement predicted that some live-stock depredations will occur in both Idaho and the Yellowstone re-gion, but at a low rate. After ten years of recolonizing Montana, the wolf packs there have taken a total of only twenty-five cattle and thirteen sheep, an average of just two-and-a-half cows and a little more than one sheep annually. We hope that the reintroduced wolves will establish a similar admirable record in Idaho and Wyo-ming.

Biologists with the two projects will monitor the movements and activities of the packs and immediately respond to any allegations of wolves killing livestock. In Montana, speedy investigations of sup-posed wolf-livestock incidents have exonerated the wolves 95 per-cent of the time. The true culprit usually turns out to be a bear, mountain lion, coyote, or the neighbor's dog.

When depredations do occur, a swift, professional response should convince local residents that the program can effectively re-solve conflicts between ranchers and wolves. A wolf proven to be a livestock killer will be relocated, placed in captivity, or destroyed, depending on the circumstances. The radio-collars worn by all of the wolves will enable the project biologists to quickly locate and cap-ture a problem animal.

A private landowner has the right to shoot a wolf caught in the act of attacking livestock. The incident must be reported within twenty-four hours and evidence must support the story. As in Mon-tana, Defenders of Wildlife will offer full market value reimburse-ment to any rancher who loses livestock to a wolf.

The fact that the Idaho and Yellowstone wolves have taken no livestock during the initial months of the programs is an important factor in influencing public attitudes about the two reintroduction projects. Later, when a wolf/livestock problem does occur, this early successful track record will help place the incident in the proper perspective.

In future years, when other states and countries consider their own wolf reintroduction programs, we can document how well the

Yellowstone and Idaho programs worked. The continued success of these projects will create endless ripple effects that could help get wolves reestablished in many other former ranges, such as in Arizona, New Mexico, Colorado, New York, New Hampshire, and Maine and perhaps even Mexico, Scotland, and Japan.

The total cost—past, present, and projected—of the thirty-year program (1973–2002) to restore gray wolves to the northern Rockies (Montana, Wyoming, and Idaho) and to eventually take them off the Endangered Species List is estimated to be about $12.7 million. That works out to less than five cents per person if divided among the number of people living in the United States. In other words, a penny every six years.

Right now it looks likely that the wolf project will achieve its ultimate goal of wolf recovery in the Yellowstone area—ten breeding pairs producing pups for three years in a row by the year 2002—ahead of schedule and under budget. This is one of the most cost-efficient government programs ever undertaken, as well as one of the few federal projects that will actually achieve its mission!

The economic benefits of having wolves back in Yellowstone are becoming obvious to local businesses. A Montana economics professor predicted that the wolves would bring in an extra $23 million annually to nearby communities. A quick look at all the wolf-related items in local stores confirms the popularity of the project. A few days ago, the manager of the Roosevelt Lodge gift shop, the store closest to Lamar Valley, told me her sales were up 44 percent over last year, an increase she attributes primarily to all the people coming to see the wolves.

Dancing on the Skyline

It is important to discuss the tremendous successes of Yellowstone's wolf reintroduction project, but to finish this story, I want to return to the Crystal Bench wolves one last time. For me, a sighting I made in early June best sums up the ultimate meaning of the project:

High on a ridge above Lamar Valley, two young grizzlies, newly separated from their mother, feed on an elk calf carcass. A light-colored wolf suddenly appears to the left of the bears. The wolf's coat identifies it as the Crystal Bench alpha female. Moving in closer to the bears, she is obviously interested in the carcass.

A few dozen feet from the grizzlies, she lies down and stares at them. Annoyed by her presence, one of the bears chases her off. Running only ten or fifteen feet, the wolf stops and looks back. The bear is already returning to the carcass. Trotting right back, the wolf returns to her original position and beds down. This causes the bear to once again chase her off, but for a shorter distance. This teasing and chasing is repeated several times.

Frustrated at their inability to drive off the wolf, the two bears abandon the carcass and move higher on the ridge. The alpha female rushes over to the carcass site and sniffs the ground. The bears must have finished off the calf, for she leaves after a few moments.

Following the bears up toward the crest of the ridge, the wolf finds both of them playing on a large snowfield. The young grizzlies rear up and grapple with each other. One slams the other down into the snow. The bear leaps up, grabs its sibling and tosses it down the slope. They race back and forth and roll in the snow, enjoying the opportunity to cool off.

At first, the wolf watches from a distance as the bears play. Then she moves closer, fifteen or twenty feet behind them, and begins prancing back and forth and leaping up in the air. Knowing that they cannot catch the wolf, the two grizzlies ignore her antics and continue to play.

All three animals move higher up on the snowy ridge and end up silhouetted against the skyline. The wolf appears to be dancing beside the two grizzlies. As they disappear over the top, the bears continue to play as the wolf dances around them.

I often think of that Crystal Bench wolf dancing on the skyline next to the grizzlies. What better symbol of Yellowstone's wolf reintroduction program? So comfortable in her new territory, the alpha female stopped to tease bears and play beside them.

No one knows what her past life was like in Alberta. Perhaps, like other wolves there, she was constantly on the alert for humans, who often tried to kill her and her family.

Her capture, processing, and long transport to the acclimation pen must have been a nightmare for her. Certainly she must have thought that all those traumatic events would lead to her death.

The first calming factor would have been the sight of her mate and their four yearlings on their release into her pen. The alpha female and the other Crystal Bench wolves eventually accepted their captivity and made the best of it. At least they were all together as a family once more.

Then, ten weeks later, they suddenly found that they could leave the pen. Once the significance of her freedom became clear, the alpha female must have felt like she had been given a reprieve, a new chance at life. The sighting the next day of the pack playing in the snow indicated they were celebrating their unexpected freedom.

As the days and weeks went by, the alpha pair and yearlings discovered that they were now living in a place that, by wolf standards, was a true paradise. The Crystal Bench wolves claimed the Lamar Valley, the area of highest concentration of prey, as their new territory. Prey animals surrounded them in nearly limitless numbers. The pack gradually came to understand that their new home was a place where humans, once their greatest enemies, seemed to leave them alone. Soon they were so relaxed in their domain that they could spend much of their time in play behavior.

In recent days, the alpha pair has fed on kills and bedded down within a half mile of the road. Despite the obvious presence of large numbers of visitors viewing them, the pair seemed totally at ease. The alpha male has been seen marking numerous bushes and trees— a sure sign that he regards Lamar Valley as his territory.

Unknown to these wolves, they have fulfilled the primary and most important goals set by the federal biologists in charge of Yellowstone's wolf reintroduction program. Above all other considerations, the biologists sought to encourage the reintroduced wolf packs to stay in the general release sites, and for each pack to stay together as a family unit. By their own free will, the wolves did just that.

The Crystal Bench, Soda Butte, and Rose Creek wolf packs are the founders of a resurrected wolf population in Yellowstone, a park whose own rangers killed off the native wolf population in the 1920s. Times have changed dramatically. Now we realize it was wrong to kill off the original wolves in Yellowstone. Now we want them back. Now we are on the side of the wolves. We want them to reoccupy all of their former ranges in the park. The wolves will do exactly that, and, in the process, give us back a restored national park, a park that truly preserves all the natural processes, including predation, of a wild ecosystem.

For nearly seventy years there has been an unnatural silence in Yellowstone—the absence of a sound that was heard in the region every day and night for thousands of years. That unnatural silence was finally broken in 1995: Wild wolves are once again howling in Yellowstone National Park!

Susan Zwinger

Becoming Water

from *Left Bank's Headwaters Issue*

The Apprenticeship.

Lie on a large log at the high-tide line by the ocean an hour before the highest high tide of the month. The waves will boom below human hearing. Take on the power of the incoming ocean in your bones.

Take notes from the great cacophony of gulls, terns, cormorants, crows, eagles, and ducks as they spiral around thousands of haystacks out from shore. The ferocious pounding that brings you fear, grants them safety, feeds the richest bird rookeries of the globe on islands off the coast of Alaska and British Columbia and Washington and Baja California. The ultimate movable feast pours down the fjords, channels, rivers, to run south along the Kuroshiwo, endless conveyor belts of organic debris.

The wave energy absorbed through a 5.5-foot-diameter Sitka spruce log polished to marble from winters of storm will pulse into your bones. Choose a log too heavy to move, whose shallow root system splays outward 9 feet in all directions, writhing like Medusa's head. In the farthest reaches of its snake-roots should hang macabre seaweeds, bits of rope, mangled ships, snarled deck chairs, all limp as dead bodies of sailors.

On top lie with your eyes closed. The impact of that first wave will make the log sigh. The next, shudder. Well past high tide, the water may still rise and rise, punched shoreward by a storm somewhere at sea. Make sure the upper end of the log has been grounded since last winter. But keep some danger.

Water will churn under your log into pockets and holes underneath; waves will slam dance and gulp unpleasantly. Water may keep rising farther than the high-water line. Make sure of escape. Your universe will be made wholly of sensation. Into you will come the rhythms of Earth: of asteroids hitting, of their explosions, of the periodic wipeouts of life, of the punctuated equilibrium of evolution. Finally, the Big Bang.

A Great Beast Wave will strike. It will shower you with spray. It will condense under your log which will move slightly on its angry back. You will flip on your stomach and grasp two large roots. You will watch the power knit and unfurl.

Prone, you will ride with John Muir on top of his conifer whipping in a Yosemite thunderstorm. You will sail with Joseph Conrad through angry seas. You may drown with Captain Ahab midst the slash of the great white tail. If you are fortunate, you will find yourself about to go down with Amelia. . . .

Step Two:

Go to the downtown library; pull huge maps of your bioregion from the drawer. Carefully trace all the edges of water, all the lakes, all the rivers onto large paper. Do not include cities or artificial borders. Move your pencil slowly, sensuously, knowing that each crook and curve is intimately known by someone who loves it.

Step back. View the waterways of the Earth as dendritic veins. Imagine the humps and lumps implied underneath as those of a muscular lover.

Apprenticeship over, work begins.

Become one giant Earth wave, with a wave length of half the planet, pulled by moon and sun, dragged by friction and gravity. Pile up on one side of the globe, then shudder to a pause and change direction. Swell up under fishermen off Viet Nam, caress skin divers in the Caribbean, strand a cruise vessel in Glacier Bay.

Become fascinatingly deadly. Travel farther north toward the poles, go to extremes. In mesotidal Puget Sound, vary only 16 feet. At Anchorage on Turnagain Arm gape 33 feet. Rush in on the south and out on the north side of the deep glacial channel creating standing waves, bore tides, walls of vertical churning water 4 feet high. Make tourists screech to a halt in their cars. Remain totally uncanny.

Try this—

Be born of a woman. Try floating around in a liquid for nine months. Or be a woman and surround liquids and cycles of liquids with an intricate nautilus of flesh. This will be hard for some of you.

Drink eight to ten glasses of water a day.

Wear down entire mountain ranges and dump them in layers. Slice whole mountains in half, leaving chains of faceted spurs up U-shaped valleys like pinking shears. Gouge long grooves in stone like horizontal fluted columns, all the way from Alaska to New Mexico. Carve whole mountains into half domes, then fill the valley with concessioners and tourists, solo free climbers, bumper to bumper traffic, then wipe the whole mess out again.

Or, gently surround Zostra marina sea grass twice a day. Protect and feed hundreds of thousands of salmonoids, Dungeness crabs, ducks, geese, and the myriad of tiny organisms that form the basis of life. Allow yourself to be named by the Coastal Salish, then by the Danish settlers, then by the Orion Company developers, and then as Padilla Bay . . . but know that none of them count.

Spread over the wings and back of the great white trumpeters who, like Lazarus, have returned from the dead, from near extinction (only 69) in the 1930s, to a healthy recovery. Then glint like diamonds as the giant birds toss you off. Or drip off the wings of cormorants stretching in great black crosses against the bright scintillation of wind across your surface. Feed thousands of brant geese and other waterfowl for whom you are a vital link.

Or, try this—

Pile up in a huge mound 200 feet high and destroy all of Valdez, Alaska, and half of Anchorage. Toss train cars across town in Seward, Alaska. Crush cities in South America and Asia simultaneously.

Or rise gracefully under surfers and kayakers, carry them along, speaking all the time to their muscles, challenge them, let them know a slight shift in weight or twitch of hips changes direction. Make them mad with desire to be out on you.

Fill human eyes with warm salt brine at least once a month. Let them weep for themselves or their dog or a child. Let them weep for all of the losses on this unusual planet.

Make captaining a ship a religion, not a profession.

Flow in and out of a million tidal pools twice a day, gently surrounding the caves and crannies crammed with delicate hydroids and isopods and nudibranchs. The Sistine Chapels of pendulant chartreuse anemones, purple sea stars, and crimson dorises. Create a biological soup as the basis of all marine life. Fill up thousands of sleek fat salmon and follow them hundreds of miles into the interior of continents. Then disgorge your detritus as they litter the land with the nutrients from sea.

Or try this—

Fill camp cook pots with small trickles of yourself seeping out from the cliffs, slipping through the mudstone and shale, flickering through ferns, coating grass blades like icicles, propelling off rock lips in white tongues of foam. Become miniature waterfalls. End up as rust-colored tannin, a forest sampler of detritus: a forest smoothie.

Steep each different part of yourself in a different plant. Make one trickle licorice flavored, sweet, having absorbed in deep leafy woods the *Abrus precatorius,* Indian licorice.

Sweet and clear, flow out from the subterranean labyrinths of Mount Olympus's glaciers. Melt with rain's hot blade cut down through the ogives and mill holes, siphoning melted glacier into your underground reasoning. Carry within you microscopic blades of sheered rock called "glacier flour," turn yourself opaque turquoise blue. Flow through the rainforest, filtered by western red cedar and western hemlock seven feet in diameter. Take into you the communion of leaves, insects, lettuce leaf lichens, ground-up birds, essence du marmot, and whatever else it offers. With this soupy-brew nourish estuaries, marshes, and bays.

Liquefy ancient forest and send it swirling far out on the Japanese current curving sharply toward the Far East with the Coriolis effect of Earth turning. Send it out on the Kuroshiwo, translated "Black Tide," toward Asia in a giant flush. Feel two-mile drift nets scraping the life from you to feed an exponentially expanding human biomass.

In your crashing waves, snap together organic particles from yourself and nuggets from the ancient forest like Lego blocks. Scavenge dissolved organic material from the rainforest, glue them into fibrils of colloidal (gelatinous) proteins. Loop these fibrils into bacterial clumps. Create with this bacteria the very algae which feeds the entire food chain.

Benthic metabolism.

Try this—

Have poets write about you as if you are alive. Scientifically, it is absolutely true, you are alive. You have a pulse, the waves, and a metabolism, your food chain. A personality, a character, a consciousness, and a sense of purpose. Not just poetically speaking, but within the perfection of the trophic food-chain spiral, the balances of life forms, and your tremendous drive toward more and more complexity and away from Chaos.

In that explosion of foam, build the bulk of whales on a molecular level.

Try this—

Turn into spray, spin rainbows. Mist down granite boulders over mosses, lichen, and a myriad of tiny yellow columbine, foam flowers, and deep pink shooting stars.

Or swallow the bodies of sailors, drunken yachters, drug smugglers, expatriates, unwatched toddlers, cement-footed mobsters, disowned spouses, humans who no longer wish to live. Dissolve them all into lovely detritus and blend them back into life. Bless them, recycle them.

Or drill deep into granite and rip it apart with your bare hands.

And be sure to delight each new child, and each human being. Follow them down streambeds. Patiently receive into you all the rocks and sticks they throw in. Do not swallow every smooth flat stone they throw at you obliquely: let one or two bounce. Humor them. Let them know in their veins that you both are connected everywhere. Enchant them. And through enchanting, change them forever.

Don Schueler

Coexisting

from *A Handmade Wilderness*

Whatever the season, Hovit always carried a pistol or a shotgun with him when he went out in the woods. For a man with only one eye, he was a pretty fair shot; anything that flew, ran, crawled, or hopped (frogs were not exempt) was an excuse for target practice. Roddy Ray, himself a relentless hunter, complained that before we bought the Place, Hovit used to shoot squirrels in the Hollow even in summer "when they don't hardly have no fat on them yet." I could well believe this, having once seen him coming back from his pasture pond carrying half a dozen blue-winged teal he had blasted out of the water. Since it was early spring, they couldn't have had much fat on them either.

Nevertheless, knowing of our enthusiasm for wildlife—live wildlife—Hovit was tactful enough to soft-pedal his penchant for killing things whenever he came by to see what Willie and I were up to, which he often did when he'd been on a binge and Lurlee was making life miserable for him at home. At such times he was glad to share with us the nuggets of nature lore he had picked up in a lifetime spent making moonshine in the great outdoors. Right here on the Place, he assured us, he had seen milk snakes sucking milk from his woods cows' teats, and hoop snakes that rolled downhill with their tails in their mouths. On one occasion he had had to run for his life from a whip snake—a folkloric relative of the slender and quite harmless coachwhip snake—that was hell bent on skinning him alive with its lashing tail. And lately he had been seeing "these real big deer, almost twice as big as the regular kind" in the neighborhood. "The government's been turnin' 'em loose," he confided, "only they don't want us to know nothin' about it."

This was pretty tame stuff, however, compared to Hovit's encounters with wildlife in the Big Swamp, where he sometimes set up a still when the revenuers made things hot for him closer to home. The Big Swamp, located about a quarter-mile beyond the northwest corner of the Place, was a boggy, heavily wooded slough into which our branch and two others drained. It wasn't really all that big except by sandhill standards; but like all swamps it closed in on itself, creating, like a well, a perception of depth out of all proportion to the surface space it had to work with. The creek that sidled through it was wide and deep enough so that even during droughty summer months you couldn't jump across. And in some places you had to do a balancing act on a network of tree roots to get around the swamp at all. During one of my exploratory forays, a misstep landed me up to my knees in gluey mud that sucked the loafers off my feet when I pulled myself free. After that, I could easily believe Hovit when he said that back in no-fence days the Big Swamp had proved a death-trap for a good many of his cows.

I also wanted to believe him when he spoke of bobcats inhabiting the Big Swamp, even though his account of them would give a naturalist pause. He explained to me that they came in two varieties. One was the familiar bobtailed kind, but the other, which he also saw frequently, was "sort'uv bushy-tailed"—the consequence, he speculated, of their fooling around with the local tomcats. However that might be, a discussion of bobcats, both standard and bushy-tailed, was just Hovit's way of warming up. In a spirit of kindly, if bleary, sharing, he would soon move on to the subject of bears and black panthers. "Now a lotta folks don't know this, Don," he would say, "but there is two kinds of bears we got around here. There is your regular big bears which ain't too common anymore, and then there is these little bears, what we call hog bears because they're 'bout the size of a good-size hog. I see 'em all the time when I go messin' around in the Big Swamp. Why, hell, I've seen 'em right up by the house a bunch of times. They're little, but they're mean and sly, y'know. I've had to shoot at two or three of 'em that was sneakin' up on me."

Hovit had also seen panthers a bunch of times, and he's not the only one. Sometimes it seems that everybody in rural Mississippi has had an encounter with these fabulous creatures at one time or another. Unlike bobcats and bears, they come in only one variety: large, long-tailed, and invariably as black as ink. Even Roddy Ray, who is not a heavy drinker, has observed black panthers "playin' like kittens, chasin' each other up and down a tree," right alongside the county road. Such sightings are always accepted as gospel truth. One of Lurlee's grandsons came barreling up to the house one day in his pickup, all excited, brandishing his shotgun, wanting to know if I had seen the black panther that a couple of young girls had spotted crossing the road, heading straight for the Place. When I told him I hadn't seen any panthers but I *had* seen a stray black mutt on the entrance drive, he blinked, registering the possibility that he might be dealing with a case of mistaken identity. But then he said, "Naw, it couldn't 'uv been a dog. The girls said that panther was *big.*" He was convinced he had come within a hair of seeing it himself, and was terribly downcast that he had missed the chance to kill it.

I knew better than to try to convince him that his black panther did not exist. The real panther, or "painter," that once roamed the southern wilderness was a subspecies of mountain lion, practically identical in all respects, including its tan color, to its western counterpart. A relict population of this southern race hangs on, just barely, in south Florida, but it has been extinct in the rest of the South, including Mississippi, since early in this century. Having only the name and the memory to work with, an older generation of southerners, growing up on Frank Buck's *Bring 'Em Back Alive* and

Johnny Weissmuller's *Tarzan* flicks, transferred the blackness of Asian and African panthers (a melanistic phase of the leopard) to the tawny animal their grandfathers had wiped out way back when.

As for the Mississippi black bear—that embodiment of wilderness that Faulkner wrote so eloquently about—there are maybe twenty or thirty of them left in the state, holed up in a couple of bottomland tracts that are nowhere near the Place. Hovit had no doubt inherited the term "hog bears" from a time when the animals were more numerous and occasionally raided someone's pigsty.

What fascinated me was the tenacity with which not just Hovit but so many of my neighbors clung to the conviction that their pillaged backwoods could still support panthers, black or otherwise, and bears, hog-size or regular, not to mention super deer or Zorro-like whip snakes. Maybe the cultivation of such bestiaries has something to do with the need of many country people to invest Nature with the sort of mystery and excitement they feel it ought to possess, the same need that populates abandoned houses with wailing ghosts. More likely, however, it is a nostalgia for a less-tamed world, one that they miss if only because, like Lurlee's grandson, they want the fun of destroying it all over again. I don't know, I think that misplaced faith and longing is sort of sad. So much of the real mystery and excitement of the natural world is still there, all around them; yet they don't seem interested in hearing about that, or discovering it for themselves.

Myself, I am endlessly surprised by the fact that the glass is still half full. Although top-of-the-line creatures like panthers, black bears, red wolves, eagles, and ivory-billed woodpeckers may be long gone from the sandhills, along with the unbroken forests that once sheltered them, most of the wildlife species that lived here one hundred years ago are still present, although some are barely hanging on. For me, seeing them, learning about them is an enthusiasm I wish were more communicable, sort of like the flu. I would love nothing better than to infect people like Hovit and Roddy Ray. But not *just* people like them. Even card-carrying Audubon types too often change their ecological tune in a hurry when they feel threatened by Lyme disease or woodchucks in their flower beds or even the squirrels that raid their bird feeders. My own feeling is that when people come into conflict with wildlife—and the odds are that this will happen occasionally to anyone who owns land in the country—the interests of the local wildlife should come first. Which, however, doesn't mean you have to passively accept any damage that might befall.

Since Willie and I were not living at the Place full time, we couldn't always react quickly when a conflict of interests did crop up. Given that circumstance, the amazing thing was how rarely problems occurred. We did keep the chickens penned up while we were gone, and the ducks usually stuck pretty close to the precarious refuge of the pond; but the geese, and especially the guineas, roamed in and out of the compound at will, noisily advertising their availability as a free lunch for any fox or hawk that happened to be passing by. Yet more often than not the local predators ignored what amounted to an invitation to entrapment. Months would often go by without a single casualty.

In the case of our resident red-shouldered hawks, the explanation was both simple and instructive: they might help themselves to bite-size baby ducks, but they weren't really programmed to attack adult poultry. On several occasions I observed one of the pair perched in a pine at the edge of the pond—a favorite observation post when they thought we weren't around—while directly below the guineas screamed their silly heads off and the ducks swam around in anxious circles, gabbling in alarm. The hawk would act as though they weren't there, its attention fixed on the pond's iris-crowded edge. Then suddenly it would swoop down and fly off with a crawfish in its talons!

For a couple of years, the broad-winged, red-tailed, and Cooper's hawks that sometimes frequented the Place seemed equally uninterested in tackling a full-grown duck or guinea, much less a bellicose goose. But one autumn evening in the early '70s, Willie and I arrived at the Place to find a recently slain mallard drake lying in the grass near the edge of the pond. The breast feathers had been neatly plucked and most of the flesh removed with almost surgical skill, clear evidence that the assailant had been a bird of prey.

"Just when I was getting to really like those hawks," Willie sighed, "they go and do something like this."

I agreed that our resident red-shoulders seemed the likely suspects, notwithstanding their previous restraint. But I proposed that we leave the duck where it was. Then, if they came back for seconds, we'd know for sure.

Next morning we were awakened by a louder than usual chorus of duck and guinea voices. When I got up and looked through the upstairs sliding doors, there was a large, fierce-eyed hawk on the lawn below making a hearty breakfast of yesterday's dead duck. Now and then he raised his head to look everywhere but up at me looking down at him.

Willie had come up behind me. "Well, leastways he's not one of ours," he whispered, sounding relieved.

The hawk was a red-tail, the one species of raptor, in the East at least, that sometimes deserves the name "chicken hawk," although the ones we occasionally sighted had never caused us any problems before. Even now I was impressed that this fellow, instead of helping himself to a nice fresh duck or guinea, which he could easily have done, was content to dine on leftovers.

Still, having set him up with a poultry smorgasbord, it seemed all too likely that he might keep coming back for more. So, not knowing what else to do, I opted for the terrorize-the-'coon routine, this time with Willie joining in. We yanked open the sliding doors and began hopping up and down and whooping and hollering like drunken Mardi Gras tourists on a Bourbon Street balcony. Downstairs, Schaeffer and Sammie, uncertain about what was going on but eager to help, added their voices to the din. The tactic worked. The scandalized hawk, a gobbet of duck still dangling from his beak, heaved himself into the air and sailed away among the pines, never to return—at least not for another meal of duck.

With the fox, we were not so lucky. Foxes are often thought of as rather furtive animals; but in fact they can be quite bold, even cocky, in their dealings with humans. They can also be very single-minded about getting what they want, as our guineas would learn to their sorrow.

Both red and gray foxes hunted the Place. The red is said to be the more clever species of the two, but the gray has the ability, almost unique among canids, to climb trees when hounds pursue it, which may explain why it is still fairly common in the sandhills and the red is not.

During the years that followed my confrontation with the angry old fox hunter, we were awakened less and less frequently by the racket of fox hounds echoing across our land. I wanted to believe that Schaeffer's gallant charges, my angry imprecations, and the impeding fence all helped to account for this welcome change. But the main reason, I suspect, was simply that the old fox hunters were dying off and they had few replacements. Running foxes, after all, was not the same as running deer, since one didn't have the satisfaction of killing the quarry oneself. And now that every little trailer and ranch house in the sandhills was furnished with a TV set, the younger generation found it more entertaining to drink beer at home than to sit in a pickup listening to the music of the hounds. Which, now that I think of it, just may be the only constructive social change that television has ever brought about.

None of that had anything to do with the behavior of our fox, however. What did was his mate's decision in the mid '70s to raise a couple of kits in a secret corner of the Place. With a family to feed, he could hardly have been expected to be as considerate of our interests as we had always been of his.

He had his modus operandi pretty well worked out. Every other day or so when we and the dogs weren't around, he arrived at the compound while it was still dark and concealed himself near the tree where the guineas were roosting. Then, when they flew down at crack of dawn, he would grab whichever one landed nearest him and carry it off. So much for the proverbial good fortune of early birds.

At first we weren't even sure we were dealing with a fox. Sammie knew, of course. After excitedly sniffing the clues—there was always a scattering of feathers, as well as a trail of down leading off toward the compound fence—he would rush up to us, tail wagging cheerfully, to report that the mystery was solved. But all we knew was that our predator was not a hawk; it could have been an abandoned, starving dog—by no means a rarity in the neighborhood—or even an unusually enterprising raccoon or possum. However, the week after the losses began, it rained, so when we arrived the following weekend I was able to discover a neat little footprint in a muddy spot near the pond. It was hardly larger than a large cat's, but the marks of the toenails were clearly visible, which wouldn't have been the case if a cat had made it. That, plus the efficient strategy of the attacks, plus the fact that we could discover no bones or other carcass remnants, convinced us that our freeloader was indeed Br'er Fox.

By the end of the fourth week, I had decided what had to be done to save not only our remaining guineas but also the ducks; for by now the fox was varying his menu by helping himself to some of them as well. However, I had a curious presentiment that something should happen before we undertook this rescue mission—that something *would* happen, if we arrived at the Place so quietly and unobtrusively that the fox would not realize we were there.

This we did. After checking out the feathery remains of two more guineas, we and the dogs kept to the house that evening—a real penance because spring was well launched at the time, and the compound was aglow with blooming azaleas, dogwood, and sweet-scented crab apple inviting us to come outside.

At first light the next morning I awoke to the lamentations of our surviving guineas and ducks. The dogs, sprawled on the living room floor, ignored the racket. Willie slept on. I pulled on a pair of jeans and, barefooted, slipped out of the house.

The casualty this time was the next-to-last of our mallard drakes. I followed the usual trail of feathery down until it faded out; then I climbed the compound fence and headed off in the direction that the trail had been headed. I crossed the middle ridge near the spot where the first house had stood and went down the opposite slope to the still raw edge of the dysfunctional Big Pond. There in the wet clay was the neat little track of our duck thief, pointed toward the narrow branch below the dam. The quill of a single iridescent feather, lying in the nearby grass, was aimed in the same direction.

I descended into the branch and made my way slowly along gray aisles of lichen-mottled sweet bays and tupelo. The spongy wet sphagnum allowed easy and silent going for my bare feet. A thin blue mist hung in the damp air like cigarette smoke. Branches overhead dripped a cold heavy dew. The rising sun was just beginning to assert its oblique presence among the trees. The atmosphere, instead of being a transparency through which light passed, had become itself a kind of light. Bronze air. In that light every dew-soaked leaf and twig was incandescently beaded like the jeweled trees in an Irish fairy tale.

The world was absolutely quiet. In that stillness I concentrated my whole being on the quarry that, until now, I hadn't quite realized I was hunting. And, as though I had summoned him, the fox—a red fox—leaped up onto a fallen log just a few yards away and for a moment posed there. He was a beautiful creature, sleek and healthy— as well as he might be, given his current diet. His orange coat, set off by jet-black leggings and a dashing white ruff, glowed against the gray-green backdrop of the branch.

I didn't move, didn't breathe. He stared at me, his eyes intelligent and curious; but he hadn't caught my scent and he hadn't heard me approach; I was to him no more than an unusually ugly and mis-shapen tree. I had the peculiar sensation that I had passed through some invisible barrier; that I had left the human world behind and become part of the otherness of this animal's "other kingdom," where what mattered were those things that are important to foxes.

What was mattering to the fox, at the moment, was a flea. He balanced himself on three legs and gave his right ear a vigorous scratching with his right hind foot. That done, he took one last, rather self-satisfied look around him, hopped off the log, and trotted off with the purposeful air of someone who has important business elsewhere.

I remained there for some time, the way one does in a theatre after seeing a memorable performance, feeling unready to go back to the world of everyday. And for weeks and months afterwards, when my wanderings took me along the edge of that small branch, I would think, "That is where I saw the fox," and my spirits would do a little jig. There is no accounting for it, this special delight in seeing an elusive wild creature in its native habitat, especially when the habitat happens to be one's own as well. As far as I was concerned, it was compensation enough for the loss of a few ducks and guineas.

Well, more than just a few, actually. At this point, the body count had become pretty grim. So Willie and I went to work that morning building three covered eight-by-eight, wire mesh pens, about thirty inches high, and equipped them with the same sort of dispensers and feeders that kept our chickens fed and watered when we were not around. Into these "safe houses" we lured the ducks, guineas, and geese with helpings of corn, and there we left them when we took off for the city that Sunday night. The next weekend we turned them loose while we were there, dragged the pens to clean patches of grass, and again confined them when we left.

We could have kept that up indefinitely, I suppose, but it was spring, and in such unprivate living quarters the birds refused to nest. So, at the end of the third week, we crossed our fingers and let the whole lot of them go back to their rambling ways. To our relief, when we returned to the Place the following weekend, we found that the strategy had worked. The fox and his vixen, no doubt miffed at finding their food supply cut off, had evidently moved their kits to a den somewhere else—something foxes tend to do anyway— and had gone back to their usual eclectic diet of rats, mice, black- berries, carrion, and the occasional grasshopper.

The fox was the single most relentless nemesis that our adult fowl had to deal with. But Willie, who liked to count his chickens before they hatched, insisted that a wild animal that devoured eggs was just as much a predator as one that devoured the birds that laid them. If one goes along with that view, I guess it could be said that egg pre- dation was an even more intractable and persistent problem.

Actually, it was a problem we didn't even know we had for a long time—months, maybe even a year. We just thought we had lazy chickens. Whenever we arrived at the Place, the first thing Willie did was head for their pen, gather the few eggs he found in the nest boxes, and then berate the hens for their poor showing. It wasn't that he cared all that much about the paltry number of eggs collected; we didn't eat that many of them anyway. But he was a staunch believer in the work ethic, and it aggravated him that "those no-account chickens been sitting on their lazy tails all week with nothing to show!" Nervously clucking, the hens would try to explain that the fault was not theirs, but to no avail.

Not, at least, until one morning when Willie came stomping into the house and told me to put some clothes on and come with him. When I asked him what was up, all he said was, "You'll see," in an aggrieved voice. I dutifully got dressed and followed him to the wire coop at the edge of the compound. From outside the enclosure, I couldn't see anything unusual about the way the little flock was be- having. Not that that proved anything; chickens have so little emo- tional range that it is difficult to interpret any but their most extreme reactions, as when, for example, one of them suddenly realizes its head has been lopped off. Once we stepped through the gate, how- ever, I did notice that one hen seemed a little agitated. She was clucking rapidly and craning her neck toward one of the nest boxes, at which Willie was also pointing an accusing finger. When I peered into it, a snake was peering lidlessly back at me—while trying frantically to unhinge his jaws from an egg he had been attempting to swallow whole. He had been caught *in flagrante delicto,* and he knew it.

It was a young gray rat snake, less than two feet long. Willie and I frequently saw these demurely patterned gray and brown snakes in the compound, but it had never occurred to us to link their relative abundance with our chronic egg shortage. I knew snakes could un-hinge their jaws to gulp down outsized prey; I had seen them do it many times in sex-'n'-violence nature films, but I hadn't realized that some of them had a taste for eggs. In fact, from what I'd read, both their nearsighted eyes and their bodies (which pick up delicate vi-brations in the ground) were specifically designed for the purpose of capturing moving prey. And yet here was this smallish snake engulf-ing something that was about as mobile and warm-blooded as a large, smooth rock. So much for my qualifications as a herpetologist.

Aside from stealing eggs (and baby chickens if they got the chance), our rat snakes were inoffensive, even helpful neighbors, pa-trolling around the house's supporting piers so efficiently that we al-most never saw a mouse inside the house itself.

However, there was an occasion when one of them precipitated a scene so embarrassing that I still cringe every time I think about it. Adelaide Dartwood, a middle-aged uptown dowager of whom we were very fond, had come to visit us in Mississippi for the first time. She was kindhearted and sentimental, and she loved small animals; but she would have been the first to admit that she was not much into nature worship. Her idea of someone having a really nice time in the out-of-doors was Marie Antoinette playing shepherdess at le Petit Trianon. She tried. She made polite little remarks about the Place, the fresh air, the sweet little birds flying around; but you could tell she found the whole scene pretty primitive. After sitting on the deck behind her sunglasses for a while and having two or three glasses of chilled wine, she felt the call of nature and retired to the bathroom.

She couldn't have been in there for more than a minute when the air for a mile around was sundered by her screams. Willie and I, along with Schaeffer and Sammie, rushed to the rescue, all of us trying to squeeze through the narrow door at the same time. We found poor Adelaide in a terrible state of disarray, no longer screaming, but wordlessly pointing at the corner of the bathtub nearest the toilet where she was still enthroned. There, curled around the old-fashioned bathtub's leg—a cast-iron ball gripped by a dragon's claw—was one of the younger members of our rat snake colony, a slender thing not more than eighteen inches long, trying his best to look as though he, the ball, and the dragon's claw were all part of the same ensemble. I made a grab for him, but he quickly slithered into the dark recesses under the tub—which understandably set our friend to screaming again. It was a pretty hectic scene for a while there—getting Adelaide out of the john, scrambling around on hands and knees searching unsuccessfully for the snake, and finally stuffing a towel under the shut bathroom door to make sure he stayed out of sight.

While wondering if our insurance covered snake fright, we did our groveling best to soothe our stricken guest. Even Schaeffer, who rarely deigned to notice anyone except Willie and me, felt implicated enough in the debacle to give her trembling hand an apologetic lick. Happily, when she finally calmed down, Adelaide was very gracious and forgiving. In time, she would even transform the episode into a humorous anecdote to be told at dinner parties in the city. But she never did visit the Place again.

As for the snake, it simply vanished, apparently exiting the house the way it must have entered, via the hole in the floor that accommodated the bathtub drainpipe. Needless to say, when we were next in town, the first thing we did was buy some pipe hole covers at the hardware store.

Keeping rat snakes out of the bathroom was one thing; keeping them out of the chicken coop now that we knew they were confirmed egg eaters was something else again. The enclosure was too large to be made effectively snake-proof. So what to do? The answer we eventually came up with was: not much. The gray rat snakes went their way and we went ours. Egg production continued to be low, but since there were always enough eggs for us, and since Willie was not keen on surprising the snakes after dark, when they usually did their poaching, we tacitly agreed to leave well enough alone.

Over the years we occasionally had other problems with predators. Every now and then during fall or winter, migrant hawks, presumably red-tails, would leave another picked-clean cadaver of a guinea or a duck on the lawn. Once a pack of half-starved stray dogs killed two geese in a single day. Come spring, raccoons or possums sometimes discovered the hidden nest of a guinea hen or a mallard. And occasionally a bird simply vanished without a trace.

In the final analysis, our best defense against predators was the attitude we adopted: our flocks of domestic fowl were an indulgence, nice to have around, but they were expendable; the Place's wildlife, including its hawks, foxes, raccoons, and snakes, was not. Sometimes, as with the fox, we were able to cut the losses by temporarily confining our free-roaming birds in portable cages. But an even more effective measure was our practice of kidnapping newly hatched broods and raising them ourselves, thereby ensuring a supply of replacements when their elders met untimely ends.

Our guineas, geese, and ducks continued to meet such ends from time to time because we chose to allow them the run of the Place. But if such losses seem as unacceptable to other owners as they no doubt did to our guineas, geese, and ducks, the solution is simple enough: a well-made enclosure, such as we built for our chickens, faced—and roofed—with a high-quality two-by-four-inch mesh, will keep any poultry safe from any predator—with the exception of an egg-filching snake.

Indeed, wire mesh is the answer to a long list of wildlife problems.

Many is the time that, leafing through the relevant pages of the late, lamented Sears, Roebuck catalog, I wished I had the talent to write a poem dedicated to the many wonderful varieties of wire mesh: to the hog wire mesh fencing (topped by barbed wire) that wildlife can jump over or slip through, but which hounds must climb; to the wire mesh poultry fencing that keeps the fox and the hawk (and in some areas the coyote and weasel and skunk) from being led into temptation; to the rat- and snake-proof wire mesh screening on cages in which ducklings, keets, and goslings are reared; to the bordering of foot-high wire mesh that discourages armadillos from digging up flower beds and young azaleas (although not, alas, lawns); and to the wire mesh cylinders that prevent cattle (and deer, in areas where they are numerous enough to be a problem) from molesting young fruit trees.

If I did write such a poem, its theme would be the same as this chapter's: Anyone who buys land in order to live close to nature has the duty to either grin and bear it when conflicts with wildlife occur, or else invest the labor and money necessary to prevent those conflicts from happening. To reach for a gun when some rolls of wire mesh would solve the problem is inexcusable.

Contributors

Rick Bass lives near Troy, Montana, with his wife, Elizabeth, and two daughters. He is the author of such fine nature books as *The Deer Pasture*, *Wild to the Heart*, *Ninemile Wolves*, and *The Lost Grizzlies*. His distinguished fiction includes *The Watch* and *Platte River*.

John Calderazzo is an English professor at Colorado State University in Fort Collins, Colorado. His nature and personal essays appear regularly in *Orion* and other literary publications.

Jerry Dennis lives in Traverse City, Michigan, and has published articles in such periodicals as *Smithsonian*, *Audubon*, *Sports Afield*, *Outdoor Life*, and *The New York Times*. His most recent books include *It's Raining Frogs and Fishes*, *A Place on the Water*, and *The Bird in the Waterfall: A Natural History of Oceans, Rivers and Lakes*. He is also an accomplished player of the bluegrass mandolin.

Susan Ewing lives in Bozeman, Montana, and publishes articles regularly in *Sports Afield* and other outdoor periodicals. She recently took a trip to Argentina in order to observe the Andean condor. Ewing is an avid big-game hunter and fisherman.

Charlene Gilmore is studying for her master of fine arts degree in creative writing at the University of Hawaii, Honolulu. This is her first book publication, and she hopes to work in the publishing industry upon graduation.

John Hildebrand is a graduate of the M.F.A. program at the University of Alaska, Fairbanks, and currently teaches English at the University of Wisconsin, Eau Claire. His books include *Reading the River*, which chronicles a trip he made in a small boat down the entire length of the Yukon River, and *Mapping the Farm: The Chronicle of a Family*, which describes life on a Wisconsin farm. His writing appears frequently in *Sports Illustrated* and other publications.

Rick Kempa makes his home in Rock Springs, Wyoming, where he works as an English and philosophy teacher at Western Wyoming College. His essays and poems have appeared in over thirty magazines and anthologies.

Carolyn Kremers lives in a cabin on Chena Ridge near Fairbanks, Alaska. She teaches part time in the English Department at the University of Alaska, Fairbanks. She has lived and worked in several remote areas of Alaska, and has traveled widely in the backcountry of the state. Her first book, *Place of the Pretend People: Gifts from a Yup'ik Eskimo Village,* appeared in 1996.

Gretchen Legler received her doctorate in English from the University of Minnesota and is currently an assistant professor of English at the University of Alaska, Anchorage. She is the author of *All the Powerful Invisible Things: A Sportswoman's Notebook* and has also published in *Orion* and other journals.

Barry Lopez is well known to readers as the author of *Of Wolves and Men, Arctic Dreams,* and other classic works of natural history. He lives in the Cascade Mountains of Oregon with his wife, an artist, and has traveled widely around the planet observing and chronicling nature.

Rick McIntyre is a career seasonal employee of the National Park Service, currently working in Big Bend National Park in the winter months and Yellowstone National Park in the summer months. He is the author of *Grizzly Cub, A Society of Wolves,* and other noted works of natural history.

David Petersen lives in the San Juan Mountains of southwestern Colorado with his wife, Carolyn. Petersen is the author of *Racks, Among the Aspen,* and *Ghost Grizzlies,* among others, and also served as editor for Edward Abbey's poems and journals.

Adrienne Ross lives in Seattle, Washington, and spends as much time as she can on the beaches and in the forests of the Pacific Northwest. She is a freelance environmental writer and is working on her first book.

Scott Russell Sanders is an English professor at the University of Indiana in Bloomington, Indiana. He is the author of *Staying Put: Making a Home in a Restless World, In Limestone Country,* and other distinguished books. In 1995 he was awarded a Lannan Literary Prize.

Don Schueler is the author of four books, including *Temple of the Jaguar* and *Incident at Eagle Ranch*. Formerly a professor of English at the University of New Orleans, he still lives at the Place in southwestern Mississippi, as well as in New Orleans.

Sherry Simpson lives in Fairbanks, Alaska, with her husband. She holds an M.F.A. degree from the University of Alaska. Simpson has worked for the daily newspapers in Juneau and Fairbanks and currently writes a weekly column for the *Fairbanks Daily-Miner*.

Stephen Trimble is a western landscape photographer and nature writer. His thirteen books include *Words from the Land,* an outstanding anthology of nature writing, *The Sagebrush Ocean: A Natural History of the Great Basin,* and most recently *Earthtones: A Nevada Album* from the University of Nevada Press. He lives in Salt Lake City with his wife and children.

Susan J. Tweit has authored three books: *Pieces of Light, Meet the Wild Southwest: Land of Hoodoos and Gila Monsters,* and *Barren, Wild, and Worthless: Living in the Chihuahuan Desert.* She lives in Las Cruces, New Mexico, with her husband and children.

Louise Wagenknecht was born and raised in Idaho, where she has worked as a seasonal firefighter for the U.S. Forest Service and Bureau of Land Management for twenty years. She and her husband maintain a small sheep ranch near Leadore, Idaho. She has a bachelor's degree in English and writes periodically on topics of interest—logging and firefighting—for *High Country News.* She is working on a book about the changes that have transformed her part of the country in the last several decades.

Terry Tempest Williams is the author of *Pieces of White Shell: A Journey to Navajoland, Coyote's Canyon, Refuge: An Unnatural History of Family and Place, An Unspoken Hunger,* and *Desert Quarter.* She has been extremely active in the fight to protect the wildlands of Utah.

Ann Zwinger lives in Colorado Springs, Colorado, with her husband. She is the author of such acclaimed books as *Beyond the Aspen Grove, Run, River, Run,* and *Downcanyon.* She is also an accomplished artist and has illustrated several of her own books with pen and ink drawings.

Susan Zwinger, daughter of Ann Zwinger, lives in the Pacific Northwest. She is the author of *Stalking the Ice Dragon,* which chronicles a trip to Alaska, and has published widely in periodicals.

Periodicals Consulted

Alaska Quarterly Review, Department of English, 3221 Providence Drive, Anchorage, Alaska 99508

American Poetry Review, 1721 Walnut Street, Philadelphia, Pennsylvania 19103

Antaeus, Ecco Press, 26 West 17th Street, New York, New York 10011

The Antioch Review, P.O. Box 148, Yellow Springs, Ohio 45387

Arizona Quarterly, Department of English, University of Arizona, Tucson, Arizona 85721

The Atlantic Monthly, 745 Boylston Street, Boston, Massachusetts 62116

Audubon, 700 Broadway, New York, New York 10003

Backpacker, 33 East Minor Street, Emmaus, Pennsylvania 18098

Chicago Review, 5801 South Kenwood, Chicago, Illinois 60637

Cimarron Review, 205 Morril Hall, Oklahoma State University, Stillwater, Oklahoma 74078

Colorado Review, 360 Eddy Building, Colorado State University, Fort Collins, Colorado 80523

Denver Quarterly, Department of English, University of Denver, Denver, Colorado 80210

Esquire, 1790 Broadway, New York, New York 10019

Florida Review, Department of English, University of Central Florida, Orlando, Florida 32816

The Georgia Review, University of Georgia, Athens, Georgia 30602

The Gettysburg Review, Gettysburg College, Gettysburg, Pennsylvania 17325

Harper's Magazine, 2 Park Avenue, New York, New York 10016

Hawaii Pacific Review, 1060 Bishop Street, Honolulu, Hawaii 96813

Hawaii Review, Department of English, University of Hawaii, 1733 Donaghho Road, Honolulu, Hawaii 96822

High Country News, P.O. Box 1090, Paonia, Colorado 81428

Indiana Review, 316 North Jordan Avenue, Indiana University, Bloomington, Indiana 47405

Kansas Quarterly, Department of English, Denison Hall, Kansas State University, Manhattan, Kansas 66506

The Kenyon Review, Kenyon College, Gambier, Ohio 43022

Left Bank, Blue Heron Publishing, 24450 NW Hansen Road, Hillsboro, Oregon 97124

Manoa: A Pacific Journal of International Writing, Department of English, University of Hawaii, 1733 Donaghho Road, Honolulu, Hawaii 96822

The Massachusetts Review, Memorial Hall, University of Massachusetts, Amherst, Massachusetts 01002

Michigan Quarterly Review, 3032 Rackham Building, University of Michigan, Ann Arbor, Michigan 48109

Minnesota Monthly, 15 South 9th Street, Suite 320, Minneapolis, Minnesota 55402

The Missouri Review, 1507 Hillcrest Hall, University of Missouri, Columbia, Missouri 65211

Montana Magazine, P.O. Box 5630, Helena, Montana 59604

Nebraska Review, Department of English, University of Nebraska, Omaha, Nebraska 68182

New England Review, Middlebury College, Middlebury, Vermont 05753

New Mexico Humanities Review, Department of English, New Mexico Tech, Socorro, New Mexico 57801

The New Yorker, 20 West 43rd Street, New York, New York 10036

Nimrod, Arts and Humanities Council of Tulsa, 2210 South Main, Tulsa, Oklahoma 74114

The North American Review, University of Northern Iowa, 1227 West 27th Street, Cedar Falls, Iowa 50613

North Atlantic Review, 15 Arbutus Lane, Stony Brook, New York 11790

North Dakota Quarterly, University of North Dakota, Box 8237, Grand Forks, North Dakota 58202

The Ohio Review, Department of English, Ellis Hall, Ohio University, Athens, Ohio 45701

Orion, 136 East 64th Street, New York, New York 10021

Outside, 1165 North Clark Street, Chicago, Illinois 60610

Pacific Discovery, Golden Gate Park, San Francisco, California 94118

The Paris Review, 541 East 72nd Street, New York, New York 10021

Prairie Schooner, Andrews Hall, University of Nebraska, Lincoln, Nebraska 68588

Puerto del Sol, Department of English, New Mexico State University, Box 3E, Las Cruces, New Mexico 88003

Santa Monica Review, Center for the Humanities at Santa Monica College, 1900 Pico Boulevard, Santa Monica, California 90405

The Sewanee Review, University of the South, Sewanee, Tennessee 37375

Sierra, 85 Second Street, San Francisco, California 94105

Sonora Review, Department of English, University of Arizona, Tucson, Arizona 85721

South Carolina Review, Department of English, Clemson University, Clemson, South Carolina 29634

South Dakota Review, Box 111, University Exchange, Vermillion, South Dakota 57069

Southern Humanities Review, Department of English, Auburn University, Auburn, Alabama 36830

The Southern Review, Drawer D, University Station, Baton Rouge, Louisiana 70803

Southwest Review, Southern Methodist University, Dallas, Texas 75275

Tampa Review, Box 19F, University of Tampa, 401 West Kennedy Boulevard, Tampa, Florida 33606

The Threepenny Review, P.O. Box 9131, Berkeley, California 94709

The Village Voice Literary Supplement, 842 Broadway, New York, New York 10003

The Virginia Quarterly Review, Department of English, University of Virginia, Charlottesville, Virginia 22903

Wilderness, 900 17th Street N.W., Washington, DC 20006

Wildlife Conservation, Wildlife Conservation Society, Wildlife Conservation Park, Bronx, New York 10460

ZYZZYVA, 41 Sutter Street, Suite 1400, San Francisco, California 94104

Permissions

Rick Bass: "Yaak: The Land that Congress Forgot," from *Montana Magazine*. Copyright 1996 by Rick Bass. Reprinted with permission of the author.

John Calderazzo: "Sailing Through the Night," from *Orion*. Copyright 1996 by John Calderazzo. Reprinted with permission of the author.

Jerry Dennis: "The Music of This Sphere," from *Wildlife Conservation*. Copyright 1996 by Jerry Dennis. Reprinted with permission of the author.

Susan Ewing: "Riding Whitewater, Seeing Shadows: Divining Hells Canyon," first publication. Copyright 1996 by Susan Ewing. Reprinted with permission of the author.

Charlene Gilmore: "Breaking Ground: A Vision of Alberta's Prairies," first publication. Copyright 1996 by Charlene Gilmore. Reprinted with permission of the author.

John Hildebrand: "Fences," from *Mapping the Farm: The Chronicle of a Family*, published by Alfred Knopf. Copyright 1995 by John Hildebrand. Reprinted with permission of the author.

Rick Kempa: "Wind," from *Puerto del Sol*. Copyright 1996 by Rick Kempa. Reprinted with permission of the author.

Carolyn Kremers: "Trapping Wolves," from *Place of the Pretend People: Gifts from a Yup'ik Eskimo Village*, published by Alaska Northwest Books. Copyright 1996 by Carolyn Kremers. Reprinted with permission of the author.

Gretchen Legler: "Gooseberry Marsh," from *All the Powerful Invisible Things: A Sportswoman's Notebook*. Copyright 1996 by Gretchen Legler. Reprinted by permission of Gretchen Legler and Seal Press.

Barry Lopez: "In the Garden of the Lords of War," from *Manoa: A Pacific Journal of International Writing* (Summer, 1996). Copyright 1996 by Barry Lopez. Reprinted by permission of Barry Lopez.

Rick McIntyre: "The Wolves of Yellowstone: Year One," first publication. Copyright 1996 by Rick McIntyre. Reprinted with permission of the author.

John A. Murray: "Island in the Stream," first publication. Copyright 1996 by John A. Murray. Reprinted with permission of the author.

David Petersen: "What the Animals Know," first publication. Copyright 1996 by David Petersen. Reprinted with permission of the author.

Adrienne Ross: "Homecoming," first publication. Copyright 1996 by Adrienne Ross. Reprinted with permission of the author.

Scott Russell Sanders: "Buckeye," from *Orion.* Copyright 1996 by Scott Russell Sanders. Reprinted with permission of the author.

Don Schueler: "Coexisting," from *A Handmade Wilderness,* published by Houghton Mifflin. Copyright 1996 by Don Schueler. Reprinted with permission of the author.

Sherry Simpson: "The Book of Being Lost," from *Sierra.* Copyright 1996 by Sherry Simpson. Reprinted with permission of the author.

Stephen Trimble: "Sing Me Down the Mountain," from *The Geography of Childhood: Why Children Need Wild Places,* published by Beacon Press. Copyright 1996 by Stephen Trimble. Reprinted with permission of the author.

Susan J. Tweit: "Weeds," from *Barren, Wild, and Worthless: Living in the Chihuahuan Desert,* published by University of New Mexico Press. Copyright 1995 by Susan J. Tweit. Reprinted with permission of the author.

Louise Wagenknecht: "Dancing with Cows" and "Strangers in the Forest," first publication. Copyright 1997 by Louise Wagenknecht. Reprinted with permission of the author.

Terry Tempest Williams: "Statement of Terry Tempest Williams, naturalist-in-residence, Utah Museum of Natural History, Salt Lake City, Utah, Before the Senate Subcommittee on Forest & Public Lands

Management Regarding the Utah Public Lands Management Act of 1995, Washington, D.C., July 13, 1995," first publication. Copyright 1996 by Terry Tempest Williams. Reprinted with permission of the author.

Ann Zwinger: "Bright Angel Trail: Coda," from *Downcanyon,* published by University of Arizona Press. Copyright 1995 by Ann Zwinger. Reprinted with permission of the author.

Susan Zwinger: "Becoming Water," from *Left Bank's Headwaters Issue.* Copyright 1995 by Susan Zwinger. Reprinted with permission of the author.